HISTORY OF THE
WORLD CUP

BY GRAHAM BETTS

HISTORY OF THE

WORLD CUP

BY GRAHAM BETTS

Sutton PUBLISHING

www.suttonpublishing.co.uk

CONTENTS

This edition first published in the UK in 2006 by Green Umbrella Publishing
exclusively for:

Sutton Publishing, Phoenix Mill, Thrupp, Stroud, Gloucestershire GL5 2BU

First published in the UK 2006

© Green Umbrella Publishing 2006

British Library Cataloguing in Publication Data.
A catalogue record of this book is available from the British Library.

Printed and bound in Italy

ISBN 0 7509 4490 0

CONTENTS

CONTENTS

Whilst the British in general and English in particular were responsible for the development of the game of football, it was the continentals that were to take the initiative in launching the World Cup. The English Football Association was the oldest such association in the world, formed in 1863 and responsible for agreeing a uniform set of rules concerning the way the game was played. Other home countries soon followed suit and, as the popularity of the game spread across the world, so other countries established their own associations.

In 1884 the British International Championship, the first international tournament came into being, featuring England, Scotland, Ireland and Wales, who would play each other once during February and March (this competition predates the launch of the Football League, so there were no League matches to have to take into account in setting the dates). The success of the competition was noted elsewhere, and by the turn of the twentieth century, there were calls for a similar styled competition, involving considerably more international teams to be organised.

By 1904 there was sufficient interest in the idea for the French FA to call a meeting of like-minded associations to

members of FIFA until the following year.

Despite a rapidly growing list of members, FIFA made little headway in organising any kind of international tournament. Indeed, the Olympic movement, which had begun in 1896, had managed to incorporate a football tournament since 1900 (there are even some reports that a tournament was played in 1896, but it seems likely that these were little more than exhibition matches), even if Upton Park FC were representing the United Kingdom in 1900 and the 1904 competition featured only three teams. Following the creation of FIFA in 1904, control of the football tournament fell under their auspices for subsequent Olympic Games, beginning with London in 1908, often considered the first official football competition of the Olympic Games. The United Kingdom were therefore the first official winners, with a side that was for once a composite but amateur side.

The following year, in 1909, tea tycoon Sir Thomas Lipton organised a tournament to contest the Sir Thomas Lipton Trophy, sometimes referred to as the first World Cup. Held in Turin, sides were invited from Italy, Germany and Switzerland, who sent their most prestigious professional sides to compete. The English FA refused to have anything to do with the competition and refused to send a side. Desperate to have a side representing the home of football, Sir Thomas Lipton invited north-east amateur side West Auckland FC, a side mostly made up of coal miners, to take part. West Auckland not only took part, they actually won the competition, and returned to Italy in 1911 to successfully defend their title, beating Juventus 6-1 in the final and being awarded the trophy outright. It should be remembered, however, that this was a competition for clubs rather than national sides, and whilst West Auckland might be fondly remembered in the north-east (and Italy) for winning the first World Cup, such recognition does not extend to FIFA.

EARLY BEGINNINGS

discuss the matter at greater length. Present at that meeting in Paris in May 1904 were representatives of France, Belgium, Denmark, Holland, Spain, Sweden and Switzerland. Despite being invited, not one of the home countries attended, their insular attitude being such that they did not even bother

sending an observer. Those that were present agreed to the formation of the Fédération Internationale de Football Association, or FIFA as it has become better known. Most importantly, FIFA agreed a statute that would give it sole responsibility for organising a world competition. A few months later the English FA hosted a meeting of home country associations and effectively rubber-stamped the FIFA directive, although they would not become

Membership of FIFA continued to grow prior to the outbreak of the First World War, only to fall again afterwards, as the British associations resigned after refusing to belong to any organisation that included Germany, Austria or Hungary (the defeated axis powers) among its members. After

rejoining, the British resigned once again, this time over disagreements with broken-time payments to amateur players.

By 1921, however, the presidency of FIFA had been taken over by French lawyer Jules Rimet and the possibility of a world championship began to become closer to reality. The success of the Olympic competition, most notably with Uruguay winning the competition in 1924 and 1928, with both competitions taking place in Europe, convinced Rimet and others, most notably Henri Delauney of the French FA, that the time was right for the launch of an international championship. It was at FIFA's 1926 meeting that Delauney pressed hardest for the creation of such a competition, not least because an international competition could no longer be retained exclusively to the Olympics because of the growing spread of professionalism – there had to be a competition for professionals. It was to take a further two years of persuasive arguments, but eventually, at the 1928 Congress, the creation of a world international tournament was put to a vote and carried by over 80 per cent of the membership.

Six countries – Italy, Holland, Hungary, Spain, Sweden and Uruguay applied to host the very first

competition, scheduled for 1930 so as to be midway between the Olympic Games of 1928 (Amsterdam) and 1932 (Los Angeles). All six countries that applied could put forward justifiable reasons why they should be given the honour of hosting the first World Cup tournament, and after Holland, Sweden and Spain withdrew their applications and threw their weight behind Italy, it effectively came down to a two horse race between Italy and Uruguay. Uruguay were reigning Olympic champions and would be celebrating their independence centenary in 1930. More importantly, they promised to underwrite the entire costs of the competition, including the travelling costs of every competing nation and as a result were awarded the inaugural competition.

FIFA commissioned French sculptor Abel Lafleur to design a trophy, a solid gold trophy that would subsequently become known as the Jules Rimet trophy in honour of the FIFA president largely responsible for the creation of the competition (Henri Delauney's involvement was never forgotten either, for the European Championship, the competition played for by the members of UEFA, is known as the Henri Delauney Trophy).

Above
Jules Rimet (3rd from left) pictured with FIFA representatives, on their way to Uruguay for the first ever World Cup.

Left
The solid gold Jules Rimet trophy.

1930
URUGUAY

Below right
1930 official World Cup poster.

Below
The French team pose aboard their ship, Uruguay bound.

Despite the enthusiasm that had initially greeted the creation of the World Cup, when it came to actually competing in the tournament enthusiasm had waned. Indeed, were it not for the personal intervention of Jules Rimet, France would not have entered. Neither too would Belgium had it not been for their representative on FIFA, Rudolphe Seeldrayers. The four home countries were ineligible owing to the fact they were not members of FIFA, and only two other European countries, Romania and Yugoslavia, bothered to send teams across the Atlantic Ocean. The Romanian team was personally selected by King Carol, who also negotiated time off work for those chosen to represent their country.

True to their word, the Uruguayans paid for the travelling expenses of the competing nations, with all four European entrants travelling on the same boat to Uruguay. For the first and only time, all matches were played in one city, the Uruguayan capital Montevideo. Indeed, it had originally been intended that all the matches would be played in one stadium, the Centenario Stadium, a brand new stadium that the Uruguayans had begun building in February 1930 but which was not completed by the time the competition was due to commence on 13th July owing to heavy rain, despite work being undertaken around the clock. Thus, matches were played at the Pocitos and Parque Central stadiums whilst work continued on the new Centenario.

There was considerable disappointment within Uruguay over the lack of European entrants for the 1930 competition, disappointment that would be paid back with interest in the years to come. As it was, there were only thirteen nations that competed for the very first World Cup; four from Europe (France, Belgium, Romania and Yugoslavia), eight from South America (Brazil, Peru, Paraguay, Argentina, Chile, Mexico, Bolivia and Uruguay) and one from North America (the United States). Since there were only thirteen entrants, for the first and only time there was no need for a qualifying tournament, with the sides being put into four groups, with the winners of each group progressing to the semi-finals.

That the Europeans had not travelled well was evidenced by the fact that only one made any real progress in the competition (Yugoslavia). The host nation left nothing to chance with their preparations, gathering together their squad eight weeks in advance of the competition and shutting them off from the outside world, the better to prepare them for the struggles ahead. Antonio Mazzali had been goalkeeper for the 1924 and 1928 Olympic winning side and was first choice for the 1930 squad, but just ahead of the competition Mazzali decided he had been removed from his family for long enough and sneaked out of the team hotel one night in order to visit them. Spotted sneaking back in, he was dismissed from the squad and sent home; the Uruguayans would leave absolutely nothing to chance in their pursuit of the trophy, including homesick players.

France and Mexico had the honour of playing the very first match in the World Cup, with France winning 4-1 and Lucien Laurent scoring the very first goal in the tournament. This was to be France's

only victory in the 1930 competition, for their group was to be dominated by Argentina, the country from just across the River Plate and potentially the biggest rivals to Uruguay. As such, most Uruguayans who witnessed any of Argentina's matches could usually be relied upon to support the opposition, with the match against the French nearly evolving into a diplomatic incident. Ten boatloads of Argentinean fans made the journey to Montevideo to cheer on their team, were searched for weapons both at the docks and on entering the ground and isolated inside the stadium. Despite the hostile atmosphere Argentina took the lead through Luisito Monti and looked to be holding on for a win. As the match headed towards its conclusion, the French rallied and looked capable of scoring an equaliser. With five minutes to go, Brazilian referee Almeida Rego blew for time, but with the Uruguayan crowd storming the pitch and the French protesting, he finally agreed to resume the match in order that it could be completed properly. The Argentineans held on to their lead, but that was not the end of the controversy that seemed to accompany them throughout the tournament. In their next match, against Mexico, they were awarded five penalties by Bolivian referee Ulysses Saucedo in a match they eventually won 6-3. Monti was back in the thick of the action in their final group match, instigating a mass brawl against Chile that eventually needed the police to bring to a halt in the 3-1 win for Argentina. As such, Argentina won their group and took their place in the semi-finals.

Group 2 was dominated by Yugoslavia, too strong a side for both Bolivia and Brazil, although the Brazilians ran them close, only going down 2-1 after falling two goals behind in the first half. Brazil beat Bolivia 4-0 in what was little more than a consolation after the Yugoslavs had already made sure of their place in the semi-finals.

They were joined by host nation Uruguay from Group 3, who beat both Romania and Peru. The clash between Peru and Romania was notable for the first sending off in a World Cup match, with Mario De Las Casas of Peru receiving his marching orders in front of a crowd of just 300, the lowest figure to have witnessed a World Cup match (qualifying matches notwithstanding). After Romania had beaten Peru 3-1 Uruguay then beat their South American opponents 1-0 thanks to a goal by Castro to end Peru's interest in the competition and set up a group decider with Romania. Despite his goal the one-armed Castro (he lost part of his arm in an accident) was dropped from the side for the deciding match, with the Uruguayans making four changes in their side. The changes obviously worked, for Uruguay won 4-0 in something of a canter, running up a three goal lead by half time to effectively finish the match as a competitive spectacle.

The fourth and final group was the group that threw up the biggest surprise, for the much fancied Belgian side were eliminated in double quick time. Not only that, they failed to win a match, finishing bottom of their group. The surprise winners were the United States, who fielded five ex-Scottish and one English professional in their side and were dubbed the shot putters by the French. Despite the ridicule and composition of their side, they were worthy winners of Group 4, beating both Belgium and Paraguay 3-0 to top their group. They were much fancied for further progression too, established as second favourites behind the Uruguayans.

The United States team did not get to live up to their reputation in the semi-final against Argentina, a match that

Above left
France prepare to play the first ever World Cup match between Mexico. Lucien Laurent scored the very first goal (bottom row, second from right).

Above right
USA take-on Belguim in Group 4.

Above
The scene is set for the final at the Estadio Centenario.

Above right
Uruguay score in the final.

Below
Uruguayan captain Jose Nazassi (left) shakes hands with 'Nolo' Fereyra of Argentina before the final of the first World Cup.

was little more than a disaster for the fancied Americans. One player broke a leg after 10 minutes, their goalkeeper badly injured before the first half was over and another left reeling after he had been kicked in the mouth. They somehow managed to arrive at half time only one goal down and seemingly still in with a chance, but they collapsed in the second half, finally going down 6-1 to a rampant Argentinean side.

A day later host nation Uruguay booked their place in the final, also with a 6-1 win over Yugoslavia. The Uruguay and Yugoslavia match was a much more one-sided game than the previous semi-final, with Uruguay racing into a 3-1 first half lead and seldom being threatened thereafter.

With no provision for a third and fourth place play-off, that meant that the next match in the competition was also the last – the final itself. Almost as soon as Argentina and Uruguay had booked their place in the final, the political bickering and back-biting began. The Argentineans wanted to play the final with a ball manufactured in Argentina, whilst the Uruguayans wished to play with a ball made in Uruguay. It was the Belgian referee Jean Langenus (who officiated the game wearing a tie!) who came up with a compromise; the first half would be played with a ball made in Argentina, then the ball would be switched for the second half to one made in Uruguay!

On 30th July 1930 a crowd of 93,000 gathered into the Centenario Stadium in Montevideo to witness the very first World Cup final. The crowd included a fair few who had crossed the River Plate from Argentina,

adding to the atmosphere, although there was also an air of hostility that hung over the ground.

Once again the Uruguayans made changes to their side, bringing back the one-armed Castro up front in place of Anselmo. Their real success and strength, however, lay in the formidable half back line of Jose Andrade, Lorenzo Fernandez and Alvaro Gestido, known as 'la costilla metallica' – the iron curtain. The majority of the side were the same players who had won the 1924 and 1928 Olympic tournaments and used to big match pressure.

Jose Nasazzi of Uruguay and Manuel Ferreira of Argentina, the two captains, shook hands before the start of the match between the two close rivals. The opening minutes were tentative as both sides tried to discover any weaknesses in their opponents, but eventually the deadlock was broken after 12 minutes when Pablo Dorado put the home side a goal ahead after slotting the ball through the legs of Botasso. The lead lasted eight minutes before Carlos Peucelle picked up a pass from Varallo and shot powerfully past Ballesteros for the equaliser. Eight minutes from half time came the most controversial moment in the match, with Stabile looking to be offside when he collected the ball shortly before scoring and putting Argentina ahead with what was his eighth goal of the competition, the highest tally in the tournament. Despite protests to the referee about Stabile being offside, the goal was allowed to stand and Argentina went in at half time 2-1 ahead.

Whether it was the change of ball at half time that turned Uruguay's fortunes around will never be known, but 12 minutes after the restart Uruguay were back on level terms thanks to a goal from Pedro Cea. The next few minutes saw the game ebb and flow as both sides tried to press for a decisive goal, with Argentina coming close thanks to their three front men Peucelle, Evaristo and Stabile. As it was Santos Iriarte scored

from 25 yards for the host nation and the stadium erupted into wild celebrations. There was still a little more than 20 minutes to play, but in the minds of the Uruguayans in the crowd, the trophy was as good as won. There were to be a few moments when that belief could have been premature, none more so than when the prolific Stabile hit the crossbar, but gradually the Uruguayans got the upper hand and held on to it. The match was given a more realistic scoreline when Castro rose to meet a Dorado cross and headed home in the very last minute, and a 4-2 win for Uruguay was probably a fair result on the basis of the match itself.

The final whistle brought with it mixed emotions. The match itself had been played in very good spirit but the announcement of the result in the Argentinean capital of Buenos Aires led to public demonstrations and many anti-Uruguayan outbursts, with the Uruguayan embassy an almost immediate target for the protestors.

The atmosphere in Montevideo was in complete contrast. A national holiday was announced for the day after the final and many danced and partied for fully three days as the enormity of what had been

achieved sank in. Despite the shortfall of European entrants, the standard of the competition had been high and the Uruguayan population had responded well to the tournament, with the total attendance for the competition hitting 434,500 for the 18 matches, producing an average of 24,139 for the tournament. There had been 70 goals scored and not one match had finished goalless. And with the host nation having ended the competition winners, it had been an altogether huge success as far as the Uruguayans were concerned.

Below left
Uruguay celebrate victory.

Below
Jules Rimet, hands the World Cup trophy to Dr Paul Jude, President Uruguayan FA.

RESULTS

Group 1

France v Mexico	4-1	
Argentina v France	1-0	
Chile v Mexico	3-0	
Chile v France	1-0	
Argentina v Mexico	6-3	
Argentina v Chile	3-1	

	P	W	D	L	F	A	P
Argentina	3	3	0	0	10	4	6
Chile	3	2	0	1	5	3	4
France	3	1	0	2	4	3	2
Mexico	3	0	0	3	4	13	0

Group 2

Yugoslavia v Brazil	2-1
Yugoslavia v Bolivia	4-0
Brazil v Bolivia	4-0

	P	W	D	L	F	A	P
Yugoslavia	2	2	0	0	6	1	4
Brazil	2	1	0	1	5	2	2
Bolivia	2	0	0	2	0	8	0

Group 3

Romania v Peru	3-0
Uruguay v Peru	1-0
Uruguay v Romania	4-0

	P	W	D	L	F	A	P
Uruguay	2	2	0	0	5	0	4
Romania	2	1	0	1	3	5	2
Peru	2	0	0	2	1	4	0

Group 4

USA v Belgium	3-0
USA v Paraguay	3-0
Paraguay v Belgium	1-0

	P	W	D	L	F	A	P
USA	2	2	0	0	6	0	4
Paraguay	2	1	0	1	1	3	2
Belgium	2	0	0	2	0	4	0

SEMI-FINALS	Argentina	6	USA	1
	Uruguay	6	Yugoslavia	1

FINAL	Uruguay	4	Argentina	2

(Dorado, Cea, Iriarte, Castro)
Ballesteros, Nasazzi, Mascheroni, Andrade, Fernandez, Gestido, Dorado, Scarone, Castro, Cea, Iriarte

(Peucelle, Stabile)
Botasso, Della Torre, Paternoster, J.Evaristo, Monti, Suarez, Peucelle, Varallo, Stabile, Ferreira, M.Evaristo

Although Italy had been one of the contenders to host the inaugural 1930 World Cup and was the only serious contender for 1934, their selection as host nation was not nearly as clear cut as it would seem. FIFA were alarmed at the rise of the Fascists and concerned that the tournament might be hijacked for political purposes (which is pretty much what happened), despite Italian claims to the contrary. It took eight meetings of FIFA before Italy was finally given the nod in October 1932, and almost as soon as the selection had been confirmed, Italian leader Benito Mussolini began using the tournament to extol the virtues of fascism.

As with 1930, there were many notable absences from the competition, chief among them the holders Uruguay. Still angry at the European snub to their competition in 1930, the Uruguayans decided against competing, the only time the holders have been missing from the competition. Also missing were all four home countries, still outside FIFA looking in, although England played Italy in a friendly international in Rome in May 1933 and drew 1-1 (prior to this match the England side had been addressed before the game by Arsenal manager Herbert Chapman, perhaps the first time a full time manager had been allowed to give any kind of tactical talk to the England team), proof that they could have competed at the highest level had they so chose.

1934
ITALY

Despite the absences, a total of thirty-two countries entered the competition, which necessitated a qualifying competition to reduce the numbers down to a more manageable sixteen to compete in the finals. Even host nation Italy had to qualify.

The qualifying competition for 1934 was not as straightforward as it would later become. Group 1, for example, featured the four North and Central American countries in the USA, Cuba, Mexico and Haiti. Cuba played three matches against Haiti, winning two and drawing one, and then three matches against Mexico, all of which were lost. Then Mexico played the USA in a play-off (although the USA had not played any matches at all!) in Rome three days before the competition proper kicked off – the

USA won 4-2 and Mexico were left with a long journey home again!

Withdrawals hit many of the other groups – Brazil qualified from Group 2 without playing a match after Peru withdrew, Chile withdrew from Group 3 giving Argentina a safe passage in similar fashion and Poland withdrew after losing at home to Czechoslovakia so giving the Czechs a ticket to the finals. Italy had only to play Greece at home and won, so qualified for their own competition, and Romania were expelled at one point for fielding an ineligible player (hence the reason why Mexico were admitted to the finals) but successfully appealed and were re-instated, prompting the USA and Mexico play-off. Records were also set, with Paddy Moore of the Republic of Ireland netting all four of his side's goals in the 4-4 draw with Belgium, although it was to be the Belgians who advanced into the finals.

Despite the success of the group matches in Uruguay four years previously, it was decided to organise the 1934 tournament on a straight knockout basis. This meant only sixteen anticipated matches for a competition scheduled to last only two weeks! The sixteen countries that had made the finals were seeded, with the stronger seeds being given a relatively easy draw against the weaker seeds. Pre-tournament favourites were host nation Italy, although there were still one or two bets on Austria, even if their 'wunderteam' had possibly peaked. Unlike Uruguay, where all the matches had taken place in one city, Montevideo, in Italy the competition was spread around the country, with matches being played in eight cities and kicking off at the same time. And just as the Europeans had struggled to adapt after a lengthy journey to South America in 1930, so the South American sides similarly suffered. Of the sixteen finalists, twelve were from Europe,

Africa's lone representative Egypt held the Hungarians 2-2 at half time but ran out of steam in the second half, finally losing 4-2 in Naples. The remaining fixtures, all European affairs, saw Czechoslovakia come from behind to beat Romania 2-1 in Trieste, Germany also come from behind to register a 5-2 victory over Belgium in Florence and Austria get the better of France with a winner in extra time, 3-2 in Turin, the first match to require extra time in World Cup history.

three from the Americas (Brazil, Argentina and the USA) and one from Africa (Egypt).

After the first round matches, there were only European countries left. Italy had a relatively easy 7-1 victory over the USA in Rome, with Angelo Schiavo netting a hat-trick. Brazil's quest for the World Cup came to an abrupt end, 3-0 down by half time against Spain in Genoa and finally losing 3-1. The losing finalists from 1930, Argentina, also went out at the first hurdle, beaten 3-2 by Sweden in Bologna, but it should be remembered that the Argentina side of 1934 was largely a reserve side, since most of their key players from four years previously had moved to Europe, including Luisito Monti, who was now a naturalised Italian!

Four days later came the quarter-finals. Austria's side had something of a struggle before finally seeing off Hungary 2-1 in Bologna to take their expected place in the semi-finals, their goals coming from Horvath and Zischek. Germany got the better of Sweden in Milan by a similar score, with Hohmann netting both their goals but picking up an injury that would ultimately rule him out of their semi-final, with disastrous results for the Germans. After the first round matches, Italy had been joined by Czechoslovakia as favourites for the competition, and they had contrasting performances in their respective quarter-finals. The Czechs' attacking play was a joy

to behold and they were well worth their 3-2 win over Switzerland, with Oldrich Nejedly adding to his growing reputation with a second consecutive goal in Turin.

The Italian clash with Spain in Florence was just that and ranks as one of the most disgraceful matches ever played in the World Cup. Spain led at half time and came in for some severe tackling, both on and off the ball during the second half before the Italians equalised. Extra time saw both sides continue to battle in an attempt to get the upper hand, but by the time the final whistle went with the score still at 1-1, only the Italians could perhaps look forward to the following day's replay with any anticipation. After the first match, seven Spaniards and four Italians were

Above left
The England football team at Victoria Station as they depart for an international friendly against Italy in Rome, 1933.

Above right
Giuseppe Meazza of Italy sets-up Enrico Guaita to score, in the World Cup semi-final against Austria at the San Siro.

Left
French defender Jacques Mairesse (left) blocks the shot of Austrian forward Anton Schall during the World Cup first-round match between Austria and France.

ruled out through injury, and with Italy having the better reserves upon which to call, the replay appeared to be something of a foregone conclusion. As it was the Spaniards rallied and only went down 1-0, the winning goal being scrambled in off a post by Enrico Guaita, another one of Italy's Argentine-born players.

Guaita repeated his performance in the semi-final, scoring the only goal of the game as Italy proved a little bit too athletic for the ageing Austrian 'wunderteam' in Milan. It was in Rome, however, that the purists played, with Czechoslovakia overcoming the Germans 3-1 in something of a master class. Leading the way was Nejedly, who scored twice to ensure his country's passage into the final.

For the first time the two beaten semi-finalists met in a match to decide third and fourth place, with Germany doing enough in the first half to put the match beyond doubt against Austria in Naples.

Four days later came the final. The stadium in Rome was not full, although 55,000 fans, including Benito Mussolini,

gathered to see whether the side assembled by trainer/manager Vittorio Pozzo could lift the trophy. Up against them was a more than competent Czechoslovakian side who had won many admirers for their play on the way to the final, backed by a considerable number of fans who had travelled to Rome by road and rail.

The political aspect raised its head before the match kicked off, with the Italian side giving the fascist salute to Mussolini before the two captains, Giampero Combi and Frantisek Planicka, goalkeepers for their respective countries, shook hands and tossed a coin to decide the kick off.

It was to be the Czechs who showed the greater determination and urgency in the opening exchanges, but the Italians held firm, superbly marshalled by Luisito Monti, whose midfield battle with Cambal was a highlight of an undistinguished match. It was 70 minutes before either side made a breakthrough, but to the dismay of the home country, it was Czechoslovakia that made it. A corner taken by Antonin Puc was partially cleared back to the same player, but by now he had advanced towards goal and from an acute angle he shot home powerfully to put the Czechs ahead with 20 minutes left to play.

The Czechs would have further chances to put the result beyond doubt, but Sobotka missed a chance that appeared easier to score and Svoboda hit the post, giving the Italians hope that they might be able to rescue the match. With just eight minutes left came the equaliser the majority of the crowd had been praying for, and what a delightful goal it was too. The former Argentinean winger Orsi gathered a pass from Guaita and set off towards goal, running through the tiring Czech defence. As he approached the goal he dummied to shoot with his left foot and then hit the ball with the outside of his right foot, sending a curling, dipping ball over the grasping hands of Planicka.

With no further score in the remaining eight minutes, the stage was now set for a climax during extra time. Although the Italians were undoubtedly fitter than their Czech counterparts, as one would expect of a side put together by Vittorio Pozzo, they were handicapped by an injury to Meazza which left him

Right
The Czechoslovakian team lines up before the 1934 World Cup final.

Below
A confident Italy before the 1934 final.

much political gain out of his brand of fascism, Nazism, during the Olympic Games in two years time.

Despite the political undertones that had accompanied the 1934 World Cup (it is claimed that Benito Mussolini exerted pressure to ensure that referees appointed to the Italian games were favourable to the host nation, with the Swedish officials for the semi-final and final meeting with the dictator prior to the game and almost all the contentious decisions going the way of the Italians – all of the referees who officiated Italy's matches during the tournament were suspended by their respective associations after the tournament), the competition was deemed to be a success. The average attendance for the tournament was only slightly down on Uruguay four years previously, with an aggregate attendance of 395,000 (with one match less) producing an average of 23,235. The 70 goals scored was exactly the same as four years previously, but the one game played less meant that the average goal count was 4.11 compared with 3.88.

Top goalscorers were Angelo Schiavo (Italy), Oldrich Nejedly (Czechoslovakia) and Edmund Conen (Germany), each of whom scored four goals. More important, of course, was the fact that more countries had applied for entry into the competition, proof that the World Cup was rapidly growing in stature. That stature was to be severely put to the test in four years time.

Left
Italian goalkeeper Giamperro Combi is beaten by a shot from Puc of Czechoslovakia during the final. Italy however went on to win 2-1.

Below
Italy carry their manager, Vittorio Pozzo following victory over Czechoslovakia after extra time in the World Cup final in Rome.

little more than a passenger hobbling out on the wing. Indeed, he was so injured the Czechs had not bothered marking him since he sustained his injury, an oversight that was to prove immensely costly.

Five minutes into extra time Meazza got the ball out on the wing, swung over a cross to Guaita which he controlled and fed off to Schiavo. Although almost out on his feet, Schiavo summoned enough energy to round a defender and then fire home just underneath the crossbar to put Italy ahead. Despite some frantic attacks from the Czechoslovakians in the remaining 25 minutes, Italy held firm to win the trophy, much to the delight of the watching Il Duce.

At the end of the match Giampero Combi received the Jules Rimet trophy in what was his 47th and final match for his country. Luisito Monti, meanwhile, collected a winners' medal to go with the runners-up variety he had collected four years previously and with it the distinction of becoming the first player to win successive World Cup medals with different countries.

Italy's footballing victory provided Benito Mussolini with his political victory, a victory he felt was down to the fascist regime. It did not go unnoticed in Berlin, where Adolf Hitler would similarly make

RESULTS

Preliminary Round

Austria v France	3-2	Germany v Belgium	5-2		
Hungary v Egypt	4-2	Sweden v Argentina	3-2		
Spain v Brazil	3-1	Switzerland v Holland	3-2		
Italy v USA	7-1	Czechoslovakia v Romania	2-1		

Quarter-Finals

Austria v Hungary	2-1	Germany v Sweden	2-1
Spain v Italy	1-1, 0-1	Czechoslovakia v Switzerland	3-2

SEMI-FINALS	Italy	1	Austria	0
	Czechoslovakia	3	Germany	1

3rd & 4th PLACE PLAY-OFF	Germany	3	Austria	2

FINAL	Italy	2	Czechoslovakia	1

(Orsi, Schiavio) | (Puc)

Combi, Monzeglio, Allemandi, Ferraris IV, Monti, Bertolini, Guaita, Meazza, Schiavio, Ferrari, Orsi

Planicka, Ctyroky, Zenisek, Kostalek, Cambal, Krcil, Junek, Svoboda, Sobotka, Nejedly, Puc

1938

Right
1938 official World Cup poster.

Below left
Adolf Hitler watching the Berlin Olympic Games in 1936.

Below right
Jesse Owens of the USA, who was massively successful at the 1936 Olympics.

Just as Benito Mussolini had done with the 1934 World Cup in Italy, so Adolf Hitler did with the 1936 Olympic Games in Berlin, but in his case even more so. The whole tournament was little more than a political exercise, designed to show the Aryan race in the greatest possible light. The success of Negro athletes such as Jesse Owens had shown that the Aryans weren't invincible, but the political undertones that accompanied everything at Berlin left a bitter taste in many mouths, not least those within FIFA. With the World Cup of 1938 just around the corner, it was imperative that they chose the correct venue for the tournament.

There were those, especially in Argentina, who believed that the World Cup should alternate between Europe and South America, and with South America having hosted the 1930 tournament and Europe the 1934 one, believed the competition would return to

1938
FRANCE

South America in 1938. This was not a view shared by FIFA, despite the growing war clouds in Europe at the time. Indeed, a number of countries were already embroiled in hostilities by the time the 1938 competition began, including Spain, racked by civil war. However, FIFA was mindful that of fifty-seven member nations, the majority of these were European. There had also been logistical problems with the 1930 tournament in Uruguay, not least the travelling that had kept most of Europe away from the

competition. Under such circumstances, therefore, it was decided to host the 1938 competition in France, a decision that was also a gesture towards FIFA's president Jules Rimet.

The decision was greeted with incredulity in South America. Uruguay refused to compete again, still smarting from the perceived European snub of 1930. Argentina also refused to enter, believing that she should have hosted the competition. The Argentine changed her mind, entered late but was accepted into qualification and then withdrew again! Brazil therefore qualified from Group 10 without playing a match. Withdrawals affected virtually every other group outside of Europe – Group 9 was to have featured the Dutch East Indies and Japan, but Japan withdrew, meaning qualification for the Dutch East Indies without playing a match. Group 11 featured only one team, the United States of America, but they withdrew! Group 12 had six teams, Colombia, Costa Rica, Cuba, El Salvador, Mexico and Surinam, but everyone bar Cuba subsequently withdrew and Cuba also qualified without playing a match!

Spain entered the competition but subsequently withdrew because of the continuing civil war. The rest of the European entries were slotted into eight groups, with three of the groups

enabling the top two to qualify and the rest the group leader. Romania managed to qualify without playing a match after Egypt withdrew. For the first time it was decided that the holders (Italy) and hosts (France) would be given automatic qualification, and also for the first time it was decided how the final qualifying positions would be distributed among the continents – Europe would be given eleven places plus the two automatic qualifiers, whilst South America, North and Central America and Asia would be given one place each.

Although this decision initially produced the required sixteen teams, not all of them competed in France. Austria qualified from a group that also featured Latvia and Lithuania, but by the time the World Cup finals kicked off, Germany had taken over the country in Anschluss and there was no longer an independent Austrian side! Their better players were incorporated into a Greater Germany and Sweden, who had been drawn against Austria in the first round, were given a bye into the quarter-finals!

Just as in Italy four years previously it was decided to organise the finals on a straight knockout basis, with Switzerland against Germany and Hungary against the Dutch East Indies kicking off the competition on 4th June 1938. Hungary

had an easy ride against the Dutch East Indies, winning 6-0 in little more than a canter. It was much closer in Paris where Switzerland met Germany (complete with Austrian players in the side), with the match ending 1-1 after extra time. The following day the remaining five matches took place and these were similarly close, with four of them going into extra time and one of these finishing all square. In Paris France overcame Belgium 3-1 to give the host nation hope that this might be their year. The match of the round took place in Strasbourg between Brazil and Poland, where both Leonidas Da Silva and Ernest Willimowski scored four goals apiece for their respective countries before Brazil finally won 6-5 after extra time. At Le Havre Czechoslovakia, another country that was feared might withdraw as a result of increasing political hostilities and pressure from the Germans managed to score three times in extra time to see off Holland.

Although there were only two members of the successful 1934 side (Meazza and Ferrari) retained by 1938, Italy did include several of the side that had won the 1936 gold medal at the Olympic Games. Despite this they had a hard time of it in their match against Norway in Marseilles, being held 1-1 after 90 minutes and scoring a late winner in extra time. Norway also had a seemingly good goal disallowed for offside that would have really shaken up the Italians.

The final match in the round involved Cuba and Romania at Toulouse, where the unknown Cubans gave a good account of themselves in drawing 3-3 after extra time. Four days later they went one better, winning the replay 2-1 with a

Above left
The Dutch East Indies before their game against Hungary.

Above right
Swiss forward Lauro Amado (centre) tries to kick the ball past German goalkeeper Rudi Raftl, round one.

Above inset
The German team gives the Nazi salute before the start of the Swiss game.

Left
Cuba and Romania exchange pennents before their game.

winning goal in the second half. The other replay saw the Swiss get the better of the Germans/Austrians, coming from 2-1 behind at half time to win 4-2 in Paris.

The quarter-finals saw Sweden play their first match of the finals in Antibes and record an easy 8-0 win over a Cuban side still trying to recover from their exploits in the previous round. Gustav Wetterstrom matched the previous accomplishments of Leonidas and Willimowski in netting four of his side's goals, but in so doing alerted potential opponents of his threat, as Sweden would discover in the semi-finals.

In Lille Hungary scored in each half to overcome the Swiss, also exhausted from their battles in the opening round. It was similarly clear cut in Paris, where the holders Italy put out the hosts France 3-1, much to the disappointment of the partisan crowd. The final quarter-final was something of a battle, with Brazil having two players sent off (Procopio and Machado) and the Czechoslovakians one (Riha). The Czechs also saw Nejedly taken off with a broken leg and goalkeeper Planicka with a broken arm. Despite this they managed to hold on for a 1-1 draw after extra time, Brazil's goal coming from Leonidas. The same player also scored in the replay, a much quieter affair that passed without incident, and saw fifteen changes from the first match line-up and resulted in a 2-1 win for the Brazilians.

Two days later Brazil lined up for their semi-final clash with holders Italy in Marseilles. Despite the fact that he was the competition's leading scorer with six goals, the Brazilians decided to rest Leonidas for the final, along with another key player in Tim! It was an act of unbelievable confidence that backfired spectacularly, Italy taking the lead through Colaussi and Meazza netting a second from the penalty spot after Domingos da Guia had pulled down Silvio Piola in a 2-1 win that put the holders back in the final.

The other semi-final in Paris saw the Hungarians work out a way of blunting the threat of Wetterstrom by cutting off his supply. With little or no threat to their own goal, the Hungarians were able to sweep forward and won 5-1, Zsengeller netting a hat trick.

Leonidas was restored to the Brazilian side for the third and fourth place play-off and showed why he should have played in the semi-final, netting twice in the 4-2 win over Sweden to take his tally for the competition to eight. Given that he and the rest of the Brazilian side believed he would have been competing in the final, it wasn't any kind of consolation to have finished the competition's top scorer.

Above
Brazil versus Czechoslovakia in the quarter-finals.

Right
Italy and France before the start of their quarter-final.

Far right
The 3rd and 4th place play-off between Brazil and Sweden.

The final between Italy and Hungary took place on the same day as the third and fourth place play-off. Almost as soon as the host nation had been eliminated interest in the competition in France had waned, with attendances dropping for the later matches. The final however saw a goodly figure of 45,000 gather to see whether the flowing football of the Hungarians could knock the holders out of their stride. Although there was still space inside the ground, the crowd outside meant the Italian coach could not enter the stadium, so manager Vittorio Pozzo ordered the driver to return to the team's hotel and wait, rather than have his players sit in a traffic jam and have their minds start to wander.

The Italian coach made it into the stadium the second time and soon showed the delay had done nothing to blunt their attitude, taking the lead after just six minutes through Colaussi's volley into the corner of the net after great approach play down the left. Despite this setback the Hungarians were soon on level terms, equalising through Titkos's powerful shot into the roof of the net barely two minutes later.

Italy took the lead again after 16 minutes, Piola (who would be acclaimed as the player of the tournament) finishing off a four-pass move inside the penalty area, and 10 minutes from half time extended it with Colaussi's second goal of the game. The second half saw the Italians sit back and invite Hungarian attacks as they opted for a more defensive formation. It appeared to be working until the 70th minute when Hungarian captain Sarosi finally found a way through and reduced the arrears to a single goal. As Hungary pushed on for a possible equaliser gaps began to appear in their own defensive formation and eight minutes from time Piola made them pay with a left foot shot from 12 yards that put the ball beyond the reach of the goalkeeper and the match beyond the Hungarians.

Vittorio Pozzo's accomplishment of winning successive World Cup competitions has been sadly overlooked in the years that have followed, largely because of the later success of the Brazilians. Pozzo effectively dismantled the 1934 winning side, with only Meazza and Ferrari being able to add winners' medals in 1938. Foni, Rava and Locatelli meanwhile were able to add winners' medals to the gold medals they had won at the Olympic Games in Berlin 1936. Pozzo claimed that his 1938 side was an even better one than the one that had triumphed in 1934. Quite how good the 1938 side could have become will never be known, for Meazza received the Jules Rimet trophy, made a fascist salute and subconsciously reminded the world that these were troubled times. It would be twelve years before another captain got his hands on the trophy.

Above left
Alfredo Foni of Italy tries to reach a cross during the World Cup final against Hungary.

Above
Italy celebrate victory, lifting the trophy for the second time.

RESULTS

Preliminary Round

Italy v Norway	2-1
France v Belgium	3-1
Brazil v Poland	6-5
Czechoslovakia v Holland	3-0

Germany v Switzerland	1-1, 2-4
Hungary v Dutch East Indies	6-0
Sweden v Austria	
Cuba v Romania	3-3, 2-1
Austria withdrew	

Quarter-Finals

Italy v France	3-1
Brazil v Czechoslovakia	1-1, 2-1

Hungary v Switzerland	2-0
Sweden v Cuba	8-0

SEMI-FINALS	Italy	2	Brazil	1
	Hungary	5	Sweden	1

3rd & 4th PLACE PLAY-OFF	Brazil	4	Sweden	2

FINAL	Italy	4	Hungary	2

(Colaussi 2, Piola 2)
Olivieri, Foni, Rava, Serantoni, Andreolo, Locatelli, Biavati, Meazza, Piola, Ferrari, Colaussi

(Titkos, Sarosi)
Szabo, Polgar, Biro, Szalay, Szűcs, Lazar, Sas, Zsengeller, Sarosi, Vincze, Titkos

A little over a year after Italy won the 1938 World Cup the world was plunged into war and organised football took something of a back seat. England, for example, did not play anyone other than Wales and Scotland for the next six years, finally meeting France at Wembley in May 1945 and then undertaking a brief tour of Switzerland for two matches in July the same year, although none of these three matches is considered a full international.

FIFA, meanwhile, with its headquarters in neutral Switzerland, had managed to keep operating throughout the war under the direction of Dr Ivo Schricker. The 1940 Congress scheduled for Luxembourg was cancelled indefinitely, and although regional and some continental meetings continued, without a full complement of members present no resolutions could be passed or agreed upon.

Much interest has been afforded the whereabouts of the World Cup trophy itself for the duration of the war. Won by Italy in 1938, the trophy was initially housed inside the Italian Football Association, most of whose officers were supporters of the Mussolini administration, including committee members Francesco and Giovanni Mauro, secretary Ottorino Barassi and the Head of Italian Sport, Consule-Generale Giorgio Vaccaro. Despite their fascist leanings, they decided to put sport above all other considerations; although they did not trust each other too much, they trusted outsiders even less, so the trophy was taken out of the offices of the Italian FA and alternated between the homes of General Vaccaro and Giovanni Mauro before finding more permanent residence in a bank vault. When the Germans occupied Italy, Dr Barassi decided to take matters into his own hands. Fearful that the Nazis might steal

1950
BRAZIL

the trophy and melt it down for its gold, he smuggled the trophy out of the bank and kept it in a shoe box under his bed!

The scheduled 1940 Luxembourg Congress was finally held six years later in July 1946. First matter on the agenda was the organisation of the next World Cup competition, for which there was only one real candidate. Most of Europe was still ravaged by the effects of war and so it was decided to hold the competition in Brazil in South America, a continent that had managed to emerge relatively unscathed from the war. This proved to be a

IV CAMPEONATO MUNDIAL DE FUTEBOL
·TAÇA JULES RIMET·
JUNHO DE 1950
BRASIL

wise choice, for it re-established the concept of switching the competition between Europe and South America, and with Brazil the reigning South American champions would ensure considerable interest. It was also decided, as a mark of respect to honour Jules Rimet's twenty-fifth anniversary as FIFA President that the trophy would be officially renamed the Jules Rimet Cup, although it was always referred to as the Jules Rimet Trophy.

The number of entries dropped from that of 1938, with only thirty-two nations entering the competition. Germany, then divided into West and East Germany, was not eligible following the Second World War, whilst a number of other European countries were still in a state of such turmoil that entering was not possible. This did not apply to the four home countries, England, Scotland, Wales and Northern Ireland, all of whom were making their first appearance in the competition. In honour of this FIFA decided that the 1949-50 Home International Championship would also serve as the qualifying

Group 5 for the World Cup. Additionally, both the winners and runners-up would be admitted to the World Cup finals in Brazil. Quite bizarrely the Scottish FA announced that they would only go to Brazil if they won the group, putting ridiculous pressure on their side in the process. After Scotland and England had both beaten Wales and Northern Ireland, it meant both sides had officially qualified by the time they met at Hampden Park on 15th April 1950, where a Roy Bentley goal gave England a 1-0 victory and top place in the group. True to their word, the Scots immediately withdrew from the World Cup finals, despite the England players, FA and Scottish players asking the Scottish FA to reconsider their decision. To their lasting shame, the Scottish FA refused, even though the granting of two places to the British group had been a unique gesture on the part of FIFA. The Scots therefore stayed at home, although given the performance and results that England managed, perhaps they made the wiser decision!

As in 1938, the holders (Italy) and hosts (Brazil) were given automatic places in the finals. A much more complex system was used to try and reduce the original thirty-two entries to the required sixteen for the finals, with Scotland's withdrawal not the last before the competition kicked off. In Group 1, for example, which originally featured Austria, Syria and Turkey, only one match was played, a 7-0 victory for Turkey at home to Syria. Austria then withdrew, Syria refused to play the return game, and Turkey seemed to have qualified for the finals

Above
Scotland and England play a Home International match at Hampden Park, Glasgow.

Left
Representatives of the Italian football federation present the Jules Rimet Cup to their Brazilian counterparts before the start of the 1950 World Cup finals.

then move forward into a final group, with the winners of that mini tournament being crowned world champions. There were to be many shocks along the way before one nation emerged triumphant.

Whilst the tournament might well have been seeing the English compete for the first time, their presence was not universally accepted – Manchester United requested that none of their players be considered for selection as the club planned a North American tour! England's preparations were little short of shambolic, training at Ascot racecourse prior to departure to Brazil, which was left as late as possible so that the players would not miss any of their home creature comforts. Of course, it backfired spectacularly because after a two day plane journey the players had no time whatsoever to acclimatise. They travelled without a doctor or chef and after discovering that many Brazilian dishes relied heavily on spices, team coach (he was still not afforded the title or even responsibilities of manager) Walter Winterbottom stood guard in the hotel kitchen and tried to supervise something more palatable to English tastes himself. It was hardly ideal preparation for a tour, let alone an assault on the World Cup!

The England players were among the crowd that witnessed the opening match of the competition as hosts Brazil took on Mexico in Rio de Janeiro. The Maracana

despite only playing one match. Then Turkey withdrew from the competition and their place in the finals was offered to Portugal, who had already been eliminated from Group 6 after a defeat and draw against Spain. Portugal refused the offer, meaning there was no one to qualify from Group 1.

In Group 3 Belgium withdrew, with Switzerland managing to qualify after two victories over Luxembourg. There were also withdrawals from the South American and Asian groups. In Group 7, featuring Chile, Bolivia and Argentina and where two countries were allocated places in the finals, both Chile and Bolivia qualified without having to play a single match after Argentina withdrew. It was a similar story in Group 8, featuring Uruguay, Paraguay, Ecuador and Peru, where Uruguay and Paraguay qualified without a ball being kicked in anger after Peru and Ecuador pulled out.

It all meant that whilst the competition finals were originally designed to feature sixteen teams, only thirteen actually qualified and agreed to attend! It also meant a bizarre set up for the final competition – four teams would compete in both Group 1 and 2, three teams would be in Group 3, and the remaining two sides would contest Group 4! There surely had to be a better format, even with the thirteen nations that were present. It was also decided that the four group winners would

Stadium was still in the process of being constructed and so resembled a building site. The infrastructure was also in much need of improvement, for the coach carrying the England team was unable to make a way through the vast crowds gathering and so the players had to walk the last part of the journey. The Brazilians may have been pre-tournament favourites (at least in the minds of the local populace) but their performance against Mexico hardly justified the expectancy despite the 4-0 victory. The English players reported they were impressed by the Brazilians but confident they could get the better of them should the need arise.

The following day England entered the fray against Chile, a side that with one exception were part-timers. The exception was George Robledo, the son of a Chilean father and Yorkshire mother and centre forward for Newcastle United. His team mates were the usual mixture of shopkeepers, postmen and assorted tradesmen and surely not in the same kind of peak physical condition as the England players, but because England had not acclimatised, they were not in peak physical condition either. Unable to adequately cope with the heat or the rarefied atmosphere, it was a laboured 2-0 win rather than the polished spectacle everyone had expected. The Brazilian crowd thought England were coasting, perhaps saving something for later battles, but the state of the players when they came off at the end told a different story; England had had to give everything to ensure victory, their goals coming from Stan Mortensen and Wilf Mannion.

Four days later came the biggest shock the football world had ever seen. Even now, more than fifty years later, it still ranks as the biggest upset in a World Cup match. England had had to travel some 300 miles out of Rio de Janeiro to the small mining town of Belo Horizonte where, although the heat was considerably cooler the pitch was bumpy and hardly an ideal venue for a World Cup match. Despite this, England were fully expected to see off the United States, who had qualified for the finals despite winning only one of their four qualifying matches and had already lost to Spain in the group matches. Indeed, so resigned to their fate were the Americans (something of a misnomer, for the team included players from around the globe who had qualified to play for America through parents, grandparents and other back door methods) that they had a difficult task in trying to keep the score down to respectable levels, they partied the night before the match! England kept the same side that had beaten Chile, which meant still no place for Stanley Matthews, perhaps the one player who could have given the Americans real problems.

A crowd of some 20,000 gathered to watch the match, all but the British miners in the crowd cheering on the Americans. The game soon settled into a predictable fashion; England attacking at will, laying siege to the American goal and firing in shots from all angles. The Americans, however, managed to get bodies in the way of most of them, and those that got through hit the woodwork. As each minute passed, the Americans grew in confidence, the English became more desperate. After 37 minutes came the unthinkable as Bahr shot from distance, a shot that Bert Williams in goal seemed to have covered, but as it made its way towards the goal, the Haitian-born forward Larry Gaetjens nipped in to deflect the ball with his head and past Williams for a goal. Despite a header from Mullen that appeared to have crossed the line before being scrambled away, England came no closer than the woodwork for the rest of the game. The final whistle was the cue for pandemonium to break out among the crowd, Gaetjens to get carried off shoulder high by team mates and fans alike and England to slink off in disgrace. So unexpected was the result that one or two British papers thought their correspondents had made a mistake and printed the result as a 10-1 win for England!

England never recovered from this result, losing their final match with eventual group winners Spain 1-0 despite recalling Stanley Matthews to the starting line-up – England's first foray into the World Cup had been concluded in double quick time.

Left
USA goalkeeper Frank Borghi saves in front of Tom Finney.

Below
The England football team arrives back at Heathrow from Rio after failure in the World Cup.

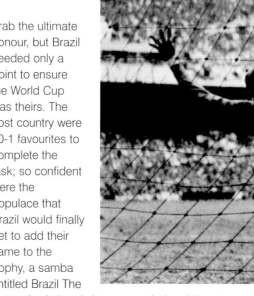

Others did not have to exert as much energy or run the risk of early elimination; Uruguay, making their first appearance in the World Cup since winning the competition in 1930, ensured they were still unbeaten after an 8-0 mauling of Bolivia at the same Belo Horizonte ground England had struggled on. It was the only match of Group 4, giving Uruguay an easy passage into the next phase.

The undoubted stars of the first group matches were hosts Brazil, who dropped only one point (against Switzerland after a 2-2 draw) and ensured their place in the final group with a 2-0 win over Yugoslavia. The final place in the second group phase was secured by Sweden, managed by Englishman George Raynor. Whilst England's preparations for the tournament had been chaotic, Raynor had left nothing to chance with Sweden's; he had ordered his players to wear lightweight boots, had the grass at their training facilities in Sweden cut to the same length as those they might encounter in Brazil and arranged for a Swedish woman living in Brazil to act as food consultant for their stay in the country. The time spent preparing for the World Cup paid dividends too, for Sweden managed to inflict a first ever defeat on Italy 3-2 and draw with Paraguay 2-2 to ensure their place in the next stage. Italy's 2-0 win over Paraguay was scant consolation – the holders were eliminated.

It had been decided that the final stage of the tournament would be a pool, with each of the four qualifiers playing each other in a League style format. As luck would have it, the top two teams met each other in the final match, giving the competition a final match worthy of the name. Whilst Brazil kicked off the group in formidable fashion, scoring four second half goals on their way to handing Sweden a 7-1 thrashing in their opening match, Uruguay and Spain ground out a 2-2 draw in Sao Paulo, with Uruguay having to come from behind before rescuing a point. The second round of matches was similarly decided; Brazil recorded a 6-1 victory over Spain, with Ademir adding a brace to take his tally for the competition to nine, a new record for the World Cup, and Uruguay came from behind again to squeeze past Sweden 3-2. It meant that going into the final two matches, Sweden and Spain were effectively competing for the wooden spoon whilst Brazil and Uruguay could

grab the ultimate honour, but Brazil needed only a point to ensure the World Cup was theirs. The host country were 10-1 favourites to complete the task; so confident were the populace that Brazil would finally get to add their name to the trophy, a samba entitled Brazil The Victors had already been recorded and the players were on £10,000 each to win.

The final matches were both played on the same day, with Sweden's 3-1 win over Spain in Sao Paolo of little interest to anyone outside Sweden or Spain but ensuring that Sweden lifted themselves off the bottom of the table and into third place. Meanwhile, the real drama was taking place in Rio de Janeiro.

The Maracana Stadium was nearer completion than it had been when Brazil kicked off the tournament but still not completely ready. For this reason the stadium, said to be capable of holding 200,000 was to be restricted to 150,000 for the final match. A paying crowd of 172,772 was reported after the match, with a further 27,000 gaining admittance for free to give a total crowd of 199,854 on the day. Despite needing only a point to ensure the trophy, Brazil played as they had in all previous matches, looking for a win to put the matter beyond doubt. Whilst Ademir was undoubtedly the real threat to Uruguay, the Uruguayan defence held firm and ensured Ademir did not have too many chances to add to his tally. Half time arrived with the game still goalless, but with Brazil having had the lion's share of possession. Two minutes into the second half the pressure finally paid off, with Ademir slipping the ball through to Friaca to open the scoring. Brazilian coach Flavio Costa, sensing that victory was all but achieved, decided on a tactical change, intending pulling Jair out of the forward line and into a more defensive role to combat any potential Uruguayan threat. The instructions, however, never reached their man, for Brazil continued to pile forward searching for additional goals to put the match beyond reach, but at the same time opening up gaps in defence that Uruguay began probing more and more.

It was right winger Chico Ghiggia who was the undoubted danger man for Uruguay, with Bigode allowing him too much room. It was from this position that Uruguay grabbed a foothold on the match, with Ghiggia taking a pass from Varela, beating Bigode with ease and crossing for Juan Schiaffino to

shoot home an equaliser after 66 minutes. Despite this wake up call, Brazil continued to press forward with much endeavour but little reward for their efforts. Uruguay by contrast were growing in stature, with Victor Andrade, whose uncle had been a member of the winning side of 1930, orchestrating matters in midfield and setting in motion many an attack. With 11 minutes to go came the decisive goal, Ghiggia again beating Bigode and setting off down the wing. Whilst the Brazilian defence moved to ensure Schiaffino, Perez and Miquez were picked up, Ghiggia suddenly changed direction and headed directly for goal, firing in a low shot that crept in between the post and Barbosa to give Uruguay an unexpected lead. Frantic Brazilian attacks in the 10 minutes or so that remained failed to produce the equaliser Brazil needed, and when English referee Jack Reader blew for time, almost 200,000 fans in the Maracana Stadium and millions more through Brazil openly wept. There were a number of reported suicides in the capital city too as the Brazilians struggled to come to terms with their unexpected defeat.

For Uruguay however, it was nothing more than a triumph, well deserved and finely achieved by a country that were still unbeaten in World Cup competition. Despite their obvious disappointment, the Brazilian crowd still remembered their sporting manners, warmly applauding as Uruguay collected and paraded the Jules Rimet Trophy around the Maracana Stadium. The scenes in Montevideo were reminiscent of 1930, with thousands pouring into the streets once the result came through to show their delight and herald the start of celebrations across the entire country.

RESULTS

Group 1

Brazil v Mexico	4-0
Yugoslavia v Switzerland	3-0
Yugoslavia v Mexico	4-1
Brazil v Switzerland	2-2
Brazil v Yugoslavia	2-0
Switzerland v Mexico	2-1

	P	W	D	L	F	A	P
Brazil	3	2	1	0	8	2	5
Yugoslavia	3	2	0	1	7	3	4
Switzerland	3	1	1	1	4	6	3
Mexico	3	0	0	3	2	10	0

Group 2

England v Chile	2-0
Spain v USA	3-1
USA v England	1-0
Spain v Chile	2-0
Spain v England	1-0
Chile v USA	5-2

	P	W	D	L	F	A	P
Spain	3	3	0	0	6	1	6
England	3	1	0	2	2	2	2
Chile	3	1	0	2	5	6	2
USA	3	1	0	2	4	8	2

Group 3

Sweden v Italy	3-2
Sweden v Paraguay	2-2
Italy v Paraguay	2-0

	P	W	D	L	F	A	P
Sweden	2	1	1	0	5	4	3
Italy	2	1	0	1	4	3	2
Paraguay	2	0	1	1	2	4	1

Group 4

| Uruguay v Bolivia | 8-0 |

	P	W	D	L	F	A	P
Uruguay	1	1	0	0	8	0	2
Bolivia	1	0	0	1	0	8	0

FINAL POOL

Brazil v Sweden	7-1
Uruguay v Spain	2-2
Brazil v Spain	6-1
Uruguay v Sweden	3-2
Sweden v Spain	3-1
Brazil v Uruguay	1-2

	P	W	D	L	F	A	P
Uruguay	3	2	1	0	7	5	5
Brazil	3	2	0	1	14	4	4
Sweden	3	1	0	2	6	11	2
Spain	3	0	1	2	4	11	1

The same FIFA Congress in Luxembourg in 1946 that had awarded the 1950 World Cup competition to Brazil had also decided that the 1954 competition would be held in Switzerland. Aside from the fact that, as a neutral country, Switzerland had not suffered any wartime damage, thus ensuring that the country's infrastructure was already in place, there was the added consideration that FIFA's headquarters were in Zurich. By the time the 1954 competition came around, FIFA would be celebrating the fiftieth anniversary of its formation, and where better to celebrate than in its own backyard.

Switzerland had the almost unheard of luxury of eight years to prepare for the competition and promised a lavish building programme that would produce stadiums worthy of the world's greatest players. Sadly that promise never materialised, for the stadiums that were built were relatively small given the growing popularity of international football. Switzerland was also unable to cope with the organisational responsibilities related to the competition, and yet, somehow, despite all of the problems, ended up with a finals competition that made a significant profit, aided in part by the minting of special commemorative coins, perhaps the first such move towards a more commercial competition. It should also be noted that the finals received some limited television coverage for the first time, also aiding the increasing popularity of the game on a worldwide basis.

A new record of thirty-eight countries entered the competition at the outset, comprising of twenty-eight countries from Europe and the so-called Near East, three from North and Central America, four from South America and the remaining three from Asia. Under the auspices of new FIFA President Rodolphe Seeldrayers of Belgium, it was decided that places in the finals would be allocated as follows; Europe would receive a total of twelve places (eleven plus Switzerland as hosts), North and Central America one place, South America two places (one plus Uruguay as holders) and Asia one place. The finals were to feature sixteen sides as before, with each of the four groups to include two seeded sides, and these seeds were selected before the qualifying competition kicked off. In the event that one of the pre-determined seeds were eliminated before reaching Switzerland, then their conquerors would assume their place as seeds. It is of course all conjecture, but it is equally possible that this decision

effectively altered the destination of the World Cup trophy itself, as we shall see.

European (and Near East, lest we forget) qualification was as complex and muddled as ever. The twenty-eight sides were placed into a total of ten groups, one with four teams, five with three teams and the remaining four with only two teams apiece! The four team group was allocated two places in the finals, the remaining nine groups one place each. Just as they had done in 1950, so FIFA dictated that the Home International Championship for the 1953-54 season would also qualify as Group 3 in World Cup qualification, with both the

championship winners and runners-up being granted places in the World Cup finals. This time, however, the Scottish FA did not add to the weight of pressure on their players by demanding that they win the championship to guarantee their participation in the finals; Scotland were going to take part even if they finished second. This was just as well, for after winning in Northern Ireland 3-1, Scotland could only scramble a draw against Wales in Glasgow. With England having beaten both Wales and Northern Ireland, it set up a final round of matches even more precarious than four years previously; if England and Wales won their respective matches against Scotland and Northern Ireland, as was widely expected, then it would come down to goal difference or possibly even the toss of a coin to decide who between Scotland and Wales would be Switzerland bound. With the Wales and Northern Ireland match scheduled for Wrexham on the 31st March 1954, Scotland would take to the field three days later against England knowing exactly what was required of them to ensure their place in the finals. Somehow, however, the Welsh contrived to lose at home 2-1, gifting Scotland a place in the World Cup finals. England's subsequent 4-2 victory in Glasgow ensured they finished with a 100% record, but by then both sides had one eye on the impending competition.

It was Groups 6 and 7 that were to effectively dictate the outcome of the final competition. The former group comprised Spain and Turkey, with the Spaniards being allocated one of the seeded places in Switzerland. All seemed to be going according to FIFA's pre-ordained plan when Spain racked up a 4-1 win at home, but Turkey pulled off something of an upset with a 1-0 victory themselves in the return. Since the idea of having the matter settled by aggregate scores hadn't yet occurred to FIFA, it meant a deciding play-off in Rome. This ended in a 2-2 draw, and so the toss of a coin was used to decide which country advanced to Switzerland and which stayed at home to lick their wounds. History does not record

who called or whether it was correct or incorrect, but the upshot was that Turkey won the right to appear in the finals, assuming Spain's seeded status into the bargain.

Group 7 featured the East European countries of Hungary and Poland. At the time, Hungary were widely regarded as quite possibly the best team in the world, a mantle they had proved with a 6-3 victory over England at Wembley in November 1953 (England's first ever defeat at home to foreign opposition, although this conveniently ignored previous defeats by the Republic of Ireland) and confirmed with a 7-1 win over the same opposition in Budapest less than a month before the World Cup finals kicked off. Whilst it was hardly the best possible preparation for England in their build-up for the finals, it did serve notice to the rest of the world that Hungary meant business. So much so Poland withdrew from the qualifying competition, giving Hungary an automatic place in the finals and seeded status into the bargain.

Aside from the goings on in Groups 6 and 7 there were no real shocks in the qualifying competition. West Germany (re-admitted to FIFA four years previously), Belgium, France, Austria, Czechoslovakia, Italy and Yugoslavia qualified out of their

Above
Baltazar of Brazil beats Mexican goalkeeper Salvador Mota in their first-round match.

Left
The president of FIFA, Jules Rimet, proclaims the official opening of the 5th World Cup, 16 June 1954.

meet for a second time in a play-off to decide who progressed into the quarter-finals. So confident were the Germans that they could beat Turkey a second time, manager Sepp Herberger deliberately played a weakened side against Hungary, drafting in six reserves and going down 8-3 in Basle. On the same day, in Geneva, Turkey duly won their second group match 7-0 to ensure their place in a play-off. Had goal difference been in operation in 1954, then Turkey would have qualified by right, but there again would Herberger have rested so many players if it had meant possible elimination? Three days later West Germany and Turkey met in Zurich for a second and decisive time, with all of the German first team back in their rightful place and romped to a 7-2 victory.

Brazil and Yugoslavia qualified from Group 1, Brazil beating Mexico 5-0 and Yugoslavia edging past France 1-0 before a 1-1 draw, after extra time, between the top two sides in the group ensured their

Above
Hungarian forward Nandor Hidegkuti (second from right) kicks the ball past German goalkeeper Heiner Kwiatkowski. Hungary beat West Germany 8-3 in the first-round.

Right
England's Billy Wright and Belgium's Jef Mermans before their match.

groups in Europe, as had been expected. Brazil won their qualifying group in South America with a 100% record, as did Mexico in North and Central America. The final place in the finals came from Asia, where the three teams (China, Japan and South Korea) were reduced to two when China withdrew. Both qualifying matches were played in Tokyo where, despite having a distinct home advantage, Japan lost the first match 5-1 and never really recovered enough to force a play-off, drawing the second match 2-2.

Thus sixteen teams had either qualified or been granted places in the World Cup finals with eight of the sides having been afforded seeded status. Each side would play only two matches in the group stage, the two seeds not being required to play each other, and extra time would be used in this phase in the event matches were level at the end of ninety minutes. If teams were level on points at the end of the group matches, then a play-off would be held, irrespective of the goals for and against columns usually used to dictate League positions.

Nowhere was this haphazard system better illustrated or exploited than in Group 2. Hungary, the team held to be the best in the world at that particular time, kicked off their campaign with a 9-0 thrashing of South Korea in Zurich. On the same day in Berne, West Germany proved that the seeding system hadn't worked with a comparatively easy 4-1 win over Turkey. The Germans expected the Hungarians to beat them in the second round of matches, just as they expected Turkey to get the better of the South Koreans, which would mean that West Germany and Turkey would have to

passage into the quarter-finals. Group 3 belonged to the World Cup holders Uruguay, who had yet to lose a match in the competition, and Austria. Both beat Scotland and Czechoslovakia in the group stage, Uruguay hitting seven

contend with and won rather easier than the 2-0 scoreline might suggest thanks to goals from Dennis Wilshaw and Jimmy Mullen. The final qualifying place out of Group 4 went to the wire, Switzerland having to repeat their earlier success against the Italians in a play-off. After beating them 2-1 in the group stage, they powered home 4-1 in the play-off to book the final place in the quarter-final.

Played over two days, with two matches on each day, the 1954 World Cup quarter-finals represented everything that was both good and bad in the competition. The opening day, the 26th June, represented the good. In Lausanne, Austria and Switzerland served up one of the greatest games in the history of the competition, a contest that ebbed and flowed and with the result in doubt right up to the final whistle. Switzerland opened with a flourish, forcing themselves into a 3-0 lead after just 20 minutes, but by half time they were behind 5-4! There were plenty of goals and action in the second half, Switzerland missing a penalty and finally ending up on the wrong side of a 7-5 defeat – home interest in the competition was brought to a conclusive end.

It was equally as good in Basle where holders Uruguay played England, only the second ever meeting between the two sides. Uruguay had won the previous encounter, played a little over a year beforehand in Montevideo, 2-1, but England had given a good account of themselves during the match. Whilst England had seemingly recovered from the mauling handed out by the Hungarians, there were still deficiencies in their game that the Uruguayans, seemingly fitter and better

without reply against the hapless Scots and Austria netting five against Czechoslovakia, similarly without reply, to ensure their places in the quarter-finals.

England were in Group 4, still smarting from two soul destroying defeats by Hungary and tinkering with team selection right up to the time they headed for Switzerland for the competition. They should have had more than enough to get past Belgium but fell behind within five minutes, recovered sufficiently to power into a 3-1 lead with 15 minutes to go and then threw it all away again by not concentrating at the back and allowing the Belgians to score twice in quick succession to force extra time. England scored again through Nat Lofthouse (his second of the match) to take the lead, only to lose it again when Jimmy Dickinson headed past his own goalkeeper. There were slight benefits however, for centre half Syd Owen pulled a muscle during the match (substitutes were still not allowed) and had, in time honoured fashion, limped out to the wing to try and cause a nuisance of himself from there. In the meantime Billy Wright had slipped into the centre half position and appeared much more comfortable in this position than any player tried since Neil Franklin's shock defection to Colombia four years previously.

Although injuries robbed England of Stanley Matthews and Nat Lofthouse for the second match against Switzerland, they still had too much for the hosts to

organised, were able to exploit. And so it proved in the World Cup clash, Uruguay taking the lead early on only for Nat Lofthouse, restored after recovering from earlier injury, to get on the end of a Stanley Matthews' created opening and level the scores. England had pressed on and dictated much of the rest of the half. But the difference between the two sides was shown inside a few seconds; Wilshaw had missed a fairly easy chance after Maspoli had beaten out a shot from Lofthouse, and in an instant the ball was down England's end and a speculative long range shot from Varela had gone past a bemused Gil Merrick in goal. Uruguay added a third shortly after half time to put themselves into a 3-1 lead. England rallied, scored through Tom Finney and pressed on looking for an equaliser, hitting the post and forcing Maspoli into a number of fine saves, but the third goal wouldn't materialise. With a quarter of an hour to go, Uruguay added a fourth goal of their own through Ambrois and ended the match as a competitive fixture; England were out and the holders were still unbeaten.

The following day came the bad. In Geneva West Germany, by now playing their best team irrespective of the opposition, had too much in hand for the Yugoslavs to contend with, winning 2-0 with a goal in each half from Rahn and an own goal. It was in Berne however that the real drama was unfolding, where Hungary

were up against Brazil. For all of the good play both sides displayed in the opening exchanges, there was still an element of ill-feeling that was creeping into the game long before matters exploded, an element that English referee Arthur Ellis was struggling to contain throughout. The Hungarians were slightly ahead on both possession and goals, having eased into a 2-1 lead when they were awarded a penalty that was duly dispatched by Lantos. This seemed to be the signal for all of the ill-feeling to come to the surface, with Nilton Santos of Brazil and Joszef Boszik subsequently dismissed for fighting, although any number of other culprits could have been

similarly sent off. Minutes later they were joined by a second Brazilian, Humberto, and fighting continued in the dressing rooms after the match, which Hungary finally won 4-2 (the match that is, not the fight!). Not for nothing has the match since entered folklore as the Battle of Berne.

Hungary was to face the other South American representatives in their semi-final, Uruguay. But this was not the Uruguay we would later encounter, this was a Uruguayan side that tried to play their way out of trouble, that believed the best form of defence was attack and still had both the air and attitude of undefeated world champions. The end result was another match to savour, played in torrential rain and watched by a ring of soldiers, there in case of any problems but not needed on the day. Hungary finally edged Uruguay out 4-2 after extra time, thus inflicting Uruguay's first ever defeat in the World Cup competition.

The other semi-final saw West Germany meet Austria in Basle where, with Italian referee Orlandini officiating, the two sides could probably swear at each other with impunity. It was a close first half, the Germans going in at the break a goal ahead, but the second half saw them turn on the style and run out 6-1 winners, with the Walters brothers netting two goals apiece.

Having gone undefeated in World Cup competition for twenty-four years, Uruguay contrived to lose successive matches, going down 3-1 to Austria in Zurich in the third and fourth place play-off.

The following day came the final between Hungary and West Germany in Berne. Hungarian manager Gustav Sebes had selection problems to contend with, with Ferenc Puskas, desperate to take part, declaring himself fit after a test in the morning, although subsequent events would prove that he might have served his country better by allowing a fitter player in to play. A crowd of 60,000 gathered at the Wankdorf Stadio for the clash, but this was not to be a repeat of the two sides' earlier meeting, an 8-3 victory for the Hungarians; the Germans were playing their best side.

It was the Hungarians who opened up first, Puskas following up a Kocsis shot that rebounded to him and netting the first goal after only six minutes. Two minutes later Hungary extended their lead, Zoltan Czibor pouncing on a sloppy back pass by Werner Kohlmeyer to knock the ball past Turek. But the Germans recovered, aided by the continual rain which drained the energy out of the unfit Puskas and left the Hungarians effectively a man down. Within two minutes, the Germans had got the first goal back, Max Morlock sprinting onto a defence-splitting pass from Schafer. They were gifted an equaliser in the 18th minute, Gyula Grosics in the Hungarian goal failing to deal with a corner from Helmut Rahn. From being two goals ahead inside eight minutes, Hungary went in level at half time. There was worse to follow.

Although the Hungarians weren't finished as an attacking force, hitting the woodwork through Hidegkuti who hit the post and Kocsis the bar, with Kohlmeyer clearing one shot off the line and Turek performing a series of heroics in the German goal, fate was beginning to take a hand. With six minutes remaining and extra time a real prospect, Rahn picked up a hurried clearance from Lantos and raced towards the edge of the penalty area where he shot low and hard. Skidding on the rain soaked pitch it picked up speed and eased past Grosics. Puskas, summoning possibly the last few ounces of energy available to him, raced up the other end and seemed to notch an equaliser, only for Welsh linesman Mervyn Griffiths to flag for offside and English referee Bill Ling award a free kick to West Germany. It was a close call for the Hungarians and they were still arguing with the officials when the final whistle blew a few moments later.

Whilst it was the Hungarians' first defeat in 30 matches, a run that extended back to 1950, it had come in the match that mattered most. For the Germans, unfancied and unseeded, it had proved that sometimes tactics on and off the field have their part to play. They had become only the third side to win the World Cup, whilst Fritz and Ottmar Walter became the first brothers to collect winners' medals.

RESULTS

Group 1

| Yugoslavia v France | 1-0 | France v Mexico | 3-2 |
| Brazil v Mexico | 5-0 | Brazil v Yugoslavia | 1-1 |

	P	W	D	L	F	A	P
Brazil	2	1	1	0	6	1	3
Yugoslavia	2	1	1	0	2	1	3
France	2	1	0	1	3	3	2
Mexico	2	0	0	2	2	8	0

Group 2

| Hungary v South Korea | 9-0 | Hungary v West Germany | 8-3 |
| West Germany v Turkey | 4-1 | Turkey v South Korea | 7-0 |

	P	W	D	L	F	A	P
Hungary	2	2	0	0	17	3	4
Turkey	2	1	0	1	8	4	2
West Germany	2	1	0	1	7	9	2
South Korea	2	0	0	2	0	16	0

Play-Off West Germany v Turkey 7-0

Group 3

| Austria v Scotland | 1-0 | Uruguay v Scotland | 7-0 |
| Uruguay v Czechoslovakia | 2-0 | Austria v Czechoslovakia | 5-0 |

	P	W	D	L	F	A	P
Uruguay	2	2	0	0	9	0	4
Austria	2	2	0	0	6	0	4
Czechoslovakia	2	0	0	2	0	7	0
Scotland	2	0	0	2	0	8	0

Group 4

| England v Belgium | 4-4 | England v Switzerland | 2-0 |
| Switzerland v Italy | 2-1 | Italy v Belgium | 4-1 |

	P	W	D	L	F	A	P
England	2	1	1	0	6	4	3
Italy	2	1	0	1	5	3	2
Switzerland	2	1	0	1	2	3	2
belgium	2	0	1	1	5	8	1

Play-Off Switzerland v Italy 4-1

Quarter-Finals

Uruguay v England	4-2
Austria v Switzerland	7-5
West Germany v Yugoslavia	2-0
Hungary v Brazil	4-2

SEMI-FINALS

| West Germany | 6 | Austria | 1 |
| Hungary | 4 | Uruguay | 2 |

3rd & 4th PLACE PLAY-OFF | Austria | 3 | Uruguay | 1 |

FINAL

| West Germany | 3 | Hungary | 2 |

(Morlock, Rahn 2)
Turek, Posipal, Kohlmeyer, Eckel, Liebrich, Mai, Rahn, Morlock, O.Walter, F.Walter, Schäfer

(Puskas, Czibor)
Grosics, Buzanszky, Lantos, Bozsik, Lorant, Zakarias, Puskas, Kocsis, Hidegkuti, Czibor, J.Toth

1958
SWEDEN

Right
1958 official World Cup poster.

Below
Stanley Matthews, Duncan Edwards and Captain Billy Wright in training for England, 1957.

Once again the South American countries felt they had a good claim for staging the World Cup and once again they were to be disappointed as Sweden was chosen ahead of any competitors. That was perhaps the only complaint that could be levelled at the 1958 World Cup competition, for everything else was superbly organised and executed.

A new record of fifty-three countries applied to enter the 1958 competition; twenty-nine from Europe, nine from South America, six from North and Central America and the remaining nine from Asia and Africa. FIFA decided that places in the finals would be allocated as follows: Europe would receive eleven places (nine to be decided by qualifying and the remaining two handed to West Germany as holders and Sweden as hosts), South America would have three, North and Central America one and a combined Asia/Africa group would be allocated the remaining place.

European qualification was relatively easy to organise with the twenty-seven countries being placed in nine groups of three teams each, the winners of each group earning a place in the finals. This meant the four home countries were to be separated for the first time ever, although England were placed in Group 1 with closest neighbours the Republic of Ireland. It also meant there was a distinct possibility that all home countries could qualify for the finals, which they ultimately did, although not before a few political manoeuvres handed Wales a second chance.

England eased through their group, beating Denmark home and away, winning at home to the Republic of Ireland and drawing in Dublin in May 1957 to maintain their two point lead over the Irishmen. Scotland won their group, Group 9, their defeat in Spain counting for little after the Spaniards had dropped a point at home to Switzerland. Northern Ireland also won their group, causing one of the biggest upsets along the way in eliminating the Italians (and Portugal into the bargain), a 2-1 win in Belfast in January 1958 lifting these Irishmen above their Italian counterparts. Only Wales of the home countries initially missed out, finishing two points behind Czechoslovakia in Group 4.

The USSR made their first appearance in the competition and won through too, beating Poland in a play-off in Leipzig in East Germany after the two nations had finished level with six points each in Group 6. Justice was seen to be done, for had goal difference been employed, the Russians would have qualified as of right.

There were no other real surprises in Europe, with England, Scotland, Northern Ireland, Czechoslovakia and the USSR subsequently being joined by France, Hungary, Austria and Yugoslavia in qualification for the finals.

The nine South American countries were similarly placed into groups of three, with the three group winners to advance. Only one group was affected by a withdrawal, Brazil and Peru

Left
The Opening
Ceremony for the
Swedish World
Cup finals.

Below
Matt Busby, talking
to Bobby Charlton
shortly after
leaving hospital
following the
Munich air disaster.

meeting each other home and away to decide Group 1 after Venezuela pulled out. A draw in Peru was followed by a slender 1-0 Brazilian victory in the return and Brazil earned her place. Argentina and Bolivia met in the deciding match in Group 2, with Argentina's 4-0 win securing a place in Sweden. There was a shock in Group 3, however, where former champions Uruguay were eliminated. Paraguay's qualification was assured thanks to a 5-0 win over the Uruguayans in the penultimate match played, Uruguay's subsequent 2-0 win in Montevideo counting for nothing as they had dropped a vital point in their opening match in Colombia.

In the North and Central American groups both Costa Rica and Mexico recorded 100% records to set up a two headed play-off that Mexico finally won, winning 2-0 in Mexico City and holding out for a draw in Costa Rica.

Only the Asian and African groups proved something of a disappointment as a host of withdrawals, mainly for political reasons, blighted the qualification process. In Sub-Group 1, Taiwan withdrew rather than play against China, with Indonesia and China subsequently needing three matches before Indonesia made it through to the next stage by virtue of having scored more goals (five) than China (four). Turkey refused to play Israel in Sub-Group 2, gifting Israel progress. In Sub-Group 3 Cyprus withdrew, handing Egypt an easy route to the next stage. Only Sub-Group 4 completed the scheduled matches, Sudan beating Syria at home 1-0 and drawing away 1-1 to move into the next round of matches. Except there weren't any, Indonesia withdrew rather than play Israel, whilst Egypt withdrew before they played Sudan. Sudan then withdrew rather than play Israel, which effectively meant Israel had qualified through three rounds without playing a match! FIFA had already decided, having noted similar withdrawals over the years, that no country other than the hosts and holders would qualify without having played at least two matches. FIFA therefore held a lottery of all the countries that had finished second in their respective groups and, after Belgium and Uruguay had declined to compete, invited Wales to meet Israel over two legs to battle for the final place in Sweden. Wales duly won home and away 2-0 and thus earned her place as the winners of the Asia/Africa group!

FIFA also dictated the formation of the four groups in the finals, which featured a team each from South America, Western Europe, Eastern Europe and Britain. The top two in each group would qualify for the quarter-finals, and in the event of the teams finishing second and third being level on points, a play-off between the two would decide which qualified in second place, with all three required play-offs featuring a team from Britain.

England, as we have seen, earned her place for the finals more than a year before the competition proper kicked off in Sweden. Stanley Matthews' long and illustrious career had finally come to an end during qualification, at least as far as England were concerned, after nearly twenty-three years an almost permanent fixture in the side. Youth, and more particularly a burgeoning crop of players emerging from the Under-23 set up, were to be the hope for the future as far as England were concerned. The bright and vibrant side that Walter Winterbottom assembled, however, had barely six months to blossom before tragedy struck. The continued domestic success of Manchester United had seen them compete in the European Cup in successive seasons, reaching the semi-finals on both occasions. It was whilst returning from Yugoslavia in February 1958, having ensured their place in the semi-finals, that the plane had stopped at Munich airport to refuel. In icy conditions the plane had struggled to take off again and, on the third occasion, overshot the runway, slammed into a house and burst into flames. Dead immediately were Tommy Taylor, Roger Byrne and David Pegg, as well as former England star Frank Swift, a journalist at the time from the News of the World. Another former England star, Johnny Berry, received injuries so severe he never played again. It got worse too, for two weeks later Duncan Edwards, something of a human powerhouse and already the proud owner of 18 caps for England, lost his valiant fight for life. He was just 21 years of age. The crash at Munich was a devastating loss for Matt Busby and Manchester United, but it was equally crushing for Walter Winterbottom and England.

It was the loss of Duncan Edwards in particular that England couldn't compensate for. No replacement could match Edwards' contribution, and robbed of a powerful goalscoring midfield player, England were a shadow of their former past. They were not

Right
West Germany
play Argentina in
the first-round.

Below
Mazzola of Brazil,
and Don Howe of
England collide in
the air during their
goalless draw
game.

Below right
Harry Gregg
Northern Ireland's
goalkeeper, fails to
stop West
Germany's Uwe
Seeler scoring the
equalising goal
during their World
Cup clash.

disgraced in Sweden, holding the emerging Brazilians, then in the early throes of introducing the world to 4-4-2, to a goalless draw in Gothenburg, the first time Brazil had featured in a goalless draw in World Cup finals competition. They also came from behind against the Russians and Austrians to earn 2-2 draws, the three points gained being just enough to earn them a second tilt at the USSR in a play-off. There they ran out of steam, going down to the only goal of the game from Iljin

and being eliminated from the competition. Brazil proved too good for both Austria and the USSR, beating the former 3-0 and the latter 2-0 to book their place in the quarter-finals.

Scotland eventually had a miserable tournament after a promising start. A 1-1 draw with Yugoslavia was a creditable result, especially as the Scots had been behind at half time, but thereafter defeats at the hands of the Paraguayans (3-2) and France (2-1) saw them out of contention. France and Yugoslavia duly qualified, France being given the top spot in the group despite finishing level on points with Yugoslavia. Their key players were the forward partnership of Raymond Kopa and Juste Fontaine, with Fontaine netting six of the eleven goals France scored in the group stages. He would go on to net more in the next phases of competition.

Holders West Germany won Group 1, but not as convincingly as many expected, winning just one of their three matches (against Argentina) and drawing the other two against Northern Ireland and Czechoslovakia. The second qualifying place was a close run thing too. Czechoslovakia's 6-1 win over Argentina at the same time Northern Ireland were holding the Germans, meant that the Irish would have to meet the Czechs in a play-off two days later. The Irish,

rearguard action for most of the match and were only finally undone by a piece of magic from a new kid on the block, Pelé.

British interest in the competition ended at the quarter-final stage, for Northern Ireland never came to grips with the French, who struggled a little in the first half but pulled well out of sight in the second, finally winning 4-0, with Juste Fontaine adding two goals to his growing tally. England's conquerors the USSR also departed at the quarter-final stage, losing to two second half goals from host nation Sweden in Stockholm. The semi-final line up was completed by holders West Germany, for whom Helmut Rahn scored the only goal of the game against Yugoslavia.

Whilst the Swedes had home advantage in their semi-final, the Germans were seasoned campaigners and determined to hold on to their trophy at all costs. They took the lead too through Schafer, and there was a blatant handball by Neils Liedholm at the start of the move that led to the equaliser. The match eventually swung in Sweden's favour when German defender Juskowiak was sent off for retaliation and in the final 30 minutes Sweden added two further goals to win a little closer than the 3-1 scoreline might suggest.

It was the clash in Stockholm that really caught the eye, where the lethal strike partnership of Raymond Kopa and Juste Fontaine were pitted against the likes of Garrincha, Didi, Vava and Pelé. The Frenchmen did their reputations no harm either, Fontaine netting one of the French goals, but Pelé was from another planet, netting three as the Brazilians hit five to earn their place in the final, although an injury to a key French

Left
Garrincha of Brazil dribbles past Welsh defender Mel Hopkins during their World Cup quarter-final.

Below
Brazilian forwards Vava and Pelé enter a melee in front of the French goal during their World Cup semi-final.

although robbed of Munich survivor Jackie Blanchflower, who suffered injuries that ended his career, were the happy-go-lucky side of Group 1. According to Jackie's brother Danny, their game plan was to equalise before the opposition scored! Northern Ireland could also lay claim to being the side that had come up with the idea of placing a 'wall' between attackers and defenders when there was a free-kick awarded, a simple technique that few sides then had an answer to. An extra time goal from Peter McParland saw the Irish sneak a 2-1 win against Czechoslovakia and a place in the quarter-finals.

The Welsh also sprang a surprise in their group, Group 3, which was dominated by host nation Sweden. Just as England had done, so the Welsh went three matches without defeat, albeit without a win either, leaving them level on points with Hungary, who had won one, lost one and drawn one of their games. This meant a play-off between the two nations, with Wales coming from a goal down to finally win 2-1 thanks to goals from Terry Medwin and Ivor Allchurch.

Wales' reward for reaching the quarter-finals was a clash with Brazil in Gothenburg. With their talisman John Charles unavailable through injury, the Welsh put up a strong

defender whilst the score was still level at 1-1 eventually worked to the Brazilians' favour.

Juste Fontaine took his tally for the competition to thirteen with a four goal burst against West Germany in the play-off for third and fourth place, France winning an entertaining and attacking game 6-3 to register their best ever showing in the competition.

The final itself was played a day later in Stockholm. The two countries had met previously, in the third and fourth place play-off in 1938 when the Brazilians had won 4-2, but this was the final and almost 50,000 fans inside the Rasunda Stadium would be cheering Sweden on. After limited television coverage of the 1954 tournament, millions around the globe were able to watch the events that were unfolding in Stockholm. The Brazilians had started the competition slowly and steadily got better with each passing game, with Pelé's explosion from the quarter-final stage onwards the real talking point. If he represented the youthful, exuberant side of Brazil, then there were the likes of Djalma Santos (playing his first match of the competition after recovering from injury), Nilton Santos and Didi, all of whom were survivors from the unsuccessful 1954 campaign, to provide the backbone.

For all this it appeared as though the rain, which was incessant throughout the match, might favour the hosts and it was they who took the lead after only four minutes, Neils Liedholm fashioning and finishing a chance for himself. Brazil had yet to touch the ball, and so Didi collected the ball from the back of the net and, as he made his way slowly to the centre circle, went round to every Brazilian player to spur them on. The impromptu pep talk worked, with Garrincha in particular working his magic down the flank to create chance after chance for Vava. Brazil were level after eight minutes, Garrincha crossing

deep for Vava to put the chance away. On half an hour the Brazilians scored an identical goal, with the same two players supplying the cross and finish.

If Vava and Garrincha had vied for the man of the match award in the first half, then Pelé made it a one horse race in the second. Ten minutes after the break he controlled the ball on his chest inside the Swedish penalty area, stepped around his man and volleyed a delightful shot straight into the goal. Others played more than a bit part thereafter, Zagallo capitalising on indecision in the Swedish defence to chase up his own cross and knock home Brazil's fourth after 68 minutes. Simonsson

reduced the arrears to two goals 10 minutes from time after good work by Gunnar Gren, but the last word had to be Pelé's. A back-heel to Zagallo set the winger clear, with Pelé matching him stride for stride, and when the cross arrived into the area, Pelé was on hand to head past Svensson for the fifth and final goal.

If there was one undying image of the 1958 World Cup, then it was the sight of Pelé in tears at the final whistle, the impact of what he had achieved at the age of seventeen hitting home. After six attempts, the only side to have competed in all the World Cup tournaments, Brazil were finally champions. And worthy champions too, in both the style of their play and the sportsmanship they displayed throughout – for their lap of honour they carried a huge Swedish national flag. The Swedish crowd might have been disappointed that their own favourites had not won, but Brazil winning was the next best thing. Brazil's first World Cup win was undoubtedly the most difficult, for no other side previously had ever won the competition on another continent. After years of stops and starts, the World Cup had finally come of age.

RESULTS

Group 1

West Germany v Argentina	3-1	Argentina v N Ireland	3-1
N Ireland v Czechoslovakia	1-0	N Ireland v West Germany	2-2
Czechoslovakia v W Germany	2-2	Czechoslovakia v Argentina	6-1

	P	W	D	L	F	A	P
West Germany	3	1	2	0	7	5	4
Czechoslovakia	3	1	1	1	8	4	3
N Ireland	3	1	1	1	4	5	3
Argentina	3	1	0	0	5	10	2

Play-Off N Ireland v Czechoslovakia 2-1

Group 2

France v Paraguay	7-3	Yugoslavia v France	3-2
Yugoslavia v Scotland	1-1	Yugoslavia v Paraguay	3-3
Paraguay v Scotland	3-2	France v Scotland	2-1

	P	W	D	L	F	A	P
France	3	2	0	1	11	7	4
Yugoslavia	3	1	2	0	7	6	4
Paraguay	3	1	1	1	9	12	3
Scotland	3	0	1	2	4	6	1

Group 3

Sweden v Mexico	3-0	Sweden v Hungary	2-1
Hungary v Wales	1-1	Sweden v Wales	0-0
Mexico v Wales	1-1	Hungary v Mexico	4-0

	P	W	D	L	F	A	P
Sweden	3	2	1	0	5	1	5
Hungary	3	1	1	1	6	3	3
Wales	3	1	1	1	6	3	3
Mexico	3	0	1	2	1	8	1

Play-Off Hungary v Wales 1-2

Group 4

England v USSR	2-2	USSR v Austria	2-0
Brazil v Austria	3-0	Brazil v USSR	2-0
Brazil v England	0-0	England v Austria	2-2

	P	W	D	L	F	A	P
Brazil	3	2	1	0	5	0	5
USSR	3	1	1	1	4	4	3
England	3	0	3	0	4	4	3
Austria	3	0	1	2	2	7	1

Play-Off England v USSR 0-1

Quarter-Finals

West Germany v Yugoslavia	1-0
France v Northern Ireland	4-0
Sweden v USSR	2-0
Brazil v Wales	1-0

SEMI-FINALS

Brazil	5	France	2
Sweden	3	West Germany	1

3rd & 4th PLACE PLAY-OFF

France	6	West Germany	3

FINAL

Brazil	5	Sweden	2

(Vava 2, Pelé 2, Zagalo)
Gilmar, D.Santos, N.Santos, Zito, Bellini, Orlando, Garrincha, Didi, Vava, Pelé, Zagalo

(Liedholm, Simonsson)
Svensson, Bergmark, Axbom, Börjesson, Gustavsson, Parling, Hamrin, Gren, Simonsson, Liedholm, Skoglund

Right
The National Stadium in Santiago Chile, where the 1962 World Cup final was held.

Below right
1962 official World Cup poster.

The 1956 FIFA Congress in Lisbon met to decide the venue for the 1962 World Cup finals tournament, with three nations submitting bids to be host country. As both the previous (1954 in Switzerland) and future (1958 in Sweden) World Cup tournaments were to be held in Europe, it was already decided that the West German application, although a sound one (they were world champions at the time they submitted their application), was going to be refused as the competition would switch back to South America. This left Chile and Argentina to contest the honour. Argentina had a better pedigree in the competition, having been runners-up in the very first tournament in 1930. They also had larger stadiums and could probably have guaranteed bigger crowds, but FIFA decided to award the competition to Chile.

Chile set about building a number of new stadiums for the tournament, with the National Stadium in Santiago the centrepiece of their construction plans. A year before the competition was due to start, however, a major earthquake rocked the country, leaving many to think that Chile would not be up to holding such a major competition. In desperation, Chilean FA President Carlos Dittborn assured FIFA 'We have nothing – that is why we must have the World Cup.' His plea touched the FIFA executive committee – the World Cup stayed in Chile.

1962
CHILE

Once again there was a new record number of entries, with fifty-six nations submitting entries for the competition. The ever expanding competition gave FIFA problems on how to whittle down the numbers to sixteen for the final competition, but it was initially announced that the places would be allocated as follows: Europe would have eight as of right, South America would have five (three places to be qualified for and the remaining two given to Brazil as holders and Chile as hosts) and North and Central America would have one place. The remaining two places would be the subject of a complex series of play-offs between winners of two European groups and the winners of groups from Africa and Asia. As both European countries won their respective play-offs, it meant no representatives from Africa or Asia and Europe lifted its total of final participants to ten.

Seven of the European groups featured three teams each, with the winners due for qualification. There was still no provision for goal difference, so in the event that two sides tied for points at the top of the group, there would be a play-off to determine who advanced. This was required for three of the groups, including Group 1, where previous hosts Sweden and Switzerland managed to beat Belgium home and away and won their respective home matches against their closest rivals. The play-off, in Berlin, saw Switzerland put out the previous tournament's runners-up with a 2-1 victory.

It required a play-off before Bulgaria were able to spring one of the major qualification surprises in Group 2. Attempting to reach the finals for the very first time, they finally beat France 1-0 in the third and crucial meeting between the two nations in Milan. The final play-off match involved Scotland, battling it out with Czechoslovakia at the top of Group 8, with the Republic of Ireland being the whipping boys of that section. Both Czechoslovakia and Scotland won their home matches against their closest rivals, requiring a third meeting, held in Brussels, before Czechoslovakia triumphed 4-2.

England were never troubled in Group 6, winning three and drawing the other in a group that featured Portugal and Luxembourg.

CAMPEONATO MUNDIAL DE FUTBOL
WORLD FOOTBALL CHAMPIONSHIP
CHAMPIONNAT MONDIAL DE FOOTBALL
COUPE JULES RIMET

CHILE 1962

Hungary registered a similar record in Group 4 in seeing off Holland and East Germany. There were 100% records from West Germany and the USSR in Groups 3 and 5 respectively, with the German victory meaning elimination for Northern Ireland.

Britain's other entrant, Wales, was in one of the groups where qualification was not quite so clear cut. Drawn against Spain, the winners of this two legged tie would then advance to meet the winners of the African sub-group home and away. A 2-1 defeat in Cardiff effectively ended Wales' interest in the competition, and although they did well to draw in Madrid 1-1 it was not enough as Spain moved on to the next stage. There they were to meet Morocco, a side who won and lost at home to Tunisia, drew the play-off and finally won through on the toss of a coin. Morocco had then met Ghana, winners of Sub-Group 3 over Nigeria, and had registered a goalless draw away and a 1-0 win at home to earn the right to meet Spain in the final. The European nation proved too strong, winning both home and away.

Group 7 had required a pre-qualifying round before the group stage proper got under way. Israel beat Cyprus at home 6-1 after a 1-1 draw and then managed to beat Ethiopia home and away to move into the group final. There they were to meet Italy, whose sub-group opponents Romania withdrew before the competition kicked off, meaning in winning home and away against Israel 4-2 and 6-0 the Italians had played only two matches to qualify for the finals.

Europe's final place in the competition proper went to Yugoslavia, who beat Poland at home 2-1 and drew away to move into the group final. Their opponent was South Korea, victors over Japan in the previous round.

South American qualification was much simpler, but that was to be expected as there were just seven countries competing for the three places available. Argentina recorded home and away wins over Ecuador to book her passage. Both Uruguay and Colombia registered home victories and away draws against their opponents, Bolivia and Peru respectively, to take the two remaining automatic places.

The final South American entrant, Paraguay, was required to meet the North and Central American group winners to contest the last place for Chile. This ultimately was Mexico, victors over the USA in Sub-Group 1 and then winners of a round robin group involving Costa Rica and Netherlands Antilles. The play-off between Mexico and Paraguay resulted in a Mexican win, victors at home by the slenderest of margins, 1-0, and holding out for a goalless draw in the second leg.

The Chilean organisers originally intended holding the final competition across nine cities, but the devastating earthquake a year before the competition was due to kick off caused a rethink, with only four cities subsequently being used. Whether it was as a direct result of the earthquake or not, attendances for most were poor, with the exception of those matches involving the hosts and holders, although the decision to raise admission prices to a much higher level than might otherwise be expected also had a detrimental effect.

It was finally decided that goal difference would be used to determine placings at the group stage. The overall format was as before; four groups of four countries each, the top two progressing into the knockout stage. Whilst the Chileans put an extreme amount of effort into the competition, it was not to be one of the best ever held, although most of the problems were beyond the capabilities of the organisers. From an attack at all costs mindset that had prevailed up to the 1958 competition, we were now seeing teams who did not want to lose; the goal tally at Chile would be one of the worst ever. In fact, with defensive football in the ascendancy, the 1962 competition ended up as one of the worst of all time from just about every consideration, with reckless tackling, on-pitch punch-ups and a host of other mishaps blighting the tournament.

Just as they had done four years previously, Brazil won two and drew the other of their three matches to top Group 3. The only point dropped came against Czechoslovakia in a goalless

draw, the closeness of the result indicating that the Czechs could be a good bet to make it all the way to the final. Czechoslovakia took second place in the group thanks to a 1-0 victory over Spain, which meant their final group match defeat by Mexico counted for little.

The winners of Group 4, Hungary, registered a similar campaign record of two wins and a draw to top the group, their victories coming over England and Bulgaria and the draw coming against Argentina. This left Argentina and England battling it out for second place and qualification for the quarter-finals. The key match was the meeting between the two sides at Rancagua, where England turned up just forty minutes before kick off, their train having been stuck behind a slow moving goods train, but settled to the task in hand quicker than their opponents. Although there were no major incidents between the two sides during the game, the physical and robust nature of some of the Argentinean tackles was an indication that the South American side often relied on literally knocking the opposition out of their stride, as England were to discover some four years later. The meeting in Chile, however, went more England's way, with Ron Flowers from the penalty spot, Bobby Charlton and Jimmy Greaves scoring the goals that put England three goals ahead. Argentina's lone response from Sanfillippo was mere consolation. Such were the vagaries of the organisation England went into their final match against Bulgaria a day after Hungary and Argentina had met in their last group matches. As the

Hungarians and Argentineans played out a goalless draw, England knew a draw or better would see them through as runners-up. In one of the most tedious displays of all in the tournament, England got no goals but did secure their point; the runners-up spot ensured them a meeting with Brazil in the quarter-finals.

The real battles were taking place in Groups 1 and 2, with the clash between the USSR and Yugoslavia leaving a Russian player with a broken leg and his dismissed assailant sent home in disgrace. With the two sides reduced to ten men for differing reasons, the Russians gained the upper hand and

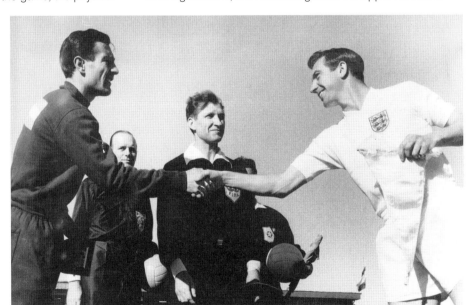

finally won 2-0. Yugoslavia recovered to win their two other matches, against Uruguay and Colombia to join their Iron Curtain comrades in the quarter-final, the USSR finishing top of the group after featuring in one of the few exciting matches of the competition, a 4-4 draw with Colombia, and then beating Uruguay 2-1.

West Germany were widely expected to dominate Group 2 and eventually did so, despite a faltering start that saw them held to a goalless draw with Italy in their opening match. The Germans recovered from this to beat both Chile and Switzerland to finish group winners. Host nation Chile had kicked off with a victory over Switzerland and so had briefly topped the group, but it was their meeting with Italy in the second round of matches that would ultimately dictate who was going to qualify out of the group. In what became known as the Battle of Santiago, Latin temperament met Latin temperament and football was the loser. Italian forward Ferrini was the first to go after only eight minutes, sent off by English referee Ken Aston for a foul but who was eventually dragged off the field, kicking and screaming by policemen. He would be joined by Chilean left winger Leonel Sanchez, who punched Humberto Maschio so hard he broke his nose. Despite the incident being picked up and beamed around the world on television, the linesman, standing only feet away, deigned to miss it. Mario David's retaliation kick at Sanchez was spotted by the officials, however, and he was sent off to join Ferrini (years later Sanchez admitted he had not been touched by the kick, but perhaps David would have been sent off for even aiming a kick at another player). With a two player advantage, Chile were able to turn this into a two goal advantage and ensure their place in the next round. Defeat in the last match, against West Germany, ensured the Germans top spot and a meeting with the Yugoslavs in the quarter-final.

All four quarter-finals were close cut affairs. In Santiago, Yugoslavia got the better of West Germany

thanks to the only goal of the game from Radakovic four minutes from time. It was a similar story in Rancagua, where presumably both Czechoslovakia and Hungary had little or no trouble from slow moving goods trains, the only goal of the game coming from Scherer to ensure Czechoslovakia's further progress. In Arica Chile made the most of the partisan crowd and some uncustomary mistakes by USSR goalkeeper Lev Yashin in overcoming the Russians 2-1, Sanchez doing all the right things in this match in scoring one of Chile's goals. The fourth quarter-final pitted Brazil, the holders and favourites, against England, who had briefly been among the favourites but had faltered through qualification. In truth, England had peaked twelve months earlier but still gave a fairly decent account of themselves in Vina Del Mar. The Brazilians were robbed of Pelé, suffering from a torn thigh muscle that would keep him out of the rest of the tournament, but in reserve they did have the likes of Garrincha, Vava and Didi. Brazil took the lead on the half hour, the five foot seven winger Garrincha out leaping the six foot one centre half Maurice Norman to head home the opener. England equalised eight minutes later, Gerry Hitchens pouncing on a rebound after Jimmy Greaves had headed against the bar. In the opening 15 minutes of the second half, however, Brazil turned on the class, grabbed goals from Vava and a second from Garrincha and effectively ended the match as a contest. A temporary halt whilst a dog ran onto the field, with Jimmy Greaves more effective in catching the rogue intruder than he was grabbing goals, enlivened the proceedings, but it was a mere sideshow for England.

The line up for the semi-finals therefore pitted the two Iron Curtain countries, Yugoslavia and Czechoslovakia together in Vina Del Mar and the two South American countries, Brazil and

Below
English referee Ken Aston sends off Italian player Mario David, while an injured Chilean player lies on the ground. This match turned out to be remarkably violent with two Italians being sent off and another having his nose broken by a punch from a Chilean player. Chile won the match 2-0.

Amarildo equalising just two minutes later, squeezing the ball in at Schroif's near post from an extremely tight angle, with Schroif fully expecting a cross and being slow to react.

On 68 minutes Brazil finally took the lead, Zito beginning the move and racing up the other end to head home Amarildo's centre. The Czechs, who had expected the main thrust of the Brazilian attack to come from the reprieved Garrincha, had battled well but could not find another way through the Brazilian defence. Their hopes were finally ended when Schroif made his second major mistake of the game, dropping Djalma Santos' lob into the area and being little more than an onlooker as Vava pounced to net a third Brazilian goal 13 minutes from time. For the Czechs, there was no way back.

Whilst the Brazilians had lacked the swagger and style of four years previously, they were not the only ones to whom such a claim could be made. The prevalence of defensive units, for whom defeat was something that was to be avoided at any cost, was sweeping across the globe. Perhaps only Brazil could be relied upon to put emphasis on attack, and they had been rewarded with successive World Cup victories. There were to be dark days before they got their hands on the trophy again.

Chile, in Santiago. Although Yugoslavia had more of the play, their inability in the final third of the pitch proved their undoing, Czechoslovakia winning 3-1 to book their place in the final. The other match saw the holders Brazil overcome a hostile atmosphere generated by the host nation Chile, winning 4-2 thanks to two goals apiece from Vava and Garrincha, but Garrincha blotted his copybook by getting himself sent off later in the game.

Chile clinched third place with a 1-0 win over Yugoslavia courtesy of a goal from Rojas. Finishing third surpassed expectations, but how much of their achievement was down to the crowd, especially in lifting the players to achieve heights previously unattainable, is a matter of some debate. Irrespective of how it was achieved, it prompted all night celebrations in the Chilean capital.

The final itself brought together Brazil and Czechoslovakia, both of whom had originally qualified from Group 3. There, as we have seen, the two sides had cancelled each other out in a goalless draw, but with both sides having second chances in the group stages, perhaps both had held something back on the day. For the final, it would be a different story. Brazil were still without the injured Pelé but were confident that his replacement, Amarildo, would give a good account of himself. The day after Brazil had secured their place in the final with victory over Chile, FIFA had met to decide the fate of Garrincha, sent off in the semi-final. Although all five players dismissed previously had been handed one game bans, Garrincha was obviously considered something of a special case – he was cleared to play in the final.

Just as they had done in Sweden, Brazil fell behind in the final, Masopust racing on to a long pass from Scherer to knock the ball past Gylmar for the opening goal on 15 minutes. Just as they had done in Sweden, Brazil recovered,

Above
Garrincha of Brazil, surrounded by Chilean players, bows his head as he leaves the field after being sent off in the World Cup semi-final.

Above far right
Zito of Brazil celebrates scoring the second goal for Brazil during the 1962 World Cup final in Santiago.

Right
Brazil pose before the World Cup final against Czechoslovakia.

RESULTS

Group 1

Uruguay v Colombia	2-1	USSR v Colombia	4-4
USSR v Yugoslavia	2-0	USSR v Uruguay	2-1
Yugoslavia v Uruguay	3-1	Yugoslavia v Colombia	5-0

	P	W	D	L	F	A	P
USSR	3	2	1	0	8	5	5
Yugoslavia	3	2	0	1	8	3	4
Uruguay	3	1	0	2	4	6	2
Columbia	3	0	1	2	5	11	1

Group 2

Chile v Switzerland	3-1	West Germany v Switzerland	2-1
Italy v West Germany	0-0	West Germany v Chile	2-0
Chile v Italy	2-0	Italy v Switzerland	3-0

	P	W	D	L	F	A	P
West Germany	3	2	1	0	4	1	5
Chile	3	2	0	1	5	3	4
Italy	3	1	1	1	3	2	3
Switzerland	3	0	0	3	2	8	0

Group 3

Brazil v Mexico	2-0	Spain v Mexico	1-0
Czechoslovakia v Spain	1-0	Brazil v Spain	2-1
Brazil v Czechoslovakia	0-0	Mexico v Czechoslovakia	3-1

	P	W	D	L	F	A	P
Brazil	3	2	1	0	4	1	5
Czechoslovakia	3	1	1	1	2	3	3
Mexico	3	1	0	2	3	4	2
Spain	3	1	0	2	2	3	2

Group 4

Argentina v Bulgaria	1-0	Hungary v Bulgaria	6-1
Hungary v England	2-1	Argentina v Hungary	0-0
England v Argentina	3-1	Bulgaria v England	0-0

	P	W	D	L	F	A	P
Hungary	3	2	1	0	8	2	5
England	3	1	1	1	4	3	3
Argentina	3	1	1	1	2	3	3
Bulgaria	3	0	1	2	1	7	1

Quarter-Finals

Brazil v England	3-1
Chile v USSR	2-1
Yugoslavia v West Germany	1-0
Czechoslovakia v Hungary	1-0

SEMI-FINALS

Brazil	4	Chile	2
Czechoslovakia	3	Yugoslavia	1

3rd & 4th PLACE PLAY-OFF

Chile	1	Yugoslavia	0

FINAL

Brazil	3	Czechoslovakia	1

(Amarildo, Zito, Vava)   (Masopust)

Gilmar, D.Santos, Mauro, Zozimo, N.Santos, Zito, Garrincha, Didi, Vava, Amarildo, Zagalo

Schrojf, Tichy, Novak, Pluskal, Popluhar, Masopust, Pospichal, Scherer, Kvasnak, Kadraba, Jelinek

1966
ENGLAND

Right
1966 official World Cup poster.

Below right
Alf Ramsey prior to the 1966 World Cup.

With the World Cup finals due to return to Europe and the English Football Association celebrating their centenary in 1963, easily the longest established football association in the world, there was only one possible venue for the 1966 tournament and England was duly ratified as the host in 1960. This, you will recall, was a time when the England manager was manager in name only, with the squad being selected by a committee and the manager, Walter Winterbottom, supposed to make the best out of the players put at his disposal. By the time preparations began for the 1966 World Cup, all that had changed. The crunch had come after the 1962 tournament, when England had faltered at the quarter-final stage once again, with the Daily Mail declaring 'If England are ever to approach the standard of the magnificent Brazilians it is vital that our whole way of soccer life, from the players and club angle, must change.'

Walter Winterbottom duly resigned after seventeen years in charge of the team and the search began for his replacement. Jimmy Adamson of Burnley, a relatively successful club manager, was widely expected to receive the call, but he chose to remain in club football in the north-west and with his family rather than spend long periods in London (where the FA were headquartered) and elsewhere checking on players. Eventually the Football Association turned to a former player, Alf Ramsey, then manager at Ipswich Town. Ramsey's credentials were impeccable, having won the League championship as a player (with Spurs) and manager (Ipswich Town) and having won 32 caps during his playing career. But Alf Ramsey would only take the job under his own terms – he and he alone would pick the squad and thereafter the team. He would allow no outside influence, as would be revealed during the tournament itself, and as he would give unhesitating loyalty to his players, he would expect it back from them. Whilst Walter Winterbottom had relied on his previous training as a former Wing Commander in the RAF to keep the players under control, Alf came across, at least to the players, as one of the lads. 'Call me Alf' he answered when asked what they should call him at one of his earliest team get-togethers.

His reign as manager got off to the worst possible start with a 5-2 defeat by France in the 1964 European Championship qualifying tournament, which duly saw England eliminated from the competition. His promise that England would win the World Cup seemed the height of folly, but Alf Ramsey had good reason to believe his side would fare well, not least because for the first time they were spared the inconvenience of having to qualify, joining holders Brazil as the two nations to have automatic qualification for the finals. In fact, both England and Brazil were put into the qualifying draw, but the draw was rigged in such a way that both countries were placed in a group on their own, thus ensuring their smooth passage into the finals!

Once again the number of entries reached record levels, with seventy-one nations submitting entries to the competition. Once again the qualifying competition threw up surprises and was rocked by mass withdrawals before sixteen nations emerged to compete in the finals. Europe again provided the bulk of the entries, with thirty-two countries, followed by a combined African, Asian and Australian section with twenty, then South America with ten and finally North, Central America and the Caribbean with nine. Europe was awarded a total of ten places in the finals

(nine plus England), South America four (three plus Brazil) and a place apiece for the combined African, Asian and Australian section and North, Central America and Caribbean.

All sixteen African countries duly withdrew, with South Africa subsequently being suspended for violating FIFA's anti-discrimination codes, which left only three teams competing in the African, Asian and Australian section! Then South Korea announced that they wished to concentrate on the 1968 Olympics (in truth they did not wish to play against bitter rivals North Korea), leaving only Australia and North Korea to compete for the one place allocated to these three continents. Home and away victories for North Korea earned them a place in the finals for the first and so far only time – they would however make a lasting impression on the final tournament.

South America's ten entrants were placed into four groups; Brazil the sole occupant of Group 14 and the remaining nine sides in three groups of three. Uruguay, Chile and Argentina had better pedigrees than any of their rivals and duly won their respective groups, although Chile needed a play-off against Ecuador before they finally emerged triumphant.

The nine North, Central American and Caribbean countries were similarly placed into three groups of three teams each, with the winners of each group then going into a final round robin tournament to decide who qualified. Jamaica, Costa Rica and Mexico duly won their groups and the final competition quickly settled into a straight battle between Mexico and Costa Rica, with the Mexicans earning a goalless draw in Costa Rica and winning 1-0 at home to take their place in the finals.

It was Europe that provided the shock, with the previous tournament's runners-up Czechoslovakia coming second to Portugal in Group 4 and being eliminated. The damage was done when the Portuguese won 1-0 in Czechoslovakia to take early command of the group and finally finished two points ahead of the Czechs. In Group 1 Belgium would have won with ease ahead of Bulgaria if goal difference had applied, but instead a play-off in Florence was required before the Bulgarians surprisingly won 2-1.

The other British entries suffered agonising qualifying competitions, with all three finishing runners-up in their respective groups. Wales were eliminated by the USSR by some four points, their rally too late to alter the course of the group. But both Scotland and Northern Ireland were in with a shout right up to the bitter end. In Group 8 Scotland ran

the Italians all the way, with both sides being tied on seven points going into the last match, which pitted the Italians against the Scots in Naples. Needing a big performance from their biggest stars, Scotland crumbled to a 3-0 defeat and an exit from the competition. Northern Ireland were similarly level on points with Switzerland going into their final matches, with the Swiss at home to Holland and Northern Ireland away in Albania. The Swiss duly beat Holland 2-1, so if Northern Ireland could get a win against Group 6's whipping boys, they would at least earn a play-off chance. The result was a disastrous 1-1 draw in Tirana, the only point Albania picked up in the competition!

West Germany, France and Hungary had relatively easy passages through the group stage to earn their place in the finals. England, of course, had the easiest passage of all in Group 10 as the only team in that group. The final European group and thus a place in the finals fell down to a three way battle between Spain, the Republic of Ireland and Syria. Syria withdrew before the competition could get under way, leaving the group down to two. The Republic of Ireland won 1-0 in Dublin, lost 4-2 in Seville but still earned a play-off, which they also lost 1-0 in Paris.

Unlike other host countries England decided to use existing grounds on which to play the competition, giving huge grants to those clubs fortunate enough to have their ground

Below
Old Trafford was among the existing grounds used for the World Cup.

selected. The only certainty was that England, regardless of what group they were placed in, would play their matches at Wembley. Group 2 would be played at Villa Park (home of Aston Villa) and Hillsborough (Sheffield Wednesday), the traditional FA Cup semi-final venues. Group 3 would be played at Goodison Park (Everton) and Old Trafford (Manchester United), whilst Group 4 was located at Ayresome Park (Middlesbrough) and Roker Park (Sunderland).

If the lasting memory of the 1966 tournament is that it was

impeccably organised, then the truth is somewhat different. The problems first began in March, when the World Cup trophy itself was the centrepiece of a stamp exhibition at the Central Hall, Westminster. Sometime during 20th March, Mothering Sunday, a thief broke into the hall and stole the trophy! The trophy, which was insured for £30,000 but held to be priceless, was the only item stolen in the raid, despite the fact that the stamps on display were worth some £3 million. Over 100 police officers from New Scotland Yard were assigned to the case, but after a week were no nearer finding the elusive trophy than they had been on day one. Then, the following Sunday, Thames lighterman David Corbett was out for

a walk with his dog Pickles on Beulah Hill, a London suburb of Norwood, when he noticed his dog sniffing at a bush. Intrigued as to what had caught the dog's attention, he peered into the bush and was surprised to see the legend 'Brazil 1962' staring up at him. The trophy was duly returned to the FA and Pickles received a medal from the National Canine Defence League whilst a dog food company donated a year's supply of canine delights. According to legend, the FA commissioned a gold plated replica trophy and kept the real thing under lock and key until it was actually needed.

Stamps were to rear their ugly heads again. The Post Office planned to release a special commemorative stamp, depicting the flags of each of the sixteen finalists, until it was pointed out by the Foreign Office that North Korea was not officially recognised by the British government! A generic series of four stamps was released instead. Finally, it had been planned that all six matches in Group 1, England's group, would be played at Wembley, but as the tournament grew closer, it suddenly dawned that the stadium was not technically available on the 15th July, when Uruguay were due to meet France, as Wembley would be staging its regular greyhound racing evening. Although the rest of the country had caught World Cup fever, the Greyhound Racing Association refused to cancel their meeting, meaning the FA had to find an alternative venue for the match. Despite the claims of Highbury and White Hart Lane, two London based grounds that could accommodate over 50,000 fans, the FA chose the White City, a venue originally built for the 1908 Olympic Games which, in a bizarre turn of events, was now used more regularly for greyhound racing!

With the trophy in place, assorted dignitaries assembled and the world watching, England kicked off the 1966 World Cup finals against Uruguay on 11th July, although once again there was a last minute scare – it had been decided that each player would have an identity card that would have to be presented to the match referee before the kick off to verify that the players turning out were who they said they were. Half the England team left theirs at their hotel, resulting in a police outrider being despatched to the Royal Garden Hotel in Knightsbridge to collect the missing cards! He got back in time to satisfy the referee and the match kicked off, although the game itself proved to be hardly worth the effort – Uruguay kept as many as ten men behind the ball, showed little sign of wanting to attack and thwarted England at every turn – the match ended goalless. Uruguay would score only two goals in their three group games, concede only one but still manage to finish second and qualify for the quarter-finals. They, more than anyone, epitomised the way the game was heading in the future. Group 1 was, however, won by England, whose 2-0 victories over both Mexico and France ensured them qualification for the next stage, although it was not all plain sailing. The match against France proved especially troublesome, with Nobby Stiles' horrendous challenge on Jacques Simon leading to calls for the player to be expelled from the tournament. It was Alf Ramsey who leapt to the player's defence, stating 'If Stiles goes, I go', which had the FA backing down. Jimmy Greaves, perhaps the finest goalscorer of the age, suffered a gash on his shin during the same match, a gash that would keep him out of the next two matches, with disastrous consequences for the player later. Another player who bowed out of the 1966 tournament was Mexican goalkeeper Antonio Carbajal, whose eleven appearances for his country in the finals had come in the 1950, 1954, 1958, 1962 and 1966 competitions, a longevity record unlikely to be challenged in the future, even allowing for the fact that goalkeepers tend to play on for longer than their outfield counterparts.

Group 2 was, just like Group 1, a head to head battle between a major European nation (West Germany) and a major South American nation in Argentina. West Germany finally emerged triumphant courtesy of a superior goal difference, although both sides had registered two wins and a draw in their three matches.

England's exploits aside, most attention was placed on Group 3, where holders Brazil were pitted against three European countries in Portugal, Hungary and Bulgaria. Brazil laboured to a 2-0 victory over Bulgaria in their opening match, scoring both from free kicks from Pelé and a slowing Garrincha. It was Pelé who suffered most, however, being the target for some tackles that bordered on assault throughout the match. Portugal thumped Hungary 3-0 in their opening match, meaning the Hungarians had to get something out of their next match if they harboured any thoughts of progression. That match pitted them against Brazil, minus the injured Pelé, and Brazil went down to their first World Cup defeat since 1954 (which was against Hungary!), beaten 3-1 at Goodison Park in front of a bewildered crowd. Portugal meanwhile scored a second 3-0 victory over Bulgaria to eliminate the East Europeans and put themselves in pole position in the group. Avoiding defeat against Brazil would ensure they topped the group, defeat would mean the possibility that three teams would tie with four points apiece. The Brazilians left nothing to chance, their ten man selection committee making nine changes to the side, including the recall of a patently unfit Pelé, and could only watch as it backfired. If Pelé had been in the wars against Bulgaria, it was

Above far left
A security guard hands over the Jules Rimet trophy to Ernie Allen at Central Hall before the World Cup.

Below far left
David Corbett smiles as he shows the spot where his dog "Pickles" found the Jules Rimet trophy.

Middle
England get the 1966 World Cup off to a start against Uruguay.

Above
Nobby Stiles kicks the ball over his head to avoid Robert Budzinski of France.

Of the four quarter-finals, only the USSR and Hungary clash at Roker Park passed without major incident or talking point. Despite their sometimes excellent play in the group matches, including their victory over Brazil, Hungary fell 2-1, undone by some poor goalkeeping by Gelei. Indeed, it was generally agreed that had the Hungarians had a goalkeeper of the Russian Yashin's calibre, they would have won, for in the likes of Albert and Bene they had strikers of true class.

For on the field action, the place to be was Goodison Park where the surprise package of North Korea raced into a 3-0 lead over Portugal, confounding all the critics who felt they would suffer a heavy defeat. Naivety did for them in the end, for Eusebio began carving great holes in the Korean defence and finally rattled in four goals, two from the penalty spot, as the Portuguese responded with five goals of their own.

At Hillsborough Uruguay started strongly against the West Germans, hitting the bar and having a good penalty claim turned down when Karl-Heinz Schnellinger handled underneath the crossbar. Despite Uruguayan protestations, English referee Jim Finney waved play on and that seemed to be the signal for the Uruguayans to lose their composure.

nothing compared to what was dished out by the Portuguese, with Vicente leaving him a hobbling passenger after half an hour and Morais finishing the job off before half time. Pelé returned later on in the game but could do little or nothing to inspire or alter events, Brazil slipping to a 3-1 defeat and elimination in all but name, which was confirmed three days later when Hungary expectedly beat the Bulgarians 3-1. This, according to the South Americans collectively, was the first conspiracy against them in the tournament.

South America's final entrant in the competition, Chile, finished bottom of Group 4, although there was not the same kind of rough treatment meted out to their players – they were woefully inept without the need for any of their opponents to resort to strong arm tactics, picking up just one point in a 1-1 draw with North Korea. The North Koreans may not have been recognised by the British government, and if truth be told wouldn't have been recognised by the British public if they spotted them walking down the street, but the Ayresome Park crowd took them to their hearts, none more so than when they handed out the biggest shock of the tournament in beating the Italians 1-0 through Pak Doo Ik to qualify for the quarter-finals and eliminate the Italians into the bargain. The USSR capitalised on the failure of the Italians, topping the group with three straight wins, whilst all the Italians had to look forward to was being bombarded by rotten vegetables when they returned home!

Above
The Bulgarian goalkeeper Georgi Naidenov leaps for the ball after the Brazilian footballer Garrincha scores at Goodison Park, Liverpool.

Above inset
Pelé writhes in pain, having been injured in a tackle during the World Cup game against Portugal.

Right
Italian goalkeeper Enrico Albertosi fails to save a shot from North Korean Pak Doo Ik.

Encouraged at almost every turn by the Germans, the Uruguayans retaliated and were promptly punished, finishing the 90 minutes having lost two men and four goals.

It was at Wembley that the real drama unfolded, where England faced Argentina. Alf Ramsey had rung the changes, dropping winger Ian Callaghan for the more all-action style of Alan Ball and brought in Geoff Hurst in place of the injured Jimmy Greaves. It was however the constant confrontations between Argentinean captain Antonio Rattin and referee Rudolf Kreitlein that ultimately dictated the outcome of the match. Rattin was quick to put himself in the face of Kreitlein at every opportunity, earning himself an early booking. Despite the warning Rattin kept up the confrontational attitude, so much so that nine minutes before half time, Kreitlein had had enough and ordered Rattin off the field. Except Rattin didn't want to go, and for fully ten minutes stood arguing with the referee, linesmen, officials and even policemen brought onto the pitch to escort him off. Eventually, accompanied by boos from the entire crowd

and a barrage of fruit, he took the long walk back to the dressing room. Even down to ten men the Argentines were a tough nut to crack, Geoff Hurst finally heading home the only goal of the game 12 minutes from the end. When the final whistle blew, Alf Ramsey raced on to the pitch in order to

Right
Bobby Charlton scores England's second goal as Portugal's Jose Carlos runs in to try and intercept during the World Cup semi-final match at Wembley.

Below
West German sriker Uwe Seeler leaps over Russian goalkeeper Lev Yashin while Vasily Danilov watches during the World Cup semi-final at Goodison Park.

Below right
England goalkeeper Gordon Banks goes the wrong way as Portuguese star Eusebio scores from a penalty, giving Portugal their only goal in the World Cup semi-final.

prevent any of his players swapping shirts with their counterparts, calling them 'animals' in his post-match interview and being ordered to retract his comments by the FA. The truth was as Ramsey described it however, for after the match a chair was thrown through the glass door in the England dressing room and several Argentine players tried to force their way in looking for a fight. Many years later it was revealed that even Bobby Charlton, normally the most placid of players, had been booked during the match, although even he couldn't remember the incident!

Once back in South America, both Uruguay and Argentina claimed there had been a conspiracy against them, with both sides having been defeated by European countries with a European official in charge. There was even talk of a South American walkout from FIFA over the issue, although nothing came of it. FIFA, however, exacted their own revenge, banning Rattin for four matches for refusing to leave the field, Onega for three for spitting in the face of an official and recommending that should Argentina apply to enter the 1970 competition it be refused unless certain assurances were made with regard to the conduct of their players and officials. Presumably those assurances were met; Argentina competed in 1970.

The tactics the West Germans had used to overcome Uruguay were again in evidence in their semi-final against the USSR, but this time the Russians gave as good as they got. Had Igor Chislenko, the Russian striker not been sent off the Russians might have registered a major surprise, but eventually goals from Beckenbauer and Haller took Germany into the final with a 2-1 victory.

After the horrors of the quarter-final, Wembley got to stage the match of the tournament in the other semi-final, that which

pitted England against Portugal. Despite the prize that was on offer, a place in the World Cup final, the match was played with exceptionally good spirit – there wasn't a foul of any description for the first 23 minutes, and Portugal didn't commit one until nearly an hour had elapsed. The Portuguese had grown in stature as the competition progressed, being installed as the new favourites after the departure of Brazil, but Alf Ramsey's tactical awareness, where Nobby Stiles shackled Eusebio without having to resort to fouling, upset the Portuguese rhythm. With

their opponents' attack blunted, England could concentrate on getting goals at the other end, and Bobby Charlton duly obliged with two, the second a thunderbolt shot that was struck so sweetly even a few of the Portuguese players shook his hand as he made his way back to the halfway line! It really was that kind of match; a feast of football, pure and simple, in what had been an unremarkable tournament up until then. English hearts were caused to flutter in the final few minutes, Eusebio reducing

the arrears to a single goal from the penalty spot after Jack Charlton had handled, but the defence held firm and the final whistle was the signal for one or two tears of joy from the England camp, disappointment from the Portuguese one.

Portugal got some consolation two days later, beating the USSR 2-1 to take third place, Eusebio adding a further goal from the penalty spot to ensure his place at the top of the goalscoring chart with nine goals.

And so to Wembley for the final. A crowd of 100,000 was crammed into the stadium and some 600 million were watching on television – what they saw and what they have debated ever since has entered folklore. Although Jimmy Greaves had recovered from injury, Alf Ramsey resisted the temptation to bring him back into the side. Whilst popular belief is that Geoff Hurst kept him out of the side, the reality is that Roger Hunt was most at risk at losing his place. Ramsey also decided against recalling any of his wingers, settling on a 4-4-2 formation that made England extremely difficult to score against. Ramsey's biggest tactical victory however, came from the German decision to assign Franz Beckenbauer to mark Bobby Charlton – Beckenbauer was certainly more than capable of doing the job but it robbed the Germans of his own attacking prowess, which had already netted him four goals.

Both sides started cautiously, perhaps afraid to make a mistake, but after 12 minutes Ray Wilson made his only one of the tournament, weakly heading out a cross to the unmarked Helmut Haller who shot home

Above
The England World Cup squad, including Martin Peters, Geoff Hurst and Bobby Charlton, relaxing the day before the final.

Left
Portuguese footballer Eusebio being led off the pitch in tears after England beat Portugal 2-1.

Above
England and West Germany enter the pitch at Wembley.

Above right
Martin Peters scores the second goal for England.

Above far right
England celebrate winning the World Cup with a lap of honour carrying the Jules Rimet trophy.

Right & inset
Geoff Hurst scores England's third goal. Was it over the line?

the opening goal. Five minutes later England drew level, Bobby Moore quickly whipping in a free kick for Geoff Hurst to head home whilst the Germans were still organising their defence. England were the stronger side thereafter and deservedly took the lead with some 12 minutes left on the clock, Alan Ball sending in a corner that ran on to Hurst. His shot was blocked, but it arched up invitingly for Martin Peters to hammer home what appeared to be the decisive winning goal.

With the clock running down, the Germans' efforts became more and more desperate. As the game moved into injury time, Jackie Charlton was harshly penalised for a foul on Held, although Charlton protested his innocence. Emmerich's free kick appeared to be helped on by Schnellinger's hand before arriving at the foot of Weber at the far post and helped over the line for an improbable equaliser.

England appeared crestfallen at being robbed so close to the prize, but Ramsey's motivational skills came to the fore. 'You've beaten them once, now go and do it again' he told them. Nearly forty years later, what happened during the first half of extra time is known the length and breadth of the country and debated still. Geoff Hurst received the ball inside the German penalty area, spun and fired a shot goalwards that cannoned off the underneath of the crossbar, bounced down onto the goal line to be greeted with cheers and cries of 'goal' from the England players and crowd. The referee Gottfried Dienst wasn't so sure but decided to consult with the nearest linesman, the Russian Tofik Bakhramov (who according to legend had fought against the Germans during the Second World War!), who had been badly positioned some 10 yards from the goal line and 50 yards from the goal but was convinced enough to signal that he thought it a goal. Had that been the last of the scoring, then the controversy

would still be raging today (and in some parts of Germany it no doubt still does!), but in the final moments, Geoff Hurst latched on to a considered clearance from Bobby Moore, ignored the presence of the chasing German defender and a few of the crowd who had run on to the pitch and fired home

the fourth and final goal (he also completed the perfect hat trick, scoring with each foot and a header). It is debatable who benefited more from the goal; Geoff Hurst, who scored it, or commentator Kenneth Wolstenholme, whose words 'There are some people on the pitch, they think it's all over – it is now', as Hurst scored, are as much a part of the 1966 folklore as Pickles, Eusebio and Rattin.

Captain Bobby Moore made his way up the steps at Wembley for the third consecutive year (he had picked up the FA Cup and European Cup Winners Cup for West Ham in 1964 and 1965) to collect the greatest prize of all, pausing to thoughtfully wipe the sweat off his hand before extending it towards Queen Elizabeth II and receiving the trophy. It was recently claimed, many years after the event, that as Bobby Moore made his way back down to the pitch, the trophy was switched with the replica commissioned by the FA, just in case a thief more audacious than the one who had swooped at Central Hall might be prowling, but with more than a 100,000 witnesses nothing untoward was likely.

Regardless of the claims of the South Americans, who believed England won as a result of a conspiracy, and the debate about the third goal in the final, England were worthy winners, growing in confidence as the competition progressed and reserving their better performances for when it really mattered. More than anything it proved the abilities of manager Alf Ramsey, who took a side that had probably only three, possibly four truly world class players and fashioned all of them into world champions. Just as he said he would when he took over as manager two years previously.

RESULTS

Group 1

England v Uruguay	0-0	
France v Mexico	1-1	
Uruguay v France	2-1	

England v Mexico	2-0	
Mexico v Uruguay	0-0	
England v France	2-0	

	P	W	D	L	F	A	P
England	3	2	1	0	4	0	5
Uruguay	3	1	2	0	2	1	4
Mexico	3	0	2	1	1	3	2
France	3	0	1	2	2	5	1

Group 2

West Germany v Switzerland	5-0	
Argentina v Spain	2-1	
Spain v Switzerland	2-1	

West Germany v Argentina	0-0	
Argentina v Switzerland	2-0	
West Germany v Spain	2-1	

	P	W	D	L	F	A	P
West Germany	3	2	1	0	7	1	5
Argentina	3	2	1	0	4	1	5
Spain	3	1	0	2	4	5	2
Switzerland	3	0	0	3	1	9	0

Group 3

Brazil v Bulgaria	2-0	
Portugal v Hungary	3-1	
Hungary v Brazil	3-1	

Portugal v Bulgaria	3-0	
Portugal v Brazil	3-1	
Hungary v Bulgaria	3-1	

	P	W	D	L	F	A	P
Portugal	3	3	0	0	9	2	6
Hungary	3	2	0	1	7	5	4
Brazil	3	1	0	2	4	6	2
Bulgaria	3	0	0	3	1	8	0

Group 4

USSR v North Korea	3-0	
Italy v Chile	2-0	
Chile v North Korea	1-1	

USSR v Italy	1-0	
North Korea v Italy	1-0	
USSR v Chile	2-1	

	P	W	D	L	F	A	P
USSR	3	3	0	0	6	1	6
North Korea	3	1	1	1	2	4	3
Italy	3	1	0	2	2	2	2
Chile	3	0	1	2	2	5	1

Quarter-Finals

West Germany v Uruguay	4-0
USSR v Hungary	2-1
Portugal v North Korea	5-3
England v Argentina	1-0

SEMI-FINALS

West Germany	2	USSR	1
England	2	Portugal	1

3rd & 4th PLACE PLAY-OFF

Portugal	2	USSR	1

FINAL

England	4	West Germany	2

(Hurst 3, Peters)

(Haller, Weber)

Banks, Cohen, Wilson, Stiles, J.Charlton, Moore, Ball, Hurst, R.Charlton, Hunt, Peters

Tilkowski, Höttges, Weber, Schulz, Schnellinger, Beckenbauer, Haller, Overath, Seeler, Held, Emmerich

The contest to host the 1970 World Cup finals was a two-horse race between Mexico and Argentina, with the latter pointing out their slightly better pedigree in the competition. They also pointed out that they had put forward a compelling case for hosting the 1962 tournament, only to be beaten by Chile in the final reckoning. There was to be further disappointment for Argentina this time too, for at the 1964 Olympic Games in Tokyo, FIFA ratified the choice of Mexico as hosts for the World Cup, a decision taken because Mexico was already hosting the 1968 Olympic Games.

The decision, extremely unpopular within Argentina, was not greeted with much enthusiasm elsewhere either, not least because it meant that competing teams would have to contend with blistering heat and high altitude. Add to this the at times volatile tournaments that had

1970
MEXICO

taken place in 1962 and 1966, especially when a South American side had faced a European one and there were those contemplating little more than a perpetual bloodbath. They needn't have worried, for the 1970 World Cup finals turned out to be one of the most exiting, adventurous and enjoyable competitions both before and since.

Both England and Mexico were spared the difficulty of having to qualify, being given safe passage as holders and hosts respectively (although just as in 1966, both were in the

hat for the qualification process, England being assigned Group 9 and Mexico Group 14, the only teams in their groups). For once the number of entrants fell, down by one from the previous tournament at seventy nations. Europe's thirty applicants were given a total of nine places (eight plus England), South America's ten countries received three places, the Central and North American Federation CONCACAF's twelve entries given two places (one plus Mexico), Asia/Oceania's seven nations afforded one place, as were the eleven African countries.

Once again Israel proved something of a problem, with many countries making it known they would not play against them. As a result, Israel were placed in the Asia/Oceania sub-group B with North Korea and New Zealand, but North Korea were eliminated from the group for refusing to play Israel. The Israelis beat New Zealand home and away to qualify for the final, a meeting with Australia. Australia's route to the final had also been rocked with political issues; their second round match against Rhodesia had to be played in Mozambique because no country recognised Rhodesia and would not travel to the country for fixtures! Australia finally won after a play-off but lost out to Israel in the final, losing 1-0 away and only drawing 1-1 at home. Israel, the country no one wanted to play, qualified for the finals in Mexico.

With the exception of England as holders, all the home countries suffered elimination in the qualifiers. Wales finished bottom of their group, with Italy shading it ahead of East Germany. Both Northern Ireland and Scotland were in with a shout of qualifying but lost out in the final round of matches; Scotland lost their last two 3-2 against West Germany and 2-0 in Austria and finished four points behind the Germans, whilst Northern Ireland went down 2-0 in Moscow and finished two points adrift of the Russians in Group 4. The Republic of

Left
The 1970 World
Cup Opening
Ceremony.

Below
Members of
England's squad in
training before the
World Cup.
With them is World
Cup Winston, a
bulldog who was
the English team
mascot.

Ireland fared no better, bottom of a group, dominated by Hungary and Czechoslovakia, that Czechoslovakia finally won after a play-off in Marseille. They were joined by Romania, Sweden (who knocked out the French), Belgium (who did for Spain and Yugoslavia) and Bulgaria (victors ahead of Poland and Holland).

The real drama came in the CONCACAF section, where the thirteen original entrants were placed into four groups, the four winners moving into a knockout stage. Haiti beat the USA home and away to book their place in the final, whilst the other tie between Honduras and El Salvador needed a third match before El Salvador finally won 3-2, but so intense had been the clash the two countries went to war for four days in the immediate aftermath! Although the skirmish became known as the Football War, there had been border disputes between the two countries previously; football provided a convenient excuse for some pent-up frustration being released.

Brazil won their group in South America with a 100% record, offering proof that they would be a force to be reckoned with come the finals. They were joined by Peru who, inspired by Brazilian manager Didi, saw off the Argentineans and Uruguay.

According to England manager Sir Alf Ramsey (he was knighted after England's triumph in 1966), he had an even better squad in 1970 than that that had won the competition four years earlier. Only six of the 1966 winners were still regulars in the side, but the likes of Gordon Banks and Bobby Moore had actually improved their reputations and stature in the game following that victory. England's preparations for the tournament commenced more than a year before the tournament kicked off with something of a fact-finding mission into South America with matches against Mexico, Uruguay and Brazil. Whilst the results were at best mediocre (England drew 0-0 with Mexico, beat Uruguay 2-1 and lost to Brazil by the same score), it was Ramsey's attitude that would cause

problems, for his abrasive style was not appreciated by either the local populace or journalists in Mexico and would be paid back with interest when the competition proper kicked off.

Problems began to mount before England even arrived, with Bobby Moore being arrested for supposedly stealing a gold bracelet from a store in Bogota, Colombia. Although the episode was quite obviously a stunt of some sort (Bobby Charlton was supposedly cast in the role of look-out man whilst the theft supposedly took place!), Moore had to spend some four days in jail and was then confined to the British Embassy before the matter was settled. When England did finally arrive in Mexico, further mud was flung in the direction of Jeff Astle, who dismounted from the plane seemingly the worse for drink, which he had taken to overcome the fear of flying.

England journeyed to their base at Guadalajara stoking up controversy in their wake. Whilst many other countries had gone on a charm offensive with the Mexican hosts, England had done what every Englishman did abroad at that time; tried to recreate a Little England. Thus supplies of beefburgers, sausages, chips and other typically English foodstuffs would protect the players' stomachs and Ramsey, known to hate almost everything that was foreign, even had a British coach and driver shipped over for the competition to drive them around!

The competition kicked off with a spectacular opening ceremony involving some 50,000 balloons and a drab match between Mexico and the USSR that was high on yellow cards but low on action – it finished goalless. The only way after that was up, and all sixteen teams played their part in turning the competition into a true feast of football.

After their stale opening, both the Mexicans and Russians improved, finishing joint group winners ahead of Belgium and El Salvador. The Russians were given top place thanks to having scored one more goal than the Mexicans, but the hosts did not concede a goal in any of their three matches.

By contrast, goals were thin on the ground in Group 2, where Italy finished group winners despite scoring only one goal! A 1-0 win over Sweden was accompanied by goalless draws against Uruguay and Israel to earn four points and top place. They would be joined in the quarter-finals by Uruguay, who only managed two goals and three points but qualified ahead of the Swedes with three points but having conceded one more goal than the Uruguayans.

England also found goals difficult to come by, opening their campaign

with a 1-0 win over Romania courtesy of a Geoff Hurst goal. The Brazilians showed how they were going to dominate the group with a 4-1 demolition of Czechoslovakia, with Pelé, much better protected than he had been in 1966, new revelation Jairzinho and centre forward Tostao, who had recovered from a potentially career-threatening eye injury, particularly impressive. Indeed, the highlight of the match was a shot that didn't go in – Pelé spotting the goalkeeper off his line and firing goalwards from the halfway line!

The two giants of Group 3 met five days later in one of the most eagerly anticipated of all World Cup matches. England's task wasn't helped by the fact that a Mexican crowd had camped outside their headquarters the night before and chanted and honked their car horns in order to disrupt the players' sleep – midway through the night the squad had to be moved to another part of the hotel. With television such a dominant part of the proceedings the kick off was scheduled for midday, a time when the heat and the sun would be at their highest. Although England in particular were not used to such conditions the two sides produced something of a classic, with the battle between Pelé and Bobby Moore perhaps one of the finest man to man clashes ever produced in world football. Moore had his best game in an England shirt, Pelé produced a few flashes of brilliance but they were both eventually eclipsed by Gordon Banks, who produced a breathtaking save from a Pelé header that even had Pelé applauding. Brazil did find a way through thanks to Jairzinho, but England also had chances; Astle missed a virtual open goal and Alan Ball hit the bar. When the final whistle sounded and Pelé and Moore swapped shirts, most of the watching world was convinced the two sides would be meeting again in the final. Both made sure

of their progress into the quarter-finals, England beating Czechoslovakia 1-0 through a penalty from Allan Clarke and Brazil beat Romania 3-2.

The fourth and final group was equally entertaining, with West Germany winning all three of their matches, scoring 10 goals in the process against Peru, Bulgaria and Morocco. The battle for second place was won by Peru, coming from behind against the Bulgarians (losing 2-0 they recovered to win 3-2 with a style reminiscent of Brazil, as one would expect with Didi as their manager) and easily overcoming the Moroccans 3-0.

The quarter-finals saw the Uruguayans finally get the better of the Russians with a goal in extra time, but it was the three other ties that provided the drama. In Toluca home interest in the competition was ended with a 4-1 victory for Italy, finally finding their goalscoring form. The match was not as one-sided as the scoreline suggests, for the two sides were level at half time and only the Italians' experience pulled them through in the second half.

In Guadalajara Brazil beat Peru 4-2 in a match that was an education in attacking football. Tostao was the hero on the day with two goals for Brazil, but the part played by Peru, especially the likes of Chumpitaz, Cubillas and Gallardo made the match the spectacle it was.

Above
Brazil's captain Carlos Alberto, and England's captain Bobby Moore prior to their World Cup match in the Jalisco Stadium.

Above right
The save, of all saves. Gordon Banks stops a header from Pelé.

Right
Jairzinho of Brazil rounds Luis Rubinos of Peru to score the fourth goal during their World Cup quarter-final.

Meanwhile, in Leon, England met West Germany in a repeat of the 1966 final, with one or two amendments. The English camp was rocked by a mysterious illness to Gordon Banks, who had a few days previously drunk a bottle of beer and then gone down with a stomach upset. That he was the only player so affected has long been the subject of speculation, but in his place Ramsey called up Chelsea goalkeeper Peter Bonetti. Both sides paraded five players who had featured in the final, with Beckenbauer again given the job of marking Bobby Charlton, but it was Alan Mullery, playing in the role previously occupied by Nobby Stiles, who opened the scoring for England. Five minutes into the second half England went further ahead through Martin Peters and it seemed to be job done as far as England were concerned, not least because no side put out by Alf Ramsey had lost a two goal lead. Although Beckenbauer forgot about marking Charlton for long enough to round Mullery and reduce the arrears, England did not appear overstretched. Then came the substitutions (this was the first competition at which substitutes were allowed, turning the game into a 13 man affair) that would haunt Ramsey for the rest of his days. Deciding both to rest key players for future matches and to introduce fresher legs, Charlton gave way to Colin Bell and Martin Peters was replaced by Norman Hunter. With Beckenbauer at last free to roam as he knew best, the Germans began creating opening after opening and Seeler got an equaliser with a freak header that eluded the stranded Bonetti, caught in no-man's land. Ramsey delivered a repeat

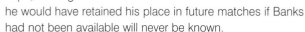

of his 'You've beaten them once' message and watched as England took the initiative in extra time, looking to have scored a good goal through Hurst (who else!) that was mysteriously disallowed before Gerd Muller scored the ultimate winner with Bonetti again little more than a spectator. Despite frantic charges at the Germans in the time remaining, no further goals were forthcoming and England slipped out of the competition, not to return for a further

twelve years. Rather than freshen Bobby Charlton for future matches, the substitution brought down the curtain on an international career that had stretched for 106 matches and brought 49 goals, a record. The West German match also saw the end of Peter Bonetti's international career after a rather more modest seven caps, although whether he would have retained his place in future matches if Banks had not been available will never be known.

The semi-finals ensured the final would be contested between teams from South America and Europe, where the only thing to be decided was which pairing. In Mexico City Italy met West Germany and produced another exciting display that belied their reputation for being a defensive outfit. Roberto Boninsegna opened the scoring for the Italians in the eighth minute and they held on to the lead for virtually the rest of the game. The German cause was not helped by serious injury to Beckenbauer, who dislocated a shoulder but eventually returned to the fray as the Germans had run out of substitutes. A minute from the end Schnellinger finally equalised, forcing the match into extra time. With both teams exhausted, especially the Germans, given that this was their second consecutive match that had required extra time, the game was always going to be decided on who made fewer mistakes. West Germany took the lead after Muller forced the ball over the line, only for Italy to respond with an equaliser from Burgnich. Riva put Italy ahead for a second time, only for the Germans to equalise once again through Muller. Two minutes

Above
England's Bobby Charlton attacks the West German goal as Franz Beckenbauer tries to intercept, in their quarter-final.

Above inset
Gerd Mueller of West Germany celebrates after scoring the winning goal in extra-time past Peter Bonetti of England.

later came the final and winning goal, Rivera putting the Italians into the final with eight minutes left to play.

In Guadalajara Brazil suffered the rarity of going behind in their match against Uruguay after Luis Cubilla half-hit a shot past Felix. Right on half time Brazil equalised through the unsung Clodoaldo and emerged in the second half the dominant force, although it was not until the game moved into the final 15 minutes that they took the lead, Jairzinho continuing his record of having scored in every match. In the final minute Rivelino gave the final scoreline a more realistic look with a third Brazilian goal. Again Pelé produced something magical, even if it didn't result in a goal, dummying the Uruguayan goalkeeper as he made to move onto a through pass – the ball trickled agonisingly past the post.

Three days later West Germany met Uruguay in Mexico City for the play-off for third and fourth place, minus the still injured Franz Beckenbauer but with a little too much experience for the Uruguayans, winning 1-0 through Overath's strike.

On paper, the meeting between Brazil and Italy in the World Cup final was as much a meeting of styles, with the defensive capabilities of the Italians, the semi-final notwithstanding, being the main reason for their progress to the final. By contrast, the Brazilians had a defence that was at best suspect, being protected largely by the delights that were the midfield and attack. It was not Brito, or Piazza or even Felix that would win the trophy for Brazil, rather what the likes of Pelé, Jairzinho and Tostao could do at the other end. In the 17th minute Rivelino sent in an inviting cross and Pelé rose to head home powerfully at the foot of the post for the game's opening goal. Italy got back into the game eight minutes before the interval after the Brazilians were guilty of sloppiness, gifting the ball to Boninsegna to round Felix and strike home an equaliser.

Capable of better, the Brazilians finally proved it in the second half. Gerson beat one defender and fired home a powerful shot from outside the penalty area with his left foot. Gerson was involved in the third goal, firing in a long ball that was headed down by Pelé into the path of Jairzinho that roared into the net, giving Jairzinho the honour of becoming the first and still only player to have scored in every match of the finals. Three minutes from time came the final goal, Pelé this time feeding captain and defender Carlos Alberto to fire home another long range effort. It was the performance that the world had wanted and the result the purists dreamed of,

but the Italians put on a display that did themselves justice – against almost anyone else they might have won, but this was the Brazilians in 1970, perhaps the best side the world has ever seen.

In winning the trophy for the third time Brazil won it for the last time – it had been decided that whoever won the competition three times would get to keep the Jules Rimet Trophy forever. Although Italy could have achieved the feat, it was Carlos Alberto who became the last captain to hold the trophy aloft, at the same time that manager Mario Zagalo became the first man to win the World Cup as a player and

Above
Franz Beckenbauer has his arm bandaged and placed in a sling after dislocating his shoulder in the semi-final against Italy.

Middle
Brazil celebrate their third goal against Italy scored by Jairzinho from a pass by Pelé in the World Cup final.

Above far right
Pelé embraces Brazilian goalkeeper Ado after winning the 1970 World Cup.

Right
Tarcisio Burgnich of Italy kicks the ball away from Pelé during the World Cup final.

Far right
Carlos Alberto lifts the Jules Rimet trophy.

manager. It was the end of the Jules Rimet Trophy (subsequently stolen in Brazil and believed to have been melted down for its gold content), the end of Pelé in the competition and the end of an era. It could not have had a more fitting finale.

RESULTS

Group 1

Mexico v USSR	0-0		Mexico v El Salvador	4-0
Belgium v El Salvador	3-0		USSR v El Salvador	2-0
USSR v Belgium	4-1		Mexico v Belgium	1-0

	P	W	D	L	F	A	P
USSR	3	2	1	0	6	1	6
Mexico	3	2	1	0	5	0	5
Belguim	3	1	0	2	4	5	2
El Salvador	3	0	0	3	0	9	0

Group 2

Uruguay v Israel	2-0		Sweden v Israel	1-1
Italy v Sweden	1-0		Sweden v Uruguay	1-0
Italy v Uruguay	0-0		Italy v Israel	0-0

	P	W	D	L	F	A	P
Italy	3	1	2	0	1	0	4
Uruguay	3	1	1	1	2	1	3
Sweden	3	1	1	1	2	2	3
Israel	3	0	2	1	1	3	2

Group 3

England v Romania	1-0		Brazil v England	1-0
Brazil v Czechoslovakia	4-1		Brazil v Romania	3-2
Romania v Czechoslovakia	2-1		England v Czechoslovakia	1-0

	P	W	D	L	F	A	P
Brazil	3	3	0	0	8	0	6
England	3	2	0	1	2	1	4
Romania	3	1	0	2	4	5	2
Czechoslovakia	3	0	0	3	2	7	0

Group 4

Peru v Bulgaria	3-2		West Germany v Bulgaria	5-2
West Germany v Morocco	2-1		West Germany v Peru	3-1
Peru v Morocco	3-0		Bulgaria v Morocco	1-1

	P	W	D	L	F	A	P
West Germany	3	3	0	0	10	4	6
Peru	3	2	0	1	7	5	4
Bulgaria	3	0	1	2	5	9	1
Morocco	3	0	1	2	2	6	1

Quarter-Finals

Uruguay v USSR	1-0
Italy v Mexico	4-1
Brazil v Peru	4-2
West Germany v England	3-2

SEMI-FINALS

Italy	4	West Germany	3
Brazil	3	Uruguay	1

3rd & 4th PLACE PLAY-OFF

West Germany	1	Uruguay	0

FINAL

Brazil	4	Italy	1

(Pelé, Gerson, Jairzinho, Alberto) — (Boninsegna)

Felix, Carlos Alberto, Brito, Piazza, Everaldo, Clodoaldo, Gerson, Jairzinho, Tostao, Pelé, Rivelino

Albertosi, Cera, Burgnich, Bertini (Juliano), Rosato, Facchetti, Domenghini, Mazzola, de Sisti, Boninsegna (Rivera), Riva

Right
1974 official World
Cup poster.

Below
Allan Clarke
making a goal
attempt during the
World Cup qualifier
match against
Poland at
Wembley, 1973.

Just as Mexico had been awarded the World Cup finals immediately after hosting the Olympic Games, so West Germany was afforded the honour in 1974. The atrocities of the 1972 Olympic Games, where eleven Israeli athletes were murdered by terrorists, cast a long shadow over all sporting events for many years to come, with security at the 1974 World Cup at the highest level ever experienced for any major sporting occasion.

After a fall at the previous competition, entrants for the 1974 World Cup reached a new all-time high at ninety-nine. Once again the bulk of these came from Europe, with thirty-three, and once again Europe was given the lion's share of places in the finals with nine (eight plus the hosts West Germany). Africa's twenty-three entrants were provided only one place, a decision that would have later ramifications for FIFA, Asia/Oceania's joint nineteen entrants were also given one place, South America's ten applicants had four places (three plus Brazil as holders) and

![1974 official World Cup poster]

FIFA World Cup 1974
Copa Mundial de la FIFA 1974
Coupe du Monde de la FIFA 1974

1974
WEST GERMANY

CONCACAF's fourteen were given the last place in Germany. There were also seven countries who applied to enter but withdrew before a ball was kicked in anger, and there were to be further withdrawals before the finals began.

Europe's thirty-three nations were placed in nine qualifying groups, five comprising four teams and the remaining four with only three teams. The group winners in the first eight groups would be given a place in the finals, whilst the winning team in Group 9 would play a play-off over two legs against the winner of South American Group 3.

Both Group 1 and Group 7 also required play-offs before the victors could take their place in the finals. Group 1 was particularly close, with three teams, Sweden, Austria and Hungary finishing on eight points and the final side, Malta, pointless. The identical goal differences shared by Sweden and Austria required a play-off in Germany that Sweden won 2-1, but it was particularly harsh on Hungary, who didn't lose a single match in qualification, finishing with a record of two wins and four draws in their six matches.

Spain and Yugoslavia were also inseparable in Group 7 on six points before Yugoslavia recorded a narrow 1-0 win in Frankfurt to take the group. Italy, Holland on goal difference,

East Germany, Bulgaria and Scotland were among the other group winners who booked their places in the finals, the Bulgarians responsible for the elimination of Northern Ireland.

By chance two of the home countries, England and Wales, were drawn in the same group, Group 5, along with Poland. If the smart money was on England to win the group in a canter, then they reckoned without the resilient Welsh. More importantly, they discounted the Poles at their peril. England's campaign got off to a shaky start in Cardiff, Colin Bell scoring the only goal of the game. The Welsh recovered in the return match, grinding out a 1-1 draw that would have severe repercussions for England later. Wales followed this up with a 2-0 win over Poland, leaving them joint top of the group with England.

A 2-0 win for Poland against England, with Alan Ball sent off put them back into contention, and a 3-0 win over Wales put the Welsh out and hauled Poland to the top of the group. It all came down to the final match, with England facing Poland at Wembley; an England win would give them the group, any other result would send the Poles to Germany. Alf Ramsey fielded a strong side, one that included three

recognised strikers in Allan Clarke, Martin Chivers and Mike Channon. Facing them was a goalkeeper described by Brian Clough as a 'clown' – Jan Tomaszewski – but the Pole was to have the last laugh. On a night when England threw everything they could into attack, Tomaszewski performed heroics in between the sticks, saving shot after shot. England were also guilty of a catalogue of misses, but as time marched on, desperation started to creep in as the expected goal feast never materialised. Twelve minutes into the second half a mistake by Norman Hunter allowed the Poles to score with their first attack and England were faced with having to score twice to qualify. They managed only one, from Allan Clarke from the penalty spot, and slid out of the competition. England's failure to qualify for the finals ultimately cost Alf Ramsey his job as manager, the fact that the Poles were better than anyone expected (as they proved in finishing third in the competition) counting for nothing.

The USSR won Group 9, knocking out the Republic of Ireland and France in the process, to take their place in the play-off against the winners of South American Group 3. Originally drawn with three teams, the withdrawal of Venezuela left Chile and Peru to battle it out amongst themselves. Although Peru were one of the surprise packages of the 1970 tournament, they lost a play-off in Montevideo 2-1 after both sides had won their home legs 2-0. The USSR drew 0-0 with Chile in Moscow but then refused to play the return leg at the designated stadium, the National Stadium in Santiago, claiming it had been used to house prisoners when a military coup had overthrown the elected left wing government. The USSR were expelled from the competition, and Chile awarded a place in the finals. They were joined by Uruguay, goal difference winners ahead of Colombia, and Argentina, easy winners of their group.

Haiti finally triumphed in the CONCACAF competition, winning a six team final group that involved each country playing the others only once in a mini tournament in Haiti! They finished with a record of four victories and one defeat, their closest rivals Trinidad & Tobago two points behind. Even more surprising was the elimination of Mexico, also two points adrift.

Left
Norman Hunter, shoulders and head down in disappointment trudges off the Wembley pitch after England's failure to qualify for the finals in West Germany. A 1-1 draw was enough to send Poland through after a spectacular display of keeping by Jan Tomaszewski.

The African competition was rocked by withdrawals, disqualifications, refusals to play and an abandonment before Zaire booked their place in Germany for the first time ever. Although their final round record read four wins out of four, in reality they only played three matches, being awarded a 2-0 win over Morocco when the Moroccans refused to play their home match in protest at the quality of refereeing in Zaire during the earlier meeting!

The final place in Germany went to Australia, winners of Sub-Group 1 and then victors over Iran and South Korea in the final round, although it took a play-off against South Korea in Hong Kong which they won 1-0 before they were confirmed as the sixteenth finalist for the World Cup.

FIFA had decided to alter the tournament for Germany. There would still be four groups of four teams, each playing the other teams in their group once. Instead of progressing into the quarter-finals, the top two in each group would go into a further group of four, again requiring matches against the other three sides. The top two sides in these groups would contest the final, the runners-up would play off for third and fourth place.

There were other changes on their way too. After Brazil's third win in the competition in 1970 they had been awarded the Jules Rimet Trophy to keep forever (it was subsequently

stolen in 1983) and a new trophy was commissioned. Designed by Silvio Gazzaniga and made from five kilograms of 18 carat gold, it depicted two human figures holding up the Earth. Whilst a number of names was considered, including the Stanley Rous Cup (in honour of the FIFA President) and even the Churchill Cup, FIFA decided upon the FIFA World Cup, meaning no country was slighted by the name. FIFA also announced that no other country would be given the trophy in perpetuity again; the winners get to keep the trophy on loan for four years and receive a replica to keep, although since the base of the trophy has no spaces for further winners after 2038, it will be interesting to see what happens to the trophy then!

Three days before the 1974 World Cup finals kicked off, FIFA gathered in West Germany to vote for the Presidency. Incumbent Sir Stanley Rous had been in the position for thirteen years and seemingly had no reason to fear for his position, but the ambitious Brazilian Joao Havelange had been hard at work canvassing support, particularly among the African countries, promising them an increase in the number of places in the finals in return for their personal votes. Since it would be impossible to accommodate increased representation by any continent without upsetting the status quo enjoyed by Europe and South America, Havelange planned to increase the number of finalists – this proved to be something of a vote winner and FIFA therefore elected the first non-European to the Presidency.

The dates for the World Cup finals had been decided after consultation with weather forecasters and fixtures drawn up by computer in order that the competition take place during the summer dry season – it rained virtually every day of the three and a half weeks, weather that ultimately suited the Northern European nations!

For the third consecutive time, the opening match of the competition resulted in a stale goalless draw, the culprits this time being Yugoslavia and holders Brazil in Group 2. This was the group Scotland, the home countries' sole survivor, were drawn in and they kicked off their campaign with a rather lacklustre 2-0 win over Zaire. When Yugoslavia rattled in nine without reply against the same opponents, it became apparent that goal difference would be vital. That Zaire were pretty clueless as to the finer points of the game came during this match; Yugoslavia were awarded a free kick just outside the Zaire penalty area and when the referee blew his whistle for the kick to be taken, it was Zaire defender N'daye who rushed at the ball and booted it away – he received a red card for his troubles! Scotland raised their game to record a goalless draw against a Brazilian side that was a mere shadow of former glories, complete with Jairzinho and Rivelino from 1970 but missing Pelé more than any other player (although he had retired from international football, he could have been persuaded to return had the manager merely asked him). It meant that Scotland had to win their final match against Yugoslavia or hope that Brazil did not beat their score of 2-0 against Zaire in order to progress. At half time it looked as though fortune was favouring the Scots; holding Yugoslavia to a goalless draw and Brazil struggling to find a way through the

Above
The new Silvio Gazzaniga designed World Cup.

Above right
Brazil play Yugoslavia in the opening match of the 1974 finals.

Left
Scotland managed a draw against Brazil.

Below
East versus West. Franz Beckenbauer poses with his East German counterpart Bernd Bransch at the start of their first-round game.

packed Zaire defence and add to their 13th minute goal from Jairzinho. Within two second half minutes it all changed, Brazil netting twice in quick succession left Scotland looking at elimination, and a late Yugoslavia goal effectively put an end to Scotland's dream. An even later equaliser from Joe Jordan was the very least Scotland deserved on the day, but they rued the misses against Zaire that had effectively seen them out of the competition.

Whilst Scotland would have done anything to have finished second in their group, West Germany in Group 1 played as though that was the exact position they were chasing – a runners-up spot in Group 1 would mean a place in Second Phase Group B, thus avoiding the much fancied Dutch in the next round. Thus their three qualifying games saw them narrowly overcome Chile 1-0 (it was in this match that the very first red card was brandished, Chile's Caszely being the unfortunate recipient) and power three goals without reply against the Australians. Their final group match brought them up against the East Germans, who were cheered on by 3,000 carefully selected fans who were allowed across the Berlin Wall on special trains and whose 1-0 win was enough to take top spot in the group – the West Germans may have lost the match but they had ultimately won the campaign.

Group 3 was widely expected to be the most open and all four sides were in with a chance of progressing into the second phase when the final round of matches kicked off. Holland managed to put behind them wrangles with their FA over match fees and bonuses to finally win the group, turning players such as Johan Cruyff, Johnny Rep and Rudy Krol into household names (and not just in Holland) after victories over Uruguay and

Bulgaria. Sweden accompanied them out of the group, a point behind after the two sides had drawn their meeting.

The final group was expected to be dominated by the Italians, but Poland were to show that their qualification ahead of England had been no fluke, winning all three of their matches against Italy, Argentina and Haiti to record the only 100% record in the group stage. This left Italy and Argentina to contest

second spot, a duel that was finally clinched by Argentina on goal difference. The two sides had ground out a 1-1 draw in their clash, but Argentina's 4-1 win over Haiti bettered Italy's 3-1 win four days previously. Haiti may not have made much of an impact on the field, but their exploits off it certainly caught the eye; Ernest Jean-Joseph became the first player to be banned for drug-taking, although the Haitian manager refused to send him home and he was finally removed from Germany by security men sent over from Haiti! Not surprisingly, Jean-Joseph never played for his country again!

Although the Dutch success so far had been based on the fluidity of their attack, the so-called 'total football' where every player was an attacker when Holland had the ball and a defender when they didn't, it was the sturdy nature of their defence, with or without the ball, that proved the foundation to their success. Conceding only one goal in their opening group matches they went one better in the second phase. Mean at the back they could then go on to overwhelm opponents at the other end; Argentina were swept aside 4-0 in their opening match whilst the Brazilians were struggling to get a 1-0 win over East Germany. Holland went one better in beating the

Above
Poland on their way to victory over Haiti.

Above right
Johann Cruyff of Holland dribbles past Argentinean goalkeeper Daniel Carnevali on his way to scoring in a quarter-final match against Argentina.

Right
Hector Yazalde (left) of Argentina scores past Haitian goalkeeper Henry Francillon as Mario Kempes falls down during the World Cup first-round.

Germans 2-0 in their next match, whilst the Brazilians saw off the Argentineans 2-1 to set up the final round of matches. Holland's superior goal difference meant the Brazilians had to win to progress and it soon became apparent that this Brazil side did not have the technical ability to do so. Instead the side that four years previously had been the epitome of the beautiful game resorted to strong arm tactics – Ze Maria appeared to have got the codes mixed up and performed a rugby tackle on Cruyff, Mario Marinho was guilty of more assaults off the ball than on and the referee finally lost patience when Neeskens was taken out by Luis Pereira, sending the Brazilian off. Although the Dutch were no angels themselves, they kept their composure enough to score twice through Neeskens and Cruyff to book their place in the final.

Group B saw another 100% record, this time from West Germany, although Poland were much stiffer opposition in this group than the Brazilians had been in Group A. West Germany kicked off the all-European group with a 2-0 win over Yugoslavia whilst Poland beat Sweden 1-0. Sweden's interest in the competition was ended with a 4-2 defeat by West Germany in what was one of the best matches of the tournament, whilst Poland's 2-1 win over Yugoslavia did much the same for the Yugoslavs. It meant that, just as in Group A, Poland needed to win to progress into the final, the Germans only needed a draw, proof that their earlier calculations on what would be the easier group to qualify from had been correct. Although the German side were often in harmony on the pitch, as their record of five victories in the competition so far would testify, it was a different matter off it, with manager Helmut Schoen and captain Franz Beckenbauer often at loggerheads over team selection and tactics. Both managed to put their differences behind them for the Poland match, a match that was delayed by more than half an hour whilst the ground staff tried to remove as much of the surface water deposited by the incessant rain as they could. A pitch that soon resembled a quagmire saw Gerd Muller score the only goal of the game, his ninth of the tournament, Hoeness have his penalty saved and the Poles miss a couple of easy chances before the West Germans booked a place in the final.

Poland duly won the battle for third and fourth place, Lato scoring the only goal of the game, his seventh of the competition. It would have been of little consolation to the English, but Poland were well worth third place and would become something of a thorn in the side of many of the world's top sides in years to come.

A day later, on 7th July 1974 West Germany and Holland lined up at the Olympic Stadium in Munich to contest the World Cup final. Whilst the Germans had been methodical in their approach to the final, at times doing just enough to beat the opposition, the Dutch had delighted all and sundry with their style of play. Whilst the Dutch were expected to supply the flair, the Germans would be relied upon for their efficiency. Unfortunately, their efficiency let them down before a ball was kicked, for English referee Jack Taylor noticed that there were no corner flags and there was an embarrassed delay whilst they were found and put into position!

There was worse for the Germans to contend with once the match got underway. The Dutch attacked straight from kick off and before even a minute had passed, Johan Cruyff was surging into the German penalty area and was promptly brought down by Berti Vogts. There had never been a penalty in a World Cup final before, Germany had yet to touch the ball but Jack Taylor had little hesitation in awarding a spot kick, his decision helped in part by the lack of real complaint from the Germans. Johan Neeskens faced up to Sepp Maier and

Above
West German Hans-Georg Schwarzenberg and Yugoslav forward Dragan Dzajic run after the ball during a quarter-final game.

decided to kick the ball straight down the middle whilst Maier was diving to his right – 1-0 to Holland.

The Germans recovered quickly from such a blow and received their reward after 25 minutes, winger Bernd Holzenbein dribbling through the Dutch defence and into the penalty area when his run was halted by Wim Jansen. It was a much less clear cut penalty than that awarded to the Dutch, with Holzenbein's exaggerated dive hardly helping, but Taylor was again pointing to the spot as Holzenbein completed his fall and roll. This time it was Paul Breitner and Jongbloed who squared up, Breitner scoring the equalising goal.

As half time loomed, both sides looked as though they would be happy to get to the interval on level terms, but with just two minutes to go before the break, Rainer Bonhof attacked down the right wing and pulled the ball back into the penalty area. It was behind Gerd Muller, but in an instant he had managed to check his run, collect the ball, turn and shoot to put the Germans ahead. Although it was his tenth goal of the competition, the four he had scored in Mexico four years previously meant he had now registered 14 World Cup finals goals, a new record ahead of Juste Fontaine. The goal was a crushing blow for Holland, with Cruyff arguing bitterly with the referee as the two teams left the field at half time, but there could be no complaints about the goal.

The Dutch pressed for much of the second half looking for their own equaliser. Neeskens shot narrowly wide and a volley was smartly saved by Maier. Germany were not a spent force in attack either, but with Franz Beckenbauer patrolling the back line like the master the world assumed him to be, further threats were averted. Jack Taylor brought matters to a close after 90 minutes, and

Above
Johann Cruyff is brought down within seconds of the game starting.

Above right
West German defender Paul Breitner ties the score at 1-1 after a penalty kick as he beats Dutch goalkeeper Jan Jongbloed.

Right
Johan Neeskens scores the opening goal from the penalty spot and sends West German goalkeeper Sepp Maier the wrong way.

West Germany were crowned world champions for the second time.

It was fitting that it should be Beckenbauer who should lift the new trophy – a member of the side that had finished runners-up in 1966 and third in 1970, he now completed his set of World Cup medals – gold, silver and bronze. Whilst he would not win another medal as a player, he had not finished with the competition, not by a long shot. For Gerd Muller, however, it was as fitting a time to bow out as any; top goalscorer in the entire history of the competition, having scored the winning goal, he announced his retirement from international football. Defences the world over breathed a sigh of relief.

RESULTS

Group 1

West Germany v Chile	1-0	Chile v East Germany	1-1
East Germany v Australia	2-0	East Germany v West Germany	1-0
West Germany v Australia	3-0	Chile v Australia	0-0

	P	W	D	L	F	A	P
East Germany	3	2	1	0	4	1	5
West Germany	3	2	0	1	4	1	4
Chile	3	0	2	1	1	2	2
Australia	3	0	1	2	0	5	1

Group 2

Brazil v Yugoslavia	0-0	Yugoslavia v Zaire	9-0
Scotland v Zaire	2-0	Yugoslavia v Scotland	1-1
Scotland v Brazil	0-0	Brazil v Zaire	3-0

	P	W	D	L	F	A	P
Yugoslavia	3	1	2	0	10	1	4
Brazil	3	1	2	0	3	0	4
Scotland	3	1	2	0	3	1	4
Zaire	3	0	0	3	0	14	0

Group 3

Sweden v Bulgaria	0-0	Uruguay v Bulgaria	1-1
Holland v Uruguay	2-0	Sweden v Uruguay	3-0
Holland v Sweden	0-0	Holland v Bulgaria	4-1

	P	W	D	L	F	A	P
Holland	3	2	1	0	6	1	5
Sweden	3	1	2	0	3	0	4
Bulgaria	3	0	2	1	2	5	2
Uruguay	3	0	1	2	1	6	1

Group 4

Italy v Haiti	3-1	Italy v Argentina	1-1
Poland v Argentina	3-2	Poland v Italy	2-1
Poland v Haiti	7-0	Argentina v Haiti	4-1

	P	W	D	L	F	A	P
Poland	3	3	0	0	12	3	6
Argentina	3	1	1	1	7	5	3
Italy	3	1	1	1	5	4	3
Haiti	3	0	0	3	2	14	0

Quarter-Finals – Group A

Brazil v East Germany	1-0	Holland v East Germany	2-0
Holland v Argentina	4-0	Holland v Brazil	2-0
Brazil v Argentina	2-1	East Germany v Argentina	1-1

	P	W	D	L	F	A	P
Holland	3	3	0	0	8	0	6
Brazil	3	2	0	1	3	3	4
East Germany	3	0	1	2	1	4	1
Argentina	3	0	1	2	2	7	1

Quarter-Finals – Group B

West Germany v Yugoslavia	2-0	West Germany v Sweden	4-2
Poland v Sweden	1-0	West Germany v Poland	1-0
Poland v Yugoslavia	2-1	Sweden v Yugoslavia	2-1

	P	W	D	L	F	A	P
West Germany	3	3	0	0	7	2	6
Poland	3	2	0	1	3	2	4
Sweden	3	1	0	2	4	6	2
Yugoslavia	3	0	0	3	2	6	0

3rd & 4th PLACE PLAY-OFF	Poland	1	Brazil	0

FINAL	West Germany	2	Holland	1

(Breitner pen, Muller) (Neeskens pen)

Maier, Vogts, Schwarzenbeck, Beckenbauer, Breitner, Bonhof, Hoeness, Overath, Grabowski, Müller, Hölzenbein

Jongbled, Suurbier, Rijsbergen (de Jong), Haan, Krol, Jansen, van Hanegem, Neeskens, Rep, Cruyff, Rensenbrink (R.van der Kerkhof)

Right
1978 official World
Cup poster.

Below
Italy celebrate
scoring against
England in their
qualifying game
for the 1978
World Cup.

After campaigning to host the World Cup on virtually every occasion the finals had been held in South America, Argentina finally got the nod for 1978. It was not a universally popular decision, for with the country being controlled by a military junta there were fears the World Cup might be used as political football (pun intended). The assassination of Omar Actis, president of the World Cup Organising Committee by guerrillas gave the fearful real cause for concern and the possibility that students, always among the most volatile of protesters, might use the occasion when all of the world's media were watching as an excuse to cause General Videla and his junta negative publicity was always present. Although it has never been proven one way or another, it was claimed that the dissidents were rounded up and held in jails around the country for the duration of the tournament – and the World Cup passed without major incident off the field.

For the first time ever the number of entrants surpassed the 100 mark, a total of 106 submitting entry forms to FIFA, although Sri Lanka subsequently withdrew when their government refused permission for the entrance fee to be paid! Europe's entries were also one down on 1974, Albania deciding against entering. The thirty-two nations that did enter were to be allocated nine guaranteed places for the finals (eight plus West Germany as holders). Africa's twenty-six entries, easily the

1978 ARGENTINA

second highest bloc, received just one place. Asia, who had eighteen entries were linked with Oceania's three and given one place. CONCACAF's seventeen entries were also given one place, with South America's ten entries given three guaranteed places (two plus Argentina as hosts). The remaining place was to be decided in a play-off between the winners of European Group 9 and the third placed side in the South American group.

For the second consecutive tournament, two of the home countries were drawn in the same qualifying group, Wales and Scotland coming out of the hat with Czechoslovakia in Group 7. Scotland got off to a bad start, going down 2-0 to Czechoslovakia, and then only narrowly beating the Welsh 1-0. When Wales then beat Czechoslovakia 3-0, it was obvious that anyone could qualify from this group – Wales were top on goal difference after each side had played two matches. Scotland overhauled them and Czechoslovakia, winning 3-1 at home against the Czechs and then 2-0 at Anfield, the home of Liverpool, against the Welsh, to book their place in Argentina.

Northern Ireland were unfortunate enough to be drawn in Group 4 against the previous tournament's runners-up Holland, who proved that 1974 had been no fluke by dropping only one point in their six qualifying matches, against Northern Ireland, recording five wins and a draw to top the group with ease. Northern Ireland didn't even finish runners-up, beaten into third place by Belgium.

Once again the drama was in England's group, Group 2, where qualification soon settled into a two-horse race between England and Italy. Led by former Leeds United manager Don Revie, Alf Ramsey having paid the ultimate price for England's failure to qualify in 1974, England's record of five wins, only one defeat and 15 goals scored against four conceded should

Left
Scotland set off for
Argentina via
Hampden Park.

Below left
Ally McLeod the
much taunted
Scottish manager.

Below
Don Revie is all
smiles, but for
England yet again
failure to qualify.

qualification. They were joined by Austria, France (who saw off the Republic of Ireland), Sweden and Spain as automatic qualifiers. Hungary topped Group 9, a point ahead of the USSR to earn their place in the play-off with the third best South American country. That turned out to be Bolivia, who were topped by Brazil and Peru in the second round group, and Hungary were a little too strong for the Bolivian side, registering a 6-0 home win and 3-2 away to win the tie 9-2 on aggregate.

Mexico had to play nine matches before they qualified for the finals, a three team round robin competition against Canada and the USA in the first round, where each side finished with an identical record of one win, two draws and a defeat but which Mexico won on goal difference (Canada beat the USA in the play-off to also advance) and then a six team mini tournament where each side played the other once. Mexico found form at the right time to register a 100% record and took the CONCACAF place for the finals.

Africa's qualifying tournament was equally complex, requiring four knockout rounds that were hit by withdrawals until three teams were left and qualification resorted to a league basis again. Having survived the first round on penalties against Morocco, Tunisia emerged triumphant ahead of Egypt and Nigeria.

The final place for Argentina was won by Iran from the Asia/Oceania group, who had to play twelve matches before winning through. Their record of ten wins and two draws, with 20 goals scored and only three conceded was enough to win both mini-Leagues they were required to play.

The format that had operated in West Germany was retained for Argentina; four groups of four teams each with the top two advancing into a second group, the winner of each of these contesting the final and the runners-up the play-off for third and fourth place. The uncertainty over the political situation did result in some notable absentees, Johan Cruyff and Paul Breitner being among the top class names who were missing from the finals, but there was plenty to keep the watching world interested as the tournament unfolded.

Scotland had been drawn in Group 4 with Holland, Peru and Iran, a group manager Ally MacLeod felt was winnable. Perhaps echoing the confidence of Alf Ramsey, McLeod made his feelings known, arranging for a massive send off for the team from Hampden Park and promising that he would be parading the trophy itself the

have been enough to see them home and dry. Unfortunately, it was the fact that they should have scored more, especially at home to Finland, which resulted in a 2-1 win (they had already won the away match 4-1) and in Luxembourg, where they only won 2-0, that cost them dear. Italy beat Finland 6-1 and Luxembourg 3-0 in between losing to England 2-0, a match they could afford to lose since they had already gained a mathematical advantage. Don Revie, perhaps sensing that there would be a price to pay for his failure to win qualification, was already looking for another job before England's elimination was confirmed, claiming he was going on a

scouting mission in Europe whilst the team was on tour in South America (supposedly to acclimatise). He turned up in Dubai where he was later confirmed as the new United Arab Emirates' coach. England handed him a ten year ban from the domestic game in retaliation.

Like Holland, Poland carried on where they had left off in 1974, also recording five wins and a draw in their group to earn

supported, some of the backing bordered on the hysterical, a nationalistic undercurrent often bubbling to the surface in a fashion never previously seen in the World Cup. Italy also had good support in Argentina, particularly in Buenos Aires where there were large numbers of Italian immigrants living, meaning the French and Hungarians were on a hiding to nothing right from the start. The fervour of the crowd sometimes appeared to influence the referees, with Argentina benefiting from some dubious decisions during the course of the tournament – Argentina could qualify easily enough on their own; they didn't need outside influences. Both Italy and Argentina kicked off their campaigns with victories, Italy beating France 2-1 after going a goal behind and Argentina recording a similar win over Hungary, who had two players sent off. Italy went one better against Hungary, registering a 3-1 win, whilst Argentina put out the French 2-1, scoring the first from a highly dubious if fortunate penalty given for handball against Tresor. The final group matches saw France record a win in their meaningless match, whilst a close match in Buenos Aires saw Bettega net the only goal of the game for Italy and win the group, but, as West Germany had figured out four years earlier, it meant they progressed into the seemingly more difficult second round group.

Pre-tournament favourites Brazil were drawn against three European sides in Group 3, Austria, Spain and Sweden. Two draws in their opening two matches meant there was a possibility they might slip out of the competition, but a single goal victory over Austria, who had already won the group,

next time they all met. Unlike Alf Ramsey, however, Ally MacLeod did not have home advantage on his side; his boasts would come back to haunt him for years after.

Once again the tournament kicked off with a goalless draw, holders West Germany held by Poland in Group 2. With Tunisia and Mexico drawn in the same group, neither the Germans nor the Poles were willing to go all out in the opening match, reasoning that they could gain enough points for future progress against the two so-called minnows. Tunisia, however, were anything but minnows, becoming the first African side to register a finals win in beating Mexico 3-1 after going a goal down and only narrowly going down 1-0 to Poland. Had they matched their performance against West Germany, where they drew 0-0, they might even have caused a major upset, but the Germans did just enough to take an unconvincing second place in the group, behind the Poles who finished off their first round campaign with a 3-1 win over Mexico. So lacklustre had the Mexicans been during the competition manager Roca refused to return home, uncertain of the reception he might be given!

Host nation Argentina, on whom so much rested, were drawn in a potentially difficult group alongside Italy, France and Hungary. Whilst Argentina were always going to be well

Above
West German goalkeeper Sepp Maier deflects a shot by a Polish player during the 1978 World Cup opening game.

Right
Dominique Rocheteau of France dribbles past Argentinean goalkeeper Ubaldo Fillol and Daniel Passarella in their first-round match.

goal win to do so. While Peru were wrapping up the group with a 4-1 win over Iran, Scotland and Holland faced each other in Mendoza. Rensenbrink gave the Dutch a 22 minute lead, but Kenny Dalglish equalised on the stroke of half time. Whatever was said in the Scottish dressing room during the interval had the desired effect, for Scotland came out and played for 25 minutes like a team possessed, Archie Gemmill putting them ahead from the penalty spot and then slaloming his way through the Dutch defence to score one of the goals of the competition to make the score 3-1 and with a little over 20 minutes left to chase the fourth goal that would earn them a place in the next phase. Alas, Johnny Rep scored another

earned them a place in the second round. Whilst the Brazilians might well have rued missed chances in earlier matches, they could also point to a quite astonishing decision by English referee Clive Thomas in their eventual 1-1 draw with Sweden; Brazil were awarded a corner virtually on half time, indeed the clock showed that time had expired three seconds previously, but as the ball came into the penalty area and Zico headed home, Thomas disallowed the goal, claiming time was up. The entire Brazilian side was still arguing with the referee as they made their way off the field.

Scotland were drawn in the final group, alongside Holland, Peru and supposed minnows Iran. The Dutch had little trouble in seeing off Iran, Rensenbrink netting a hat-trick that included two penalties in the 3-0 win. Meanwhile, in Cordoba, Scotland got off to a flying start when Joe Jordan put them ahead against Peru. That was as good as it got, for Scotland underestimated the Peruvians, conceded two long range efforts from Cubillas, one of the stars still around from 1970, missed a penalty and finally lost 3-1. Ally MacLeod's boasting before the tournament, that Scotland would win the competition, meant that the (British) media viewed this as a 'major shock'. Those who knew better realised that Scotland were not as good as they thought they were and Peru were not as bad as Scotland thought they were. Worse was to follow, with winger Willie Johnston being found guilty of taking an illegal substance, expelled from the squad, sent home in disgrace and banned for a year by FIFA. Just when Scotland thought it couldn't get any worse they hit rock bottom, held to a 1-1 draw with Iran despite again taking the lead, this time two minutes before half time from an own goal. With Holland being held to a goalless draw against Peru, there was still a slim hope that Scotland might somehow qualify for the next stage, but they would need little short of a miracle and a three

thunderbolt shot to bring the Scots back down to earth and put Holland through on goal difference. Perhaps if Scotland had not claimed they were going to win the competition the media might have complimented them on their brave efforts, but Ally MacLeod's boasts meant they went home to derision and MacLeod's career never recovered.

The final round of matches in Groups 3 and 4 meant that for the second phase, Group A featured four European countries in Holland, Italy, West Germany and Austria, whilst Group B contained all three South American survivors and Poland as odd men out. In Group A Italy were unable to turn better support into goals against West Germany, having to settle for a share of the spoils in a goalless draw. On the same day Holland finally hit top gear, thumping the luckless Austrians 5-1, the scoreline almost worth an extra point in itself. Four days later came the second round of matches, with Italy beating Austria 1-0 and the Dutch and Germans finishing all square at 2-2. The Germans twice took the lead, but a mixture of their inability to successfully defend and the Dutch ability to prise them open meant they were effectively out of contention. That was confirmed in their third and final match when they lost to near neighbours Austria 3-2, the winning goal coming in the very last minute of the game. The winner take all match in Buenos Aires went the way of the Dutch, who again recovered from being a goal down to

overcome Italy 2-1 in a game they only needed to draw, such was the superiority of their goal difference.

Goal difference was needed to settle Group B, but the manner in which it was achieved would leave a stain on the game for many years after. Unimpressive in their opening group matches, Brazil finally woke up and produced the form with which their name had become synonymous, putting three past Peru without reply. On the same day Argentina could only score twice against the Poles, again without reply, although Poland missed a penalty, their concentration perhaps being put off by the referee's insistence on re-positioning the ball just as Kazimierz Deyna was about to take the kick. Despite the miss, Argentina were already a goal behind Brazil in the run towards the final. By chance the two sides met in the second round of matches, Brazil managing to put aside the hostility of the home crowd and emerging with a credible 0-0 draw. Although Poland beat Peru 1-0 to lift themselves within a point of both Brazil and Argentina, they were not considered serious rivals for a place in the final. So it proved against Brazil in their final group match, for despite drawing level just before half time, Brazil turned on the magic to score twice in the second half and take the game 3-1. Astonishingly, it had been decided that Argentina would kick off their final match, against Peru, almost four hours behind Brazil, thus knowing exactly what was required of them to progress into the final. FIFA explained away this anomaly by declaring that television commitments had prevented both matches being scheduled together, but in light of subsequent events, it was not a convincing argument. Needing to win by four clear goals to progress, Argentina scored six against Peru, a result that raised even more eyebrows when it was revealed that Peruvian goalkeeper Quiroga was actually born in Argentina! The players of both sides denied any collusion and Quiroga was not blamed personally for any of the goals, but one Brazilian paper noted that 'If Brazil had won 50-0 against Poland, Argentina would

have beaten Peru 52-0!' Even Brazilian manager Claudio Coutinho got caught up in the hysteria, claiming that his country were 'moral winners' of the Cup, which prompted Argentinean manager Cesar Luis Menotti to declare 'I congratulate Brazil on their moral victory. Now, I hope Coutinho will congratulate us on our 'real' win?' Brazil duly beat Italy to claim third place in the competition, but there was still a bitter taste in the mouth at the end of the match.

Whilst not as blatant, Argentina employed gamesmanship in the final itself, remaining in their dressing room for a good five minutes after the Dutch had taken to the field. The Argentinean players then objected to the plaster cast being worn by Rene Van De Kerkhof, anything that might unsettle the Dutch players before the match itself kicked off.

Argentina settled quicker, although in truth the Dutch side were below par on the day, and Mario Kempes, one of the Argentina players who had really caught the eye during the competition, netted the opening goal after 38 minutes. The Dutch finally sparked into action in the second half, deservedly equalising with eight minutes left on the clock through substitute Dirk Nanninga. Five minutes later they could have won it, Rensenbrink's shot cannoning off the post with Fillol in the Argentine goal beaten. As if reprieved, Argentina raised their game in extra time, Kempes putting the home side ahead again on 105 minutes and Daniel Bertoni putting the matter beyond all doubt with a third five minutes from the end.

It is not known whether Claudio Coutinho congratulated his Argentine counterpart after their victory. Whatever the circumstances of their win, Argentina's side, whilst not a great

Above
The Brazilian team pose before their game against Italy in a quarter-final.

Above right
Mario Kempes scores his second goal for Argentina and duly celebrates.

Left
The scoreboard confirms Argentina as the 1978 World Cup winners.

Below
Cesar Menotti in relaxed mode smoking his usual cigarette.

one in terms of individual flair, were a great team, superbly led on the field by Daniel Passarella and guided off it by Cesar Luis Menotti. It was the striking abilities of Mario Kempes, however, that had enabled Argentina to finally win the trophy after nearly fifty years of trying.

RESULTS

Group 1

Italy v France	2-1	Argentina v France	2-1
Argentina v Hungary	2-1	Italy v Argentina	1-0
Italy v Hungary	3-1	France v Hungary	3-1

	P	W	D	L	F	A	P
Italy	3	3	0	0	6	2	6
Argentina	3	2	0	1	4	3	4
France	3	1	0	2	5	5	2
Hungary	3	0	0	3	3	8	0

Group 2

West Germany v Poland	0-0	West Germany v Mexico	6-0
Tunisia v Mexico	3-1	Tunisia v West Germany	0-0
Poland v Tunisia	1-0	Poland v Mexico	3-1

	P	W	D	L	F	A	P
Poland	3	2	1	0	4	1	5
West Germany	3	1	2	0	6	0	4
Tunisia	3	1	1	1	3	2	3
Mexico	3	0	0	3	2	12	0

Group 3

Brazil v Sweden	1-1	Brazil v Spain	0-0
Austria v Spain	2-1	Brazil v Austria	1-0
Austria v Sweden	1-0	Spain v Sweden	1-0

	P	W	D	L	F	A	P
Austria	3	2	0	1	3	2	4
Brazil	3	1	2	0	2	1	4
Spain	3	1	1	1	2	2	3
Sweden	3	0	1	2	1	3	1

Group 4

Holland v Iran	3-0	Scotland v Iran	1-1
Peru v Scotland	3-1	Scotland v Holland	3-2
Holland v Peru	0-0	Peru v Iran	4-1

	P	W	D	L	F	A	P
Peru	3	2	1	0	7	2	5
Holland	3	1	1	1	5	3	3
Scotland	3	1	1	1	5	6	3
Iran	3	0	1	2	2	8	1

Quarter-Finals – Group A

Italy v West Germany	0-0	West Germany v Holland	2-2
Holland v Austria	5-1	Holland v Italy	2-1
Italy v Austria	1-0	Austria v West Germany	3-2

	P	W	D	L	F	A	P
Holland	3	2	1	0	9	4	5
Italy	3	1	1	1	2	2	3
West Germany	3	0	2	1	4	5	2
Austria	3	1	0	2	4	8	2

Quarter-Finals – Group B

Brazil v Peru	3-0	Argentina v Brazil	0-0
Argentina v Poland	2-0	Brazil v Poland	3-1
Poland v Peru	1-0	Argentina v Peru	6-0

	P	W	D	L	F	A	P
Argentina	3	2	1	0	8	0	5
Brazil	3	2	1	0	6	1	5
Poland	3	1	0	2	2	5	2
Peru	3	0	0	3	0	10	0

3rd & 4th PLACE PLAY-OFF	Brazil	2	Italy	1

FINAL	Argentina	3	Holland	1

(Kempes 2, Bertoni)   (Nanninga)

Fillol, Olguin, Galvan, Passarella, Tarantini, Ardiles (Larossa), Gallego, Kempes, Bertoni, Luque, Ortiz (Houseman)   Jongbloed, Poortvliet, Krol, Brandts, Jansen (Suurbier), Neeskens, Haan, W Van de Kerkhof, R Van de Kerkhof, Rep (Nanninga), Rensenbrink

Right
England manager
Ron Greenwood
pictured with Laurie
Cunningham
before the 1982
World Cup.

Below
1982 official World
Cup poster.

Although Joao Havelange had based his campaign for the presidency of FIFA on increasing the numbers of participants in the finals tournament, the idea that the competition could be increased in size had been considered many years before. Indeed, the previous president Sir Stanley Rous had claimed that the competition would be more manageable with twenty-four teams than the sixteen who had competed for the cup since 1954. As was noted previously, however, Joao Havelange had secured votes from the African and Asian countries in particular by promising an increase in the number of finalists and an increase in places for those continents.

Spain was awarded the right to host the expanded 1982 World Cup finals, selecting fourteen cities at which the fifty-two matches would be played. The expanded competition also attracted a record number of applications for entry, with 108 nations entering out of the 147 who were members of FIFA.

Whilst the increase in the number of finalists was primarily designed to reward the so-called minnow continents, both Europe and South America benefited as well – Europe's thirty-three entrants were to be afforded a total of fourteen places in the finals (thirteen plus Spain as hosts) and South America's ten would result in four places (three plus Argentina as holders). Each of the remaining sectors were given two places apiece – Africa (out of twenty-eight entrants), CONCACAF (fifteen entrants) and Asia (eighteen entries). Israel, who had been moved from one sector to another with regularity in previous years, were admitted into the European section.

1982
SPAIN

Europe's entries for the qualifying competition were placed in seven groups, six of five teams and one of three. The top two sides in the larger groups together with the winner of Group 7 (the smaller group) would qualify for the finals. Once again two of the home countries were drawn in the same group, Scotland and Northern Ireland contesting Group 6 with Sweden, Portugal and Israel. Despite dropping points here, there and everywhere, both Scotland and Northern Ireland managed to retain enough to qualify, Northern Ireland achieving second place in the group with a slender 1-0 home win over Israel to lift themselves above Sweden. Scotland topped the group, the highlight being home and away victories over Sweden.

Wales were drawn in a particularly tough group alongside the USSR, Czechoslovakia, Iceland and Turkey and the group soon settled down into a three-way battle between Wales and the two Iron Curtain rivals to earn qualification. Wales won all four of their opening matches to take pole position but then stumbled, drawing two and losing two of the remaining matches to finish on ten points. The USSR won the group with fourteen points, taking nine out of ten points in their final five matches to overhaul Wales. Czechoslovakia finished their campaign with ten points as well, the final point coming in a 1-1 draw with the USSR, but with a slightly better goal difference than Wales to take second spot and qualification.

England, meanwhile, were grouped with Hungary, Romania, Switzerland and Norway and should have had little difficulty in qualifying for the finals for the first time since 1970. If they were favourites for the group then they didn't show it, turning in exceptional performances such as a 3-1 win in Hungary and then abysmal displays such as their 2-1 defeat in Norway, a result that prompted the epic radio announcement from Borge Lilleelien immediately after the match finished 'We have beaten England. Lord Nelson, Lord Beaverbrook, Sir Winston Churchill, Sir Anthony Eden, Clement Atlee, Henry Cooper, Lady Diana. We have beaten them all. Maggie Thatcher your boys took a hell of a beating.' England just about had the last laugh, Switzerland's surprise victory in Romania allowing England to finish second in the group behind Hungary, the placings confirmed with a 1-0 victory at

Wembley against the Magyars. Manager Ron Greenwood had twice tried to resign during the campaign but was talked out of it by his players. Those same players who had struggled to qualify owed their manager a decent finals tournament in return.

The only major failure in qualification came from Holland, runners-up in both the previous campaigns, who finished fourth in their group behind Belgium, France and the Republic of Ireland. It was hard on the Irish, beaten out of qualification on goal difference by the French, but their inability to do better than a 3-2 win over Cyprus in their opening match ultimately proved their undoing.

Group 1 had seen West Germany and Austria finish ahead of Bulgaria, Albania and Finland, the Germans finishing with a 100% record. Poland also topped their group with a 100% record, although they were only required to play four matches and finished ahead of East Germany and Malta to earn their place in the finals. Europe's qualifiers were completed by Yugoslavia and Italy from Group 5, giving the continent a particularly strong list of qualifiers.

South America again opted for three mini Leagues, the winner of each group to qualify. Brazil had little trouble in Group 1, drawn against Bolivia and Venezuela and won all four matches. Peru finished top of Group 2, ahead of Uruguay and Colombia, and the final South American place went to Chile, who dropped only one point against Ecuador and Paraguay.

African qualification was accomplished by a knockout competition, with the two surviving sides earning a place in Spain. Egypt were helped along two stages by withdrawals (Ghana and Libya) before losing to Morocco. Morocco then lost to Cameroon in one of the 'finals' for qualification, Algeria winning the other against Nigeria. Both qualifiers would perform well in Spain, proof of the growing abilities of the continent in football terms.

A mix of mini Leagues and knockout competitions was used to whittle down the Asian and Oceania contingent, with Kuwait finishing top of the final group to earn one of the allocated places in the finals. The other was between New

Zealand and the People's Republic of China, re-admitted to FIFA in 1979, and required a play-off after both sides had finished level on points and goal difference, New Zealand finally emerging triumphant with a 2-1 win in Singapore.

CONCACAF's two places in the finals were decided by a series of mini Leagues, Honduras and El Salvador qualifying out of Group 3 three points ahead of their nearest rivals and then finishing in identical positions in the final round ahead of Mexico, Canada, Cuba and Haiti.

Along with an increase in finalists came yet another format for the World Cup finals. The 24 teams would be placed into six groups of four teams each, with the top two in each group then going into a further four groups of three teams apiece. The winner of each group would then advance to the semi-finals, meaning that the side winning the cup would need eight matches to accomplish the feat. As the competition loomed close, there was a real fear that the numbers might drop owing to withdrawals by the three British sides – England, Scotland and Northern Ireland – over war that was then raging against Argentina in the Falkland Islands. Argentinean troops had invaded the islands in April of that year and after diplomatic measures had failed to remove them, the British had gathered a Task Force to forcibly remove them from the islands. Scotland were most likely the first British opponents who would face the Argentineans in the World Cup, assuming both sides survived the first stage, prompting questions in the

Above
British troops arriving at the Falklands Islands during the Falklands War, 1982.

House of Commons over whether the three nations should be competing in a football competition at a time when British troops were being killed thousands of miles away. The British Task Force completed the expulsion of the Argentinean troops on 12th June, and all three sides pledged they would compete in the competition regardless.

The traditional curtain raiser, featuring the holders Argentina was the first surprise of the competition, beaten 1-0 by Belgium in Barcelona thanks to a goal from Erwin Vandenbergh, the first goal scored in the opening World Cup match since 1962. Argentina coach Cesar Luis Menotti came under instant fire from his hard to please critics over his reliance on many of the players who had won the tournament in 1978, the implication being that many of them were already past their best, but there was still Diego Maradona to delight the crowds. Argentina picked themselves up to beat both Hungary and El Salvador to ensure progress into the next stage, finishing second in the group behind Belgium. Hungary's elimination was the real surprise in Group 3, especially as they had kicked off their campaign with a 10-1 win over El Salvador to establish a new record score for the competition, with Laszlo Kiss registering the quickest ever hat-trick in just seven minutes in scoring in the 70th, 74th and 77th minutes of match, and that after coming on as a substitute!

Goals were particularly hard to come by in Group 1 where Poland, Italy, Peru and Cameroon were battling. After the first four matches, only two goals had been scored, both of these coming in the 1-1 draw between Peru and Italy. Poland finally broke the trend, hammering in five second half goals against Peru to take the group with four points. A day later Italy kicked

off against Cameroon knowing that a draw would take them through on goals scored and this was duly accomplished with Francesco Graziani netting for the Italians in the 1-1 draw. Cameroon were thus eliminated without losing a match whilst Italy progressed without winning one. Even more galling for Cameroon was that Roger Milla had a perfectly good goal disallowed against Peru that would have seen them through, but both Milla and Cameroon's day would come again.

Group 2 had been expected to be dominated by the West Germans, but complacency almost proved their undoing. A 2-1 defeat by Algeria in their opening match, was a result that ranks alongside the USA's shock 1-0 win over England in 1950 and North Korea's similar result against Italy in 1966. This was no scrambled victory either, for Algeria took the lead through Rabah Madjer on 54 minutes, survived a German equaliser from Karl Heinz Rummenigge on 68 minutes and still had enough energy left to score the winner through Lakhdar Belloumi soon after. That quickly had media interest focusing on the so-called African minnows. They were found out in their second match, beaten 2-0 by an Austrian side that booked their place in the second stage at the same time, having already beaten the disappointing Chileans 1-0 in their opening match. Algeria duly recovered to lead Chile 3-0 at half time in their final match before partially running out of steam in the second half, finally winning 3-2. That put them in second place in the group, behind Austria but ahead of the West Germans. Just as had happened four years earlier when Argentina played Peru knowing exactly what score would earn them a place in the next stage, so West Germany and Austria took to the field a day after Algeria knowing a 1-0 German win would

ensure both German speaking countries progressed. In one of the most distasteful games ever played in the World Cup finals, Germany scored their goal through Horst Hrubesch and then effectively stopped competing. With boos and jeers ringing out from the 41,000 crowd, neither side showed any inclination to add to the score, leading many to label the match the Anschluss game and the belief that the two sides had agreed to a 1-0 win for the Germans beforehand. Despite Algerian protests to FIFA over this supposed collusion, FIFA refused to do anything other than ensure that in future World Cups the final matches would kick off at the same time, which was of little or no consolation to he Algerians.

England's stuttering qualification for the finals hardly had them installed as pre-tournament favourites and they weren't helped by long-term injuries to Kevin Keegan and Trevor Brooking, both named for the squad despite the fact that neither was expected to be fit until at least the second stage, assuming England lasted that far. A goal after only 27 seconds from Bryan Robson in the opening match against France settled England down and Robson added a second and Paul Mariner the other in the 3-1 win. The French just about recovered to beat Kuwait 4-1 and earn a draw with Czechoslovakia to qualify for the next stage, but their match against Kuwait was surrounded in some controversy when the Kuwaiti players stopped after hearing a whistle they believed was blown by the referee Miroslav Stupor. It turned out to have been someone in the crowd and whilst the Kuwaitis were motionless, France nipped in to score through Alain Giresse. Although the goal was subsequently disallowed, the Kuwaiti protests were so fierce, with Kuwaiti FA president Prince Fahid marching onto the pitch to remonstrate with the referee, they were subsequently fined £6,000, hardly a fortune to the oil rich kingdom! England had ensured their progress with a 2-0 win over Czechoslovakia thanks to goals from Mariner and Trevor Francis. They finished the first stage campaign with a single goal victory over Kuwait thanks to a Trevor Francis goal, but were considerably aided in their quest by the fact that the World Cup coincided with Ramadan and some of the more religiously observant among the Kuwaiti side had taken to the field on empty stomachs and refusing to take on board refreshments at half time. Equally, the England players lost nearly a stone in weight during the match.

Above
Bryan Robson of England scores the first and the fastest ever goal in a World Cup match during their game against France.

Left
Kevin Keegan pictured in 1982.

second place therefore was between Scotland and the Russians, with Scotland starting well in racing into a five goal lead against New Zealand in their opening match. Lack of concentration allowed New Zealand to net two of their own before the final whistle, goals that were ultimately to prove costly to the Scots. A 3-0 win by the USSR over New Zealand a day after Brazil had thumped Scotland 4-1 meant Scotland had to win their final match against the USSR to qualify for the next stage for the first time ever. Despite goals from Joe Jordan and Graeme Souness they were pegged back to a draw and slid out of the competition – Great Britain's three sides had just become two.

Brazil's reward for winning Group 6 was a place in the most difficult of all second stage groups, alongside Argentina and Italy. Neither had been impressive in the opening rounds, but when it mattered most Italy finally found form, inspired largely by Paolo Rossi, who had returned to the side after being banned for two years following a bribery scandal. He wasn't on the score sheet in the clash against Argentina, that honour going to Marco Tardelli and Antonio Cabrini who scored the goals that saw off Argentina in the group opener, Argentina finishing the match with ten men. A few days later their side was

Spain as host country had been expected to dominate Group 5 but were unconvincing almost throughout, opening their campaign held by Honduras in a match in which they had been expected to better Hungary's ten goal tally against El Salvador. Only a penalty from Lopez Ufarte saved them from bigger embarrassment. Honduras also proved an obstacle for Northern Ireland, who followed up their satisfying goalless draw with Yugoslavia with a 1-1 draw against the Central American side. Spain got the better of Yugoslavia in their meeting, winning 2-1 in Valencia, and Yugoslavia finally ended Honduras' interest in the competition with a 1-0 win in Zaragoza. A day later Spain faced Northern Ireland in the final group match, a Gerry Armstrong goal earning the Irish two points and top place in the group, Spain just holding on to second spot courtesy of having scored one more goal than Yugoslavia. Northern Ireland's performance was made all the more heroic by having to play for most of the second half with only ten men following the dismissal of Mal Donaghy.

If it were hoped Spain might do well, it was expected of Brazil who came to the tournament with one of the strongest sides they had ever assembled. They certainly proved too good for their group opponents, beating the USSR 2-1, Scotland 4-1 and New Zealand 4-0. The battle for

Above
Zico and the rest of Brazil play Scotland.

Right
Marco Tardelli of Italy holds onto Paz of Argentina during their World Cup quarter-final.

similarly reduced in numbers, Diego Maradona earning a red card after a wild swing at a Brazilian player, but by then the damage had been done as Brazil swept into a 3-1 lead. That set up a final group match between Italy and Brazil to decide the group, with Brazil firmly installed as favourites to progress.

Had they a goalkeeper and centre half the equal of their many fine strikers and midfield players they might have won the match, but Paolo Rossi had three efforts at goal and scored with each, each time restoring Italy's lead in a match they had to win to move into the semi-finals. Brazil equalised twice but couldn't manage a third and went out.

Italy's semi-final opponents emerged from Group A where Belgium were cast in the role of whipping boys, losing 3-0 to Poland in their opening match and then 1-0 to the USSR. That gave Poland pole position in the group going into the final match, a draw enough to earn them a place in the semi-final. A match as drab and dull as Brazil and Italy's clash had been pulsating, Poland settled for a draw and got it without too much trouble, the Russians lacking the ability and know-how on breaking down the Polish defence.

In Group C England faced West Germany in the World Cup for the third time with honours even, England having won in the final in 1966 and West Germany the quarter-final four years later. Honours ended even after the game too, a goalless draw that was only just better entertainment than the Poland and USSR clash. Karl Heinz Rummenigge hit the bar in the game's only real chance, both sides knowing that defeat would effectively end their interest in the cup. The Germans raised their game three days later to beat their Spanish hosts 2-1 thanks to goals from Pierre Littbarski and Klaus Fischer to put themselves top of the group. England needed to beat Spain by two clear goals to progress into the semi-final but managed none, their lack of a world class striker proving their ultimate undoing. As time ticked away Ron Greenwood gave way to desperation and brought on both Keegan and Brooking, neither of whom was fully fit. They managed to galvanise the

Above left
Paolo Rossi proved to be an inspiration for Italy against Brazil in their quarter-final.

Above
Not even the great Socrates could prevent Italy from progressing to the semi-final.

Left
Alberto Tarantini comforts Diego Maradona as he walks off the field after being sent off during the World Cup quarter-final between Brazil.

The final place in the last four went to France, who beat Austria 1-0 in the Group D opener thanks to Bernard Genghini's first half strike. The Austrians came from behind to earn a draw in the match against Northern Ireland in the second match, meaning the Irish needed to beat France to progress. The French however finally hit form, with Alain Giresse and Dominique Rocheteau both netting twice in their convincing 4-1 win.

If the tournament up to then had been unimpressive, all that was to change with the semi-finals. In Barcelona the rapidly improving Italians proved their victory over Brazil was no fluke with a commanding 2-0 win over Poland, reformed bad boy Paolo Rossi netting both. In Seville France and West Germany played out the match of the tournament, a match that had just about everything – six goals, a controversial incident involving the German goalkeeper, a German comeback and a penalty shoot out. It was all square at half time, Michel

England side as they laid siege to the Spanish goal, firing in some 24 shots on goal against the Spanish two. The best chances fell to Keegan and Brooking who might both have scored had they been fully fit, but they didn't and England slid out despite conceding only one goal in the competition.

Platini scoring for France from the penalty spot and Pierre Littbarski netting for the Germans, the closeness of the sides being shown in a stalemate second half. Extra time saw the French step up a gear, powering into a 3-1 lead through Marius Tresor and Alain Giresse and seemingly with one foot

Above
Kevin Keegan of England glances a header narrowly wide. It wasn't meant to be... as England go out of the World Cup.

Right
Michel Platini of France executes a bicycle kick in front of Norhern Ireland's goalkeeper Pat Jennings.

in the final. They might have added to their tally too, Patrick Battiston bearing down on the German goal and knocking the ball past Harald Schumacher, intent on retrieving it the other side of the opponent. He never got a chance, taken out by a disgraceful and blatant foul that saw the Frenchman taken off on a stretcher. Bizarrely, Dutch referee Charles Corver didn't think it a foul, awarding West Germany a goal kick! Reprieved, the Germans came back through goals from Karl-Heinz Rummenigge and Klaus Fischer to take the game into the lottery of a penalty shoot out. If Brazil had been moral winners in 1978, then France were their equivalent in 1982, West Germany winning the shoot out 5-4 after Didier Six and Maxime Bossis' penalties were saved in what was the first penalty shoot out in World Cup history.

France fielded a largely reserve side for the third and fourth place play-off against Poland, but the Poles had too much experience on the day, finally winning 3-2. France would eventually receive their just reward in two years time in the European Championship, but for many they deserved better than fourth place in the 1982 World Cup.

Karl Heinz Rummenigge had not been fully fit throughout the competition and was left out of the final. Italy were also short with Giancarlo Antognoni missing from their starting line-up and Francesco Graziani being lost soon after the match kicked off. Goalless at half time, Paolo Rossi broke the

Left
French defender Patrick Battiston lies on the ground as Michel Platini and Didier Six surround him while waiting for the medical staff to arrive.

Below
Harald Schumacher of West Germany saves the decisive penalty kick from Maxime Bossis of France during the World Cup semi-final. West Germany won the match 5-4 on penalty kicks.

deadlock 12 minutes after the break with his sixth goal of the tournament. Twelve minutes later Marco Tardelli added a second and Italy were virtually home and dry, the two goal cushion seldom being troubled by the West Germans. With nine minutes left on the clock Alessandro Altobelli scored a third Italian goal to finish the game as a contest, although Paul Breitner scored a consolation goal two minutes later. Captain Dino Zoff, at 40 the oldest player to captain a World Cup winning side, collected the cup that moved Italy up to joint place in the merit table, it being their third trophy win alongside Brazil.

It is difficult to know whether the new format was a success. Certainly the expanded competition increased the number of so-called minnows who featured in the finals and, as the likes of Algeria, Cameroon and Honduras to a certain extent showed, the gap between the established and up and coming nations was getting smaller each year. On the negative side, however, there were now too many meaningless matches in the World Cup finals, with some sides going out knowing exactly what they needed to do in order to progress into the next phase – the West Germany and Austrian arrangement being the best example. Whilst the world had expected the

Above
Paolo Rossi (left) celebrates scoring Italy's first goal against West Germany in the 1982 World Cup final.

Above right
Marco Tardelli celebrates scoring the second goal against West Germany.

Right
Alessandro Altobelli of Italy scores the third and final goal for Italy as they win the World Cup.

Far right
Scirea and Dino Zoff of Italy hold the World Cup trophy aloft.

likes of Zico, Socrates and Maradona to dominate the 1982 World Cup, it was Paolo Rossi who took the plaudits on a player level and the French as a team. Italy's success proved that it is not always the best team that wins the World Cup, it goes to the team that hits form at the right time. In July 1982, that team was Italy.

RESULTS

Group 1

Italy v Poland	0-0	Poland v Cameroon	0-0
Peru v Cameroon	0-0	Poland v Peru	5-1
Italy v Peru	1-1	Italy v Cameroon	1-1

	P	W	D	L	F	A	P
Poland	3	1	2	0	5	1	4
Italy	3	0	3	0	2	2	3
Cameroon	3	0	3	0	1	1	3
Peru	3	0	2	1	2	6	1

Group 2

West Germany v Algeria	1-2	Algeria v Austria	0-2
Chile v Austria	0-1	Algeria v Chile	3-2
West Germany v Chile	4-1	West Germany v Austria	1-0

	P	W	D	L	F	A	P
West Germany	3	2	0	1	6	3	4
Austria	3	2	0	1	3	1	4
Algeria	3	2	0	1	5	5	4
Chile	3	0	0	3	3	8	0

Group 3

Argentina v Belgium	0-1	Belgium v El Salvador	1-0
Hungary v El Salvador	10-1	Belgium v Hungary	1-1
Argentina v Hungary	4-1	Argentina v El Salvador	2-0

	P	W	D	L	F	A	P
Belgium	3	2	1	0	3	1	5
Argentina	3	2	0	1	6	2	4
Hungary	3	1	1	1	12	6	3
El Salvador	3	0	0	3	1	13	0

Group 4

England v France	3-1	France v Kuwait	4-1
Czechoslovakia v Kuwait	1-1	France v Czechoslovakia	1-1
England v Czechoslovakia	2-0	England v Kuwait	1-0

	P	W	D	L	F	A	P
England	3	3	0	0	6	1	6
France	3	1	1	1	6	5	3
Czechoslovakia	3	0	2	1	2	4	2
Kuwait	3	0	1	2	2	6	1

Group 5

Spain v Honduras	1-1	Honduras v Northern Ireland	1-1
Yugoslavia v Northern Ireland	0-0	Honduras v Yugoslavia	0-1
Spain v Yugoslavia	2-1	Northern Ireland v Spain	1-0

	P	W	D	L	F	A	P
N Ireland	3	1	2	0	2	1	4
Spain	3	1	1	1	3	3	3
Yugoslavia	3	1	1	1	2	2	3
Honduras	3	0	2	1	2	3	2

Group 6

Brazil v USSR	2-1	USSR v New Zealand	3-0
Scotland v New Zealand	5-2	USSR v Scotland	2-2
Brazil v Scotland	4-1	Brazil v New Zealand	4-0

	P	W	D	L	F	A	P
Brazil	3	3	0	0	10	2	6
USSR	3	1	1	1	6	4	3
Scotland	3	1	1	1	8	8	3
New Zealand	3	0	0	3	2	12	2

Quarter-Finals – Group A

| Poland v Belgium | 3-0 | Poland v USSR | 0-0 |
| Belgium v USSR | 0-1 | | |

	P	W	D	L	F	A	P
Poland	2	1	1	0	3	0	3
USSR	2	1	1	0	1	0	3
Belgium	2	0	0	2	0	4	0

Quarter-Finals – Group B

| West Germany v England | 0-0 | Spain v England | 0-0 |
| West Germany v Spain | 2-1 | | |

	P	W	D	L	F	A	P
West Germany	2	1	1	0	2	1	3
England	2	0	2	0	0	0	2
Spain	2	0	1	1	1	2	1

Quarter-Finals – Group C

| Italy v Argentina | 2-1 | Italy v Brazil | 3-2 |
| Argentina v Brazil | 1-3 | | |

	P	W	D	L	F	A	P
Italy	2	2	0	0	5	3	4
Brazil	2	1	0	1	5	4	2
Argentina	2	0	0	2	2	5	0

Quarter-Finals – Group D

| Austria v France | 0-1 | France v Northern Ireland | 4-1 |
| Austria v Northern Ireland | 2-2 | | |

	P	W	D	L	F	A	P
France	2	2	0	0	5	1	4
Austria	2	0	1	1	2	3	1
N Ireland	2	0	1	1	3	6	1

SEMI-FINALS	Poland	0	Italy	2
	West Germany	3	France	3

West Germany won 5-4 on penalties

3rd & 4th PLACE PLAY-OFF	Poland	3	France	2

FINAL	Italy	3	West Germany	1

(Rossi, Tardelli, Altobelli)
Zoff, Bergoni, Cabrini, Collovati, Scirea, Gentile, Oriali, Tardelli, Conti, Graziani (Altobelli) (Causio), Rossi

(Breitner)
Schumacher, Kaltz, KH Forster, Stielike, B Forster, Breitner, Dremmler (Hrubesch), Littbarski, Briegel, Fischer (Muller)

Right
An expectant
Mexican supporter
awaits the Opening
Ceremony for the
1986 World Cup.

Below
1986 official World
Cup poster.

The increase in the number of finalists in 1982 from sixteen to twenty-four may have been well received by the African and Asian football federations, who saw their allocation of places in the finals double, but it was something of a logistical nightmare for many others. The World Cup was due to return to South America in 1986 and Colombia was awarded the competition in 1980. When they saw the expanded competition for 1982, as observers having failed to qualify in their own right, there were doubts that they would be able to host the tournament. Although work began on renovating a number of stadiums and despite initial assurances that all would be ready by 1986, with three years to go the money had run out and work ground to a halt. With the Colombian government either unable or unwilling to assist, in 1983 the Colombian FA regretfully informed FIFA that they would be unable to host the competition.

Whilst there were a number of European countries willing to host the tournament in their place, FIFA was adamant that the competition should be staged in South America. Fortunately Mexico offered their facilities, which was gratefully accepted by FIFA – the 1986 World Cup would take place in South America after all. Mexico's own preparations were not all plain sailing either, for a devastating earthquake in September 1985 left more than

1986
MEXICO

20,000 dead and caused considerable damage around the country. Fortunately the stadiums planned for the competition

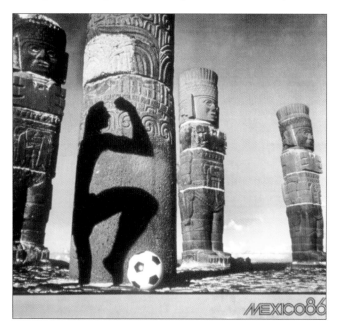

were largely unaffected meaning the competition could go ahead as planned, but Mexican recovery from the after effects of the earthquake were such that there were still a large number of citizens living in tent cities around the country, the inhabitants of which felt aggrieved at the amount of money being spent on a football competition whilst they were still trying to rebuild their lives. According to contemporary reports, the Mexican police did an effective job in ensuring any protests were quickly quelled.

Mexico not only stepped in late in the day as hosts, they were also awarded Colombia's automatic place in the finals, joining Italy as holders as the two countries that qualified as of right. There was an initial list of 119 countries that applied to enter the competition, a new record that was subsequently stretched to 121 following late entries. Once again the bulk came from Europe, thirty-three entries, which were granted an initial fourteen places (thirteen plus Italy). South America's ten

four matches to establish an early lead in the race for qualification, recording victories over Finland at home and Turkey and Northern Ireland away before dropping their first points in the competition with a goalless draw in Romania. The remaining four England matches saw them win only one, at home to Turkey, but draws in Finland and at home to Romania ensured these opponents could not get close to toppling England. The battle for runners-up spot and therefore a place in the finals came down to a three-horse race between Northern Ireland, Romania and Finland. The Finns ran out of games without having got into second spot, leaving the Irish and Romanians to battle it out. By the time the two countries went into their final matches, Northern Ireland were in second spot, two points ahead of the Romanians but with a slightly worse goal difference – they needed a point in their last match to ensure qualification, on the same night Romania were in Turkey playing the group's whipping boys. Northern Ireland's opponents were England at Wembley, where the Irish did enough to earn a point after a goalless draw. In answer to predictable complaints that the result had been squared before the game both sides could point to goal scoring chances – Pat Jennings in the Irish goal in particular made a number of spectacular saves – he deserved his place in Mexico more than anyone.

countries were awarded four places for the finals, Africa's twenty-nine entries would be whittled down to two, as would Asia's twenty-six and CONCACAF's eighteen countries (of which one place was allocated to Mexico as hosts). The final federation, Oceania, which had three entries, had no guaranteed place, just a play-off with the thirteenth placed European side.

Europe's thirty-two sides were placed in seven groups, four of which contained five sides with the top two qualifying, and the remaining three groups with four teams apiece. The winning team would qualify as of right, the runners-up of Groups 1 and 5 meeting in a two-legged play-off and the runner-up in Group 7 meeting the winner of the Oceania competition over two legs.

The four British sides were drawn in two groups; England and Northern Ireland in Group 3 and Scotland and Wales in Group 7. England picked up seven points from their opening

Both Scotland and Wales were in the running to qualify from Group 7, alongside Spain. Wales had recovered from a disastrous start that saw them lose their first two matches, in Iceland (their only win in the group) and away in Spain, but they came back to register consecutive wins against Iceland, Scotland and a thumping of Spain. Scotland were their usual inconsistent selves, beating Iceland and Spain and then losing to Spain and Wales. By the time the final matches came round, all three contenders had six points, with Wales due to play Scotland at home and Spain welcoming Iceland a few days later, by which time they would know exactly what they would have to do to qualify. Scotland got a vital draw that put them on top of the group on goal difference and assured of at least a place in the play-off against the winners of the Oceania group, although the elation at the result was severely dampened when manage Jock Stein suffered a heart attack as he walked down the tunnel at the end of the game and died soon after. Spain duly beat Iceland 2-1 to take the group and condemn Wales to elimination once again.

The major surprise of the European qualification programme was the elimination of Holland, missing out on automatic qualification from Group 5 when they finished second, three points behind Hungary (despite a victory in Budapest in their final group match) and then missing out on away goals in a play-off with the runners-up of Group 1, Belgium, their 1-0 defeat being followed by a 2-1 win. West Germany, France and Denmark were the other European group winners, being joined in qualification by runners-up Portugal, Bulgaria and the USSR.

Scotland's reward for finishing second in Group 7 was a two-legged tie against Australia, winners of the Oceania group, with Scotland winning the home leg 2-0 at Hampden Park and drawing 0-0 in Sydney.

Brazil, Argentina and Uruguay won their respective South American groups to earn automatic qualification, leaving four sides still battling through a series of play-offs to settle the remaining place in Mexico. That finally went to Paraguay, victors over Colombia (who thus missed out on qualifying for the tournament they were originally selected to host) and Chile.

Africa chose a straight knockout competition, with the two semi-final winners to collect the continent's places in the finals. Algeria, one of the surprise nations in the 1982 competition, and Morocco emerged as eventual winners, although once again the competition was rocked by withdrawals.

CONCACAF's were slotted into three qualifying groups, the winners of these going into a final round robin competition. Despite fierce competition, Canada finally won through to the finals for the first time in their history, registering three wins and a draw in their first group and two wins and two draws against Honduras and Costa Rica in the final stage.

The final two places for the tournament went to Iraq and South Korea from Asia after a complex series of groups and knockout rounds. South Korea only got through on away goals against the Japanese, Iraq had a rather more convincing 3-1 aggregate win over Syria.

FIFA, in their infinite wisdom, changed the format of the finals competition once again. The twenty-four competitors were slotted into six groups of four teams each, with the top two in each group going forward to the second stage. In addition, they would be joined by the four best third placed teams, after which the competition would revert to a straight knockout. Whilst a number of much fancied teams would ultimately rely on third place and a superior record over their

competitors in other groups to qualify, it did mean that after two weeks of intensive football, all that had been achieved were that eight sides had been eliminated.

The competition kicked off on the last day of May, the earliest the World Cup has been held, with Bulgaria

Above
Diego Maradona of Argentina celebrates his goal during the World Cup first-round match against Italy.

Right
Hugo Sanchez of Mexico is booked in their match against Paraguay.

surprisingly holding the holders Italy to a 1-1 draw in Group A. Argentina made a bright start to their opening match, powering into a two goal lead against South Korea and finally winning 3-1, although the Koreans were not disgraced. The clash between the two giants of the group resulted in a 1-1 draw, a scoreline that perhaps was of more benefit to the Italians, notoriously slow starters. Italy duly made sure of their progress into the next stage with a 3-2 win over South Korea, as wary and mindful of their opponents in 1986 as they had been complacent against North Korea thirty years previously. Argentina wrapped up the group with a 2-0 victory over Bulgaria, a result that also confined the Bulgarians to instant elimination.

Host nation Mexico dominated Group B, their attack spearheaded by Hugo Sanchez, something of a local hero who plied his trade in the Spanish League. A fine opening result saw them beat the much-fancied Belgium 2-1 in Mexico City. Four days later Mexico let slip a lead against Paraguay and had to settle for a draw, but this was the only point dropped in the group stage, Iraq being beaten 1-0 in the final match. Paraguay surprisingly took the runners-up spot, beating Iraq and holding the Belgians to a draw, but Belgium slipped through into the next stage with a victory over Iraq that ensured they were one of the third placed best performing sides.

Group C was expected to be between France and the USSR for qualification to the next stage and so it proved. With two wins and a draw apiece between them the group came down to goal difference, with the Russians' 6-0 hammering of the hugely disappointing Hungarians being more than enough to ensure top place. Although Canada didn't score or collect a single point, they proved a troublesome side to beat, as France, who only won 1-0 with a second half goal from Papin would confirm.

It was Northern Ireland's fate to be drawn in Group D with Brazil, who as expected won all three matches without conceding a goal to top the group. They were fortunate, however, in their opening match where the officials missed a Spanish shot from Michel that crashed against the crossbar and dropped behind the line and also managed to give goalscorer Socrates onside to head home the only goal despite being clearly offside. Spain recovered to take second spot and also buried the ghosts of 1982 with a victory over

Northern Ireland before a convincing 3-0 win over Algeria in their final match. Northern Ireland's only point in what was Pat Jennings' last appearances for his country came in their opener against Algeria; needing to beat Brazil in their final match to ensure progress they went down to a 3-0 defeat.

Group E, featuring West Germany, Denmark, Uruguay and Scotland, on paper perhaps the strongest group, was quickly dubbed the 'group of death'. It was not the West Germans, however, who dominated, but Denmark, who won all three matches, including a 2-0 win over West Germany in their final match to top the group. Even though they had lost their two opening matches, Scotland still had a chance of qualifying for the next stage with a victory over Uruguay, but the Uruguayan intent was spelt out early on with Jose Batista being sent off after only 55 seconds and thereafter kept all ten men behind the ball in order to ensure a 0-0 draw and progress into the next stage. It was perhaps this group, more than any other, that showed the peculiarities of the new format – Uruguay finished third with only two points, having scored only two goals and conceded seven, but still advanced into the next stage!

If Group E had been the 'group of death', then Group F, with England, was the 'group of sleep'. After four matches only two goals had been scored, although all four teams still harboured

hopes of qualifying for the second round. England's campaign had started disastrously, beaten 1-0 by Portugal who scored some 14 minutes from time with virtually their first attack of the afternoon. It didn't get much better in the second match either, held 0-0 by Morocco in the searing midday heat, but it was the loss of Bryan Robson through a dislocated shoulder and Ray Wilkins, sent off after petulantly throwing the ball at the referee that was ultimately to change England's fortunes. Whilst much of the media was calling for the head of manager Bobby Robson, he rang the changes for the must win match against Poland, bringing in Peter Reid to bolster the midfield and Peter Beardsley to work alongside Gary Lineker up front. With Glenn Hoddle orchestrating matters in midfield, England finally came good, Gary Lineker netting a hat-trick in the 3-0 win. After a promising start Portugal had soon faded, beaten by Poland in their second match and then losing to Morocco 3-1 in Guadalajara. Whilst England qualified in second place in Group F and Poland eventually had to settle for a place as one of the best third placed teams, the group was won by Morocco, who thus became the first African nation to qualify for the second stage of the World Cup.

After a cagey start in which sides had been more anxious to avoid elimination, the World Cup finally woke up in the second round, where the competition reverted to a straight knockout. Host

nation Mexico were willed on by the crowd in their 2-0 victory over a Bulgarian side that, despite appearing in the second round, had yet to win a World Cup finals match! On the same day in Leon, Belgium won a thrilling match against the USSR, coming from behind to win 4-3 in extra time after the two sides had finished 2-2 in normal time.

A day later it was the turn of the South Americans to take centre stage, with Brazil's four goal demolition of Poland one of the performances of the competition so far. Although they

Above
England captain Bryan Robson is helped off the pitch after dislocating his shoulder playing against Morocco.

Above right
Ray Wilkins is sent off, for throwing the ball towards the referee.

Right
Gary Lineker kicks the ball past Polish defender Stefan Majewski on his way to scoring a hat-trick.

Middle
Careca of Brazil celebrates after scoring against Poland in the second-round.

Left
Yannick Stopyra of France celebrates after scoring the second goal for his team past Italian goalkeeper Giovanni Galli.

Below
Gary Lineker in action for England against Paraguay.

were still reliant on a number of old faces, including Socrates and Zico, Brazil were still too strong for the disappointing Poles, adapting to the heat quicker than their European opponents. Uruguay's performances against Denmark and Scotland in the group matches had both resulted in a sending off and FIFA made it quite plain that a repeat performance against Argentina would earn them expulsion from the competition, irrespective of the outcome. It was therefore something of a subdued Uruguayan side that went down to a single strike from Pasculli.

France relied heavily on many of the players that had earned them the European Championship crown in 1984 during the 1986 World Cup, with the likes of Michel Platini beginning to move into top gear by the time the knockout stage commenced. A goal in each half against Italy gave them a comfortable 2-0 win over the holders, as disappointing in their final match of 1986 as they had been impressive in their final match of 1982. West Germany had more than a scare or two in their match against Morocco and only scraped through thanks to a late goal from Matthaus.

The final round of matches saw England overcome Paraguay rather more easily than the 3-0 scoreline suggested. A further two goals from Gary Lineker would not have gone unnoticed by the rest of the world, but it was his partnership with Peter Beardsley, who scored the other England goal, that was driving the team forward. The final second round match threw up a major surprise, with the Danes, who had been superb in their three group matches, but who appeared to abandon all thoughts of defence and were swept away 5-1 by Spain. Level at half time 1-1, Denmark couldn't get to grips with Butragueno in the second spell, who netted four of Spain's goals to earn a quarter-final clash with Belgium.

The match of the quarter-finals was undoubtedly Brazil's clash with France in Guadalajara, where the old masters met the new. An intriguing match between two adventurous sides resulted with nothing between them after 90 minutes had ended 1-1 and Zico had missed a penalty. Extra time finished

goalless, leaving the lottery of the penalty shoot out to decide who would progress into the semi-finals. France held their nerve, despite a miss from Michel Platini, to win 4-3 and send the Brazilians home despite not having lost a match during normal time.

Mexico suffered the same fate on the same day, held to a goalless draw by the stuttering West Germans and then falling to pieces in the penalty shoot-out, beaten 4-1.

Twenty-four hours later came one of the most eagerly awaited clashes of the competition, with England up against Argentina in Mexico City. Although it was four years since the Falklands War, diplomatic relations between the two countries still remained cut. Sporting relations on Argentina's side were still influenced by the ill-tempered clash between the two sides in the same stage in 1966 – there was an added flavour to their 1986 meeting! The match passed without incident, diplomatic or sporting during the first half, but burst into life five minutes into the second half. An attempted clearance by Steve Hodge flew up into the England penalty area, with Diego Maradona on the Argentina side and Peter Shilton in the England goal coming together about eight yards from the England goal line to contest the ball. Peter Shilton at six foot had a considerable height advantage over his Argentinean opponent, but only if Maradona attempted a legal challenge for the ball. Maradona undoubtedly picked up a couple of extra inches with his leap,

but the ball was directed towards the England goal by his hand, as was witnessed by virtually everyone in the stadium but the two people who mattered, the referee and linesman. Despite fierce protests from the England team, who surrounded the referee Ali Ben Naceur almost to a man, the goal was allowed to stand. Five minutes later Maradona scored one of the goals of this and any other tournament, collecting the ball inside his own half and going on a run that took him past four England players and around Shilton before stroking home a second. England threw caution to the wind, throwing on wingers in Chris Waddle and John Barnes who carved open the Argentina defence for Gary Lineker to slide in at the far post to reduce the arrears. A few minutes later Barnes created a similar chance, but this time Lineker missed by the narrowest of margins and that was effectively England's last chance at rescuing the match. Post-match interviews with Maradona centred on his illegal goal, which he claimed was scored by 'the Hand of God.' It has almost been forgotten that his second goal, a truly memorable effort, showed that he, more than any other player on earth, could produce moments of magic and sublime skill and had no need to revert to what was basically cheating. It was little or no consolation that Gary Lineker's strike

Above
French Captain Michel Platini celebrates scoring against Brazil in their quarter-final.

Middle
England and Argentina walk out for their World Cup quarter-final match.

Right
Hugo Sanchez of Mexico, is surrounded by West German defenders Andreas Brehme (3) and Karlheinz Foerster during their World Cup quarter-final.

Left
Diego Maradona handles the ball past Peter Shilton to the amazement of the England players.

Below
Andreas Brehme of Germany scores from a free kick as French players form a wall in front of goalkeeper Joel Bats during their World Cup semi-final.

enabled him to finish the competition as top goalscorer with six – England were out.

The fourth quarter-final match also required a penalty shoot out to settle matters, Spain coming from behind against Belgium to force extra time. A much tighter penalty shoot out finally saw the Belgians win 5-4, but it was particularly hard on Spain, one of the impressive sides of the competition.

Belgium's reward was a semi-final clash against Argentina in Mexico City where Maradona scored twice, neither of which was as controversial as his first nor as magical as his second against England, but were enough to earn Argentina a place in the final.

The other clash in Guadalajara between France and West Germany was a repeat of the 1982 semi-final. Although the Germans had been largely unimpressive up to now, fortunate to have progressed through two rounds after scoring only one goal, they worked out a plan to beat the French that worked to perfection. Michel Platini was kept quiet in midfield, the defence more than took care of anything the French could throw at them and at the other end goals from Brehme and Rudi Voller took them into their fifth final.

The match for third and fourth place was an exciting lash between Belgium and France in Puebla, with France going one better than four years previously with a 4-2 win, something of a last stand for the side built around Michel Platini.

The final between Argentina and West Germany was expected to be the match in which Maradona lived up to his reputation as one of the finest players in the world, and he would eventually make a considerable contribution to the game. Argentina were the much stronger and better side for some 75 minutes, leading through goals from Brown in the first half and Valdano in the second and seemingly coasting to the trophy for the second time in eight years. Then the Germans woke up, scoring twice inside eight minutes through Rudi Voller

and Karl Heinz Rummenigge to bring the scores level, an unlikely scoreline given the amount of possession Argentina

Above
Rudi Voeller of Germany scores a header past Argentinean goalkeeper Alberto Pumpido during the World Cup final.

Above right
Argentina along with Diego Maradona with the World Cup trophy.

Right
Jorge Burruchaga beats German goalkeeper Harald Schumacher to score the winning goal during for Argentina.

downside, however, was more meaningless matches in the opening group stages than previously, with two sides able to progress into the second round with only two points on the table. That was an issue FIFA would have to attend to in the future.

RESULTS

Group A

Bulgaria v Italy	1-1	South Korea v Bulgaria	1-1
Argentina v South Korea	3-1	South Korea v Italy	2-3
Italy v Argentina	1-1	Argentina v Bulgaria	2-0

	P	W	D	L	F	A	P
Argentina	3	2	1	0	6	2	5
Italy	3	1	2	0	5	4	4
Bulgaria	3	0	2	1	2	4	2
South Korea	3	0	1	2	4	7	1

Group B

Belgium v Mexico	1-2	Iraq v Belgium	1-2
Paraguay v Iraq	1-0	Iraq v Mexico	0-1
Mexico v Paraguay	1-1	Paraguay v Belgium	2-2

	P	W	D	L	F	A	P
Mexico	3	2	1	0	4	2	5
Paraguay	3	1	2	0	4	3	4
Belgium	3	1	1	1	5	5	3
Iraq	3	0	0	3	1	4	0

Group C

Canada v France	0-1	Hungary v Canada	2-0
USSR v Hungary	6-0	USSR v Canada	2-0
France v USSR	1-1	Hungary v France	0-3

	P	W	D	L	F	A	P
USSR	3	2	1	0	9	1	5
France	3	2	1	0	5	1	5
Hungary	3	1	0	2	2	9	2
Canada	3	0	0	3	0	5	0

Group D

Spain v Brazil	0-1	Northern Ireland v Spain	1-2
Algeria v Northern Ireland	1-1	Northern Ireland v Brazil	0-3
Brazil v Algeria	1-0	Algeria v Spain	0-3

	P	W	D	L	F	A	P
Brazil	3	3	0	0	5	0	6
Spain	3	2	0	1	5	2	4
N Ireland	3	0	1	2	2	6	1
Algeria	3	0	1	2	1	5	1

Group E

Uruguay v West Germany	1-1	West Germany v Scotland	2-1
Scotland v Denmark	0-1	Scotland v Uruguay	0-0
Denmark v Uruguay	6-1	Denmark v West Germany	2-0

	P	W	D	L	F	A	P
Denmark	3	3	0	0	9	1	6
West Germany	3	1	1	1	3	4	3
Uruguay	3	0	2	1	2	7	2
Scotland	3	0	1	2	1	3	1

Group F

Morocco v Poland	0-0	Poland v Portugal	1-0
Portugal v England	1-0	England v Poland	3-0
England v Morocco	0-0	Portugal v Morocco	1-3

	P	W	D	L	F	A	P
Morocco	3	1	2	0	3	1	4
England	3	1	1	1	3	1	3
Poland	3	1	1	1	1	3	3
Portugal	3	1	0	2	2	4	2

Second Round

| USSR v Belgium | 3-4 | Argentina v Uruguay | 1-0 | Morocco v West Germany | 0-1 | Denmark v Spain | 1-5 |
| Mexico v Bulgaria | 2-0 | Brazil v Poland | 4-0 | Italy v France | 0-2 | England v Paraguay | 3-0 |

Quarter-Finals

Brazil v France — 1-1
France won 4-3 on penalties

West Germany v Mexico — 0-0
West Germany won 4-1 on penalties

Argentina v England — 2-1

Spain v Belgium — 1-1
Belgium won 5-4 on penalties

SEMI-FINALS

| France | 0 | West Germany | 2 |
| Argentina | 2 | Belgium | 0 |

3rd & 4th PLACE PLAY-OFF

| France | 4 | Belgium | 2 |

FINAL

| Argentina | 3 | West Germany | 2 |

(Brown, Valdano, Burruchaga)   (Voller, Rummenigge)

Pumpido, Cuciuffo, Olarticoechea, Ruggeri, Brown, Giusti,
Burruchaga (Trobbiani), Batista, Valdano, Maradona, Enrique

Schumacher, Berthold, Briegel, Jakobs, Forster, Eder, Brehme,
Matthaus, Allofs (Voller), Magath (Hoeness), Rummenigge

had enjoyed previously. With extra time looking likely, Maradona turned provider to set Jose Burrachaga free just inside the German half of the field. Burrachaga ran half the length of the field, drew Harald Schumacher from the German goal and slotted home the winner in what had ended up as a dramatic final. Two minutes from time Burruchaga was substituted by Marcelo Trobbiani, his only appearance for his country in the World Cup, so his two minutes of action gave him the best possible return!

Diego Maradona's first goal against England notwithstanding, Argentina were probably worthy winners of a competition that could justifiably claim to be the World Cup, containing as it did more of the so-called emerging footballing nations in the finals. The

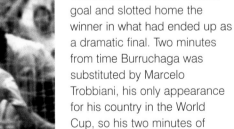

The World Cup finals tournament of 1990 saw the competition return to Italy, despite competition from England, Greece and the USSR, thus becoming the first nation to be officially awarded the finals on two separate occasions (Mexico having hosted the 1986 tournament following Colombia's withdrawal as host). As such Italy was spared the inconvenience of having to qualify but given added pressure from an expectant nation.

There were 112 original entries into the World Cup, although India subsequently withdrew from the Asian tournament. Europe's thirty-three entries were to be whittled down to fourteen qualifiers (thirteen plus Italy as hosts), South America's ten nations down to four (three plus Argentina as holders), Africa's twenty-four entrants were given two places in the finals, as were Asia's twenty-five and CONCACAF's fifteen. Only Oceania, who had four original entrants and subsequently had Israel placed in their group, had no qualifiers as of right, but the winner of the competition would meet the winner of South American Group 2 in a play-off over two legs.

1990
ITALY

Europe's entrants were put into seven groups, four with five teams and three with four, with the group winners of every group winning qualification. Additionally, the runners-up in six of the groups would also qualify, with only the runners-up of Group 1 ultimately missing out. That role befell Denmark, who led Romania by a point going into the very last match of the competition, which saw the Danes visiting Bucharest in a crucial play-off. Needing only a point to earn their place in Italy, the Danes slumped to a 3-1 defeat and missed out at the final hurdle.

England in Group 2 posted one of the best defensive records of the qualifying competition in not conceding a single goal and netting 10 of their own (only South Korea in Asia, whose group record

saw them score 25 goals without reply did better). Despite this record England could only finish second in the group with three wins and three draws, finishing a point behind Sweden. The dropped points came in stalemates home and away against Sweden and in Poland, now seemingly cast as perennial opponents, but England still managed to finish four points ahead of the Poles to banish any thoughts of 1974 revisited.

The Scots in Group 5 also finished runners-up to earn qualification, four points behind group winners Yugoslavia but, most crucially, a point ahead of the much fancied French who missed out. Once again Scotland contrived to almost throw away qualification, struggling home and away against Cyprus, even though they won both games. The French rally came too late, for with three games to play Scotland needed only a point to ensure they went through and finally got it in a 1-1 draw at home to Norway.

By contrast Wales and Northern Ireland struggled throughout in their respective groups, Wales finishing bottom of the pile in Group 4 and Northern Ireland second bottom in Group 6. In truth both countries knew they were going to be hard pressed to qualify when the draw had been made, Wales coming out with Holland, West Germany and Finland, whilst the Irish were paired against Spain, Hungary, Malta and their close friends and foes the other side of the Irish border. The Republic of Ireland, now managed by former England player Jack Charlton and

seeking qualification for the finals of a major tournament for the first time, finally got through, winning 2-0 at home to Hungary to give themselves the best possible chance; victories at home to Northern Ireland and away in Malta gave them second spot in the group behind the Spaniards.

Aside from France the other notable absentees were Portugal, who finished third in Group 7 behind Czechoslovakia and group winners Belgium, who joined Sweden, England, West Germany, Holland and Yugoslavia as European qualifiers without losing a single match.

Both the South American and CONCACAF tournaments were rocked with controversy and got caught up in ongoing unstable political situations. In South America the nine teams having to qualify were placed in three groups, with the winners of two going to the finals automatically and the third, the winner of Group 2, being given a play-off spot against the Oceania winner. Uruguay in Group 1 won through by the narrowest of margins, goal difference against Bolivia after both sides had won three and lost the other of their four matches. Colombia finished a point ahead of Paraguay in Group 2 to earn the play-off spot against the winners of the Oceania group and thus on their way to making up for the disappointment of four years earlier. The real drama came in Group 3, which quickly developed into a battle between Brazil and Chile for the automatic qualification spot. Going into the final match the sides were level on points, although Brazil had a distinct goal difference advantage. Having already drawn in Chile 1-1, Brazil were widely expected to do enough in their own Maracana Stadium to make the finals, but Chile made more than a game of it, holding the home side to a goalless first half. The drama unfolded in the second spell, Brazil taking the lead through Careca on 49 minutes, leaving the Chileans two goals to find in the remaining 40 or so minutes. The Brazilian crowd thought the matter was already settled and began celebrating, throwing flares onto the pitch. Many of these landed in or near the Chilean goal, and one appeared to hit goalkeeper Roberto Rojas, who suddenly collapsed and then stood up with blood on his face. The Chilean team walked off in protest, prompting a FIFA investigation into the matter. It appeared that Brazil were in real danger of being expelled from the competition, but the final verdict found them innocent – Rojas had not been hit or injured by a flare and had tried to fool the authorities, which earned him a lifetime ban. Several other Chilean officials were also banned and the match was awarded to Brazil 2-0, giving them passage into the finals. The investigation did not reveal, however, how Rojas had come to have blood on his face nor did it attempt to do anything about the flares, which were rapidly becoming a real danger at grounds around the world.

Expulsion also hit the much fancied Mexicans, who were found to have falsified the age details of four players in the World Youth Championships and were handed a ban from FIFA from June 1988 for two years. Mexico had already received a bye in the first round of the CONCACAF qualifying competition; their expulsion handed their second round opponents Costa Rica a similar bye into the group stage. There they made the most of their good fortune, winning the group on goal difference ahead of the United States, who also qualified for the finals. The Guatemala and El Salvador fixtures were not played, the political situation in El Salvador having deteriorated to such an extent that a match against Costa Rica had been abandoned. Neither side would have qualified had either match been played, but it was a reminder that football was not above politics.

Israel topped the Oceania group, despite winning only one of their four matches, their three draws enabling them to finish a point ahead of Australia in second place. That earned them a play-off against Colombia, with Colombia scoring the only goal of the two legs in the home tie in Barranquilla to take the final place in the competition.

Whilst the other twenty-three nations battled to make it to the finals, hosts Italy had their own problems to contend with. As 1989 gave way to 1990, there seemed a real possibility that the stadiums, many of which were merely being renovated, some being completely built from scratch, might not be ready in time, a mixture of bad planning and corruption having taken their toll, but fortunately all was ready, at least on the building side when the world gathered to watch the kick off on 8th June

Left
The Robsons – Bryan and Bobby pictured before the 1990 tournament.

Below
Joao Havelange, the President of FIFA in 1990.

got the call to rejoin the national side (he had been a member of the 1982 World Cup squad). Despite his advancing years (and there was considerable speculation that he might have been older than he claimed!) Roger was too sprightly for the Romanians and celebrated each goal with a little jig around the corner flag! With Cameroon having sown up Group B in the shortest possible time, Argentina, Romania and the USSR were left scrabbling for crumbs, with Romania and Argentina just about qualifying for the next stage at the expense of the Russians. The USSR slipped out of the competition at the first hurdle, despite a 4-0 thrashing of Cameroon in their final match, once again failing to live up to expectations. Argentina may have made it through to the next stage but it was something of a costly exercise,

Above
Biyick of Cameroon scores for his side in the opening game of the World Cup versus Argentina.

Right
Roger Milla celebrates his goal against Romania and performs his trademark jig around the corner flag, surrounded by his team.

in Milan. Things did not go entirely smoothly on the day, with FIFA President Joao Havelange waiting for the President of the Organising Committee to make his speech, and vice versa, with the result no speeches were made. Given the long winded speeches the world has had to suffer in the past, this may well have been the best result!

The opening match of the competition in the San Siro stadium turned out to be the match the world had been waiting for, with holders Argentina up against the emergent African country Cameroon. The South Americans were widely expected to win in a canter, but on the day the Africans were more than a match for their seemingly more illustrious rivals. Naivety was perhaps Cameroon's worst enemy, for just on the hour Andre Kana-Biyick was sent off for a foul on Claudio Caniggia, but rather than capitulate, Cameroon defended even more resolutely. Not only that, some six minutes later Francois Oman-Biyick headed past Pumpido to set up an unlikely win. Two minutes from time Benjamin Massing became the second Cameroon player to leave the field following a waist high assault on the unfortunate Caniggia (it was later described 'The intent was not so much to break Caniggia's legs but more to separate them from the rest of his body') but the nine men held on for their historic win.

If the world thought Cameroon's win over Argentina was the end of the shocks, then there were further surprises in store from the Indomitable Lions, who followed up this result with an even more impressive 2-1 win over Romania in their second group match. Star of the show was two-goal hero Roger Milla, a 38 year old striker who was in semi-retirement and playing local football on the island of Reunion when he

goalkeeper Pumpido breaking a leg after nine minutes of the 2-0 win over the USSR, bringing his World Cup tournament to a quick end.

In Group A Austria were expected to do so much better than achieve one win. That came against the United States, making their first finals' appearance since 1950 when they beat England 1-0. They were not to get the chance of springing similar surprises this time around, losing all three of their matches, but their time would eventually come. The group came down to a straight battle between hosts Italy and Czechoslovakia, with Italy winning the group with three straight wins. Goals were still something of a problem for Italy, who registered two 1-0 victories (against Austria and the USA)

and a 2-0 win in topping the group, the very least the Italian nation expected.

Scotland were once again drawn against Brazil in Group C, alongside Sweden and Costa Rica, but three points might have been enough to have earned them a place in the second stage for the first time in their history. Two of the required points were earmarked against Costa Rica, but as Cameroon had already shown, the gap between the original powers and the minnows was shrinking at a fantastic pace – Costa Rica won the match 1-0. Scotland finally got points on the board with a 2-1 win over the disappointing Swedes in their second match, whilst Brazil made sure the group was all but theirs with a 1-0 win over Costa Rica. The final two matches in the group paired the Brazilians with Scotland and Costa Rica against Sweden; Brazil had already won the group, whilst Costa Rica and Scotland were level on points. Even if Costa Rica won, Scotland could still qualify for the next stage if they got a point from their match, and for an hour and a quarter, all seemed to be going Scotland's way – Sweden had the lead against Costa Rica and Scotland were containing the Brazilians. As always happens in such circumstances, the picture changed inside 10 minutes or so, with Costa Rica scoring twice to take a lead they ultimately held

against Sweden and Muller scored for Brazil to put Scotland to the sword. Once again they had fallen at the first hurdle.

As expected West Germany were the dominant force in Group D, topping the group with five points, one ahead of Yugoslavia in second place and dropping their only point against Colombia. German intent

Colombia as one of the best third place teams in the group stages.

Third place was also good enough in the remaining two groups. In Group F Uruguay finished third behind Spain and Belgium, gaining their required win with a 1-0 victory over South Korea in their final group match to sneak into the second round. In truth, however, this was a poor a Uruguayan side as had been seen in the World Cup

had been shown in the very first match, a 4-1 win over the much-fancied Yugoslavs, and in their 5-1 demolition of the United Arab Emirates in their second match; there was to be no chance of an Algerian-like upset here. In the event both Yugoslavia and Colombia followed them out of the group,

finals, scoring just two goals in their three group matches, finishing with a deficit goal difference and still managing to qualify! No such problems for the Spaniards and Belgians, who scored five and six respectively and finished first and second in the group.

The final group, which featured England, was one of the most tense or boring, depending upon which side of Hadrian's Wall you sit. After four matches, all four teams were level on points and goals scored, England and the Republic of Ireland drawing 1-1 (England took the lead but their foot off the gas, allowing the Irish back into the game), Egypt coming from behind to rescue a point against the Dutch, who then played out a goalless draw against England a day before the Irish and Egyptians recorded their own stalemate. With the prospect of the drawing of lots facing the four teams

Above
West Germany prepare to face Columbia at the San Siro stadium.

Right
Ruben Sosa of Uruguay and Francisco Perez of Spain fight for the ball during their World Cup game.

should a further two draws be recorded, something had to give, with Mark Wright scoring the only goal of the game for England in the match with Egypt to put them in the driving seat. A late equaliser from Niall Quinn for the Republic of Ireland gave them second spot in the group, level on points and goals scored with the Dutch, but both sides progressed into the second round. More worrying for both the Irish and Dutch was the fact that neither had yet won a match; Holland were expected to do so much better.

After the cat and mouse play that usually accompanied group matches, it was now down to sudden death cup tie football from here on in. It did not take long for the shocks to come, with Cameroon's 2-1 victory over Colombia the pick of the bunch. After 90 minutes of goalless action the game came to life in extra time, with Roger Milla grabbing both goals to effectively put Cameroon through to the quarter-finals. Although Colombia rallied, it was too late, undone as much by the antics of Rene Higuita, the Colombian goalkeeper (one of the goals came when he attempted to dribble the ball up to the halfway line, lost it to Milla and despite a frantic lunge at the opposing player, could only watch as Milla strolled the ball into an empty net, laughing his head off as he did so) as they had by their own inability to score at the right end.

Czechoslovakia made sure there was no upset in their second round clash with Costa Rica, although they were pegged back 10 minutes into the second half before the Costa Ricans ran out of steam and Czechoslovakia ran out 4-1 winners.

A day later came the clash of the round in Turin, with Argentina pitted against the Brazilians. Despite the 100% record in group matches and the presence of the likes of Branco and Careca, this was not the Brazil of old, with goalkeeper Taffarel identified as perhaps the weak link. Whilst Brazilian sides of the past had often played with a weak goalkeeper, the prevailing thought of attack, attack, attack had

usually provided enough cover to protect the defence, but this time there was little forward enterprise. With the match heading for extra time, Caniggia made the most of the space around him to fire home the only goal of the game 10 minutes from time.

There was an equal battle royal taking place in Milan, where old foes West Germany came up against Holland, something of a re-run of the 1974 final. The score ended with a similar 2-1 win for the Germans too, Holland's consolation goal coming two minutes from time from Ronald Koeman. Far worse, however, was the dismissal of Frank Rijkaard for twice spitting at Rudi Voller, and even claims of racial taunts did not make Rijkaard's action any more palatable.

The Republic of Ireland qualified from the group stage without winning a match, and managed to advance into the quarter-finals without scoring a goal, at least in the regulation 120 minutes of normal and extra time against the Romanians. Fortunately, Romania couldn't find the net either, and that set up a penalty shoot out, which the

Irish won 5-4 to set off one of the biggest parties Genoa had ever seen.

The host nation had no need of penalties in their tie with Uruguay, finally scoring twice in the second half to earn a place in the quarter-final. Although the Uruguayans were well organised defensively, the lack of enterprise from Enzo Francescoli and Ruben Sosa up front proved their undoing. By contrast, the emergence of Salvatore Schillaci, who had only one season of Serie A with Juventus behind him, at just the right time, offered the Italians hope that this might once again be their year.

There was a dour struggle in Verona where Spain met Yugoslavia. The Yugoslavs were one of the most improved sides of the competition; the Spaniards one of the most disappointing. A side that could boast the likes of Butragueno up front and a goalkeeper the Brazilians would have killed for in Zubizarreta deserved to progress further in the competition, but the solid, functional Yugoslavs finally did for them in extra time, Stojkovic scoring two minutes into the additional period to win the match 2-1.

England's clash with Belgium was equally tense, with the game ebbing and flowing and being largely dictated by the mercurial talents of Paul Gascoigne in the English midfield. The

Above
Rudi Voller doesn't look too happy, after being spat at by Frank Rijkaard of Holland.

Middle
Pedrag Spasic of Yugoslavia pulls on the shirt of Emilio Butragueno (L) of Spain in their second-round game.

Right
David O'Leary of the Republic of Ireland scores the decisive penalty against the Romanian's.

Belgians were no slouches either, with Enzo Scifo inspiring his side to hitting the woodwork twice on the few occasions they managed to find a way past the likes of Des Walker and Mark Wright. Extra time came and almost went, with the prospect of a penalty shoot out looming when a Gascoigne free kick floated into the Belgian penalty area. David Platt was the first to react, watching the ball drift over his shoulder, spinning and catching a perfect volley that sailed past Preud'homme in the Belgian goal. With 119 minutes on the clock, there was no time for Belgium to mount a reply; England were into the semi-finals.

Argentina's run of good fortune continued into the quarter-finals. Whilst they may have kept Stojkovic quiet at the back, they offered little or nothing up front, the midfield efforts of Diego Maradona failing to provide anything for Caniggia to latch on to. Ninety minutes of huff and puff failed to produce a goal, as did a further 30 minutes, leaving the lottery of a penalty shoot out to decide who would progress into the semi-final. Here Argentina held their nerve, winning 3-2, although they barely deserved it.

If the Argentine pushed their luck to the limit in their match, then it finally ran out for the Irish in their match with Italy. Resolute at the back, the Irish

needed more creativity up front, but whilst Niall Quinn and John Aldridge and their eventual replacements Tony Cascarino and John Sheridan provided plenty of stamina, the final thrust was always missing. A lone strike from Schillaci, almost pre-ordained, did for them in the end.

A single goal was enough to see the West Germans into the semi-finals following their clash with Czechoslovakia, the only strike coming from the penalty spot from Matthaus

Above
David Platt of England scores a dramatic winning goal against Belgium to send England through to the quarter-finals.

Left
Pat Bonner goalkeeper for the Republic of Ireland saves a ball from Aldo Serena of Italy during their quarter-final match.

midway through the first half. The Czech effort wasn't helped by the dismissal of Moravcik, but the Germans were seldom troubled.

If the three other quarter-finals were relatively drab and devoid of goals, then the same could not be said of England's match with Cameroon. The Cameroon side had brightened a decidedly dull World Cup tournament and proved right from the start with victory over Argentina that they were not just here to make up the numbers. England, however, had improved as the tournament progressed, their dour draw with the Republic of Ireland in their opening match a dim and distant memory. David Platt, a substitute in England's clash with Belgium was in the starting line-up for the Cameroon match and carried on where he had left off, putting England ahead with a header on the 25 minute mark. Cameroon never gave up, virtually laying siege to Peter Shilton's goal, but the English defence held firm until some 20 minutes into the second half when Gascoigne brought down Milla inside the area for a Cameroon penalty. Kunde duly despatched the kick to bring Cameroon level, and four minutes later Ekeke chipped Shilton to put Cameroon ahead for the first time in the match. Staring defeat in the face, manager Bobby Robson abandoned the sweeper system, although how much of this was due to managerial influence off the pitch and sheer instinct on it is open to debate. In the event, Paul Gascoigne's runs and passes created a host of chances, some clear cut, others not so, but the Cameroon defence ran out of legitimate options on how to contain either him or striker Gary Lineker. Eventually their luck ran out, and eight minutes from the end of normal time Lineker was brought down in the box for an England penalty. Lineker retained his composure to draw England level from 12 yards and, just on the stroke of half time in extra time, repeated the feat after he had again been brought down. Although Cameroon launched a succession of attacks on the England goal in search of an equaliser, England held firm to take their place in the semi-finals, their first such appearance since 1966.

Both semi-finals were the subject of gamesmanship before a ball was kicked. Diego Maradona whipped things up against the Italians, claiming that he was effectively playing a home match (the semi-final was to take place in Naples, with whom Maradona played his club football) and that, as Napoli residents did not consider themselves Italian, perhaps they

Above
Thomas Berthold of West Germany and Ivo Knoflicek of Czechoslovakia both jump to head the ball during their quarter-final.

Right
David Platt heads in his first goal for England against Cameroon in their World Cup quarter-final.

but the pressure of being the home side, with all the expectation that went with it, seemed to affect the players. Slowly Argentina got back into the game, Maradona beginning to run things in midfield and setting up a succession of chances. Eventually one went in, Caniggia heading the first goal Italy had conceded in the entire competition on 67 minutes after goalkeeper Walter Zenga had been caught badly out of position. Both sides had chances to settle the match before the final whistle went on 90 minutes, and extra time was played out nervously, neither side wanting to make a mistake at such a crucial stage in the competition. That left it to the penalty shoot out to decide who advanced into the final and who missed out, with the Argentine experience from the previous round giving them a slight advantage. Just as in the shoot out against Yugoslavia, the hero was Argentine goalkeeper Sergio Goycoechea (who, it will be recalled, was only in the side after first choice Pumpido broke his leg earlier in the competition), guessing correctly to keep out Donadoni and Serena - the host nation were not to make the final after all.

Left
Claudio Canniggia of Argentina heads the ball past Walter Zenga the Italian goalkeeper in their World Cup semi-final.

Below
Goycoechea the Argentinean goalkeeper saves the vital penalty against Italy to take them through the final.

should support Argentina instead! It didn't work, virtually the whole of the ground cheering on the Azzuri towards the final. The pre-match histrionics were slightly better than the match itself, with Italy starting strongly but fading just when they could least afford it. Gianluca Vialli, widely expected to be one of the key Italian players in the entire tournament, had another anonymous match and was replaced on 70 minutes by Serena. The Italian hero once again was Salvatore Schillaci, who netted the opening goal on 17 minutes. That should have settled Italian nerves,

A day later came the second semi-final, the clash between long time foes England and West Germany. Although England had won the 1966 final against the Germans (continuing a run that had seen them avoid defeat in every match since hostilities of a football kind commenced in 1930), they had failed to get the better of them in major competitions since, losing in the World Cup quarter-finals in 1970, the European Championship quarter-finals in 1972 and drawing the World Cup second group stage in 1982. Despite this, the informed view was that whilst the Germans had been impressive in their group matches, they had started to run out of steam as the competition progressed, scraping through with single goal victories against Holland and Czechoslovakia. As of course had England against Belgium and Cameroon, but England had been woeful against the Republic of Ireland and improved match on match since, with Paul Gascoigne in particular becoming a major influence on each game he played. If the general standard of play in the entire competition prior to England's match with West Germany had been cautious, then the same could not be said for this match. At last, in effectively the penultimate match of the competition, it came to life, with both sides attacking the other in an attempt to win on goals scored. England had the better of the first half, Gascoigne coming close with a low volley and Shilton being rarely troubled in goal even if the Germans had plenty of possession. The opening goal finally came just short of the hour mark, a goal somewhat out of keeping with what had passed previously. Stuart Pearce fouled Thomas Hassler just outside the England penalty area and the German laid off a short free kick to Andreas Brehme. His shot, whilst on target, looked to have been covered by Shilton, but it hit the on-rushing England defender Paul Parker, looping up high over the England wall and Shilton before nestling in the back of the goal. It was a blow that would have crushed most sides, but this England side were made of sterner stuff. Rather than kick and rush in a desperate search for an equaliser, England played as they had for the first hour, maintaining possession, picking their moment to move forward. The equaliser came with nine minutes left on the clock, Parker crossing from deep on the right, causing panic in the German defence and there was Gary Lineker, still as sharp as four years previously, to stroke the ball home past Illgner.

Whilst there were no further goals in the remaining nine minutes there was one crucial incident. Man of the moment Paul Gascoigne had played most of the tournament on the edge but had kept his enthusiasm and exuberance in check until a few moments from time. Weaving his way past two Germans he temporarily lost control and tried to retrieve the ball before Berthold could use it to any affect. It was not a malicious tackle, indeed later replays showed it to be

Above right
Gary Lineker scores the equaliser for England during the World Cup semi-final against West Germany.

Right
Lineker celebrates scoring his goal.

even if he couldn't make it to the final, he was going to make damn sure his England team mates would. Extra time came and there was no let up in the action or tension, Chris Waddle hitting the post for England, Buchwald doing likewise for the Germans. Eventually, just as 24 hours previously, time ran out and we were left with a penalty shoot out to settle the matter. After six strikes England and Germany could still not be separated, Lineker, Platt and Beardsley's successes being repeated by Brehme, Matthaus and Riedle. Then Stuart Pearce saw his penalty strike the legs of Illgner and Thon gave Germany the advantage with his successful strike. Chris Waddle stepped up to try and bring England level and sent his

no more than innocuous, but a combination of Berthold writhing around as though in pain and the German bench leaping to their feet convinced the Brazilian referee that it was

worthy of a yellow card. Unfortunately it was Gascoigne's second of the tournament and meant that should England reach the final, he would have to sit it out. The realisation hit Gascoigne first, with tears beginning to well up in his eyes. For a few moments he was of little help to England, running around as though lost in his own world, about to miss out on the biggest match of his career. Eventually he calmed down and, as he later explained, played to ensure that

kick sailing high over the bar and into the sky (a couple of days later, when the England team were back home, Waddle was one of the guests on a breakfast television show. He received a call from a viewer in Derby who claimed that Waddle's kick had landed in his back garden – did he want the ball back!), England were out.

Given the way they had played, the third and fourth place play-off between England and Italy would have

Above
Stuart Pearce shows his disappointment after his penalty kick miss.

Far left
Paul Gascoigne receives a yellow card and knows he will miss the final should England beat Germany.

Left
David Platt leaps above the Italian defence in the third and fourth place play-off.

made a better final. With little or nothing resting on the outcome, both sides played with a little more adventure than had been presented to the world in the previous three weeks or so. Baggio opened the scoring on 70 minutes, Platt equalised 10 minutes later and six minutes from time Schillaci netted the winner from the penalty spot (where else!). It was his sixth goal of the competition, enabling him to finish top scorer in the competition and came against Peter Shilton in what was his 125th and final match for England. England went home to something of a hero's welcome, fourth place being their best showing since winning in 1966. They also picked up the FIFA Fair Play Award, testament to their attempts to play the game as it was intended throughout the competition.

England's plane was landing in Luton as West Germany and Argentina began their preparations for the final. For the Germans it was a third successive final, the first time any side had achieved the feat. Against them was Argentina, the holders, the first time a side had reach the final to try and defend their title since Brazil in 1962. It was also the first repeat final, for both sides had faced each other four years previously in Mexico City. Sadly, the build-up proved to be better than the match, one of the worst ever witnessed in such a prestigious competition. For this the blame must lay solely with Argentina, a side who were as cynical in 1990 as they had been adventurous in 1978 and 1986. They had collected over twenty yellow cards on their run to the final, the worst

disciplinary record of any of the finalists, and it did not improve in the final itself. In a match forgettable as far as action was concerned, West Germany did more of the attacking without ever really looking likely to score, but at least they were prepared to try and score – Argentina appeared to have set their stall out on holding on for a third penalty shoot out. Eventually even the referee lost patience with the malicious nature of Argentina's play, brandishing a red card in front of substitute Pedro Monzon, who became the first player to be dismissed in a final. Another Argentine foul, this time by Roberto Sensini on Rudi Voller resulted in a penalty, which

Above
West Germany attempt to block a free-kick against Agrentina in the World Cup final.

Above right
Andreas Brehme scores the winning and only goal for West Germany from the penalty spot.

Right
Celebrations for West Germany as they display the World Cup.

Andreas Brehme put away for what turned out to be the only goal of the game six minutes from time. There was still time for Argentina to completely lose their heads, Gustavo Dezotti joining Monzon for an early bath and nearly being joined by a few others as the Argentine players surrounded the referee to make their point. It had been that kind of final, in that kind of tournament. The fact that West Germany had joined Brazil and Italy as three times winners of the competition, or that German coach Franz Beckenbauer had become the first man to captain and manage a World Cup winning side was lost among the recriminations from Argentina.

The 1990 competition is widely held as one of the worst of all time, with fewer goals, more cautions and more penalty shoot outs than anything previously. Indeed, Italy 1990 is usually mentioned in the same sentence as Chile 1962, it was that bad. There were moments to savour however, with England's matches against Belgium, Cameroon and West Germany providing most of the action and drama in the competition. Cameroon were a revelation, Costa Rica didn't disgrace themselves and even Egypt had a chance of qualifying for the next stage

going into the last group matches – none of the so-called minnows had reason to feel downhearted. There was a certain irony, however, in the similarities between the very first match in the competition and the very last – one side finished with only nine men and Argentina lost 1-0! Justice was done, and in front of the largest television audience in the world, well and truly seen to be done!

RESULTS

Group A

Italy v Austria	1-0	Austria v Czechoslovakia	0-1
USA v Czechoslovakia	1-5	Italy v Czechoslovakia	2-0
Italy v USA	1-0	Austria v USA	2-1

	P	W	D	L	F	A	P
Italy	3	3	0	0	4	0	6
Czechoslovakia	3	2	0	1	6	3	4
Austria	3	1	0	2	2	3	2
USA	3	0	0	3	2	8	0

Group B

Argentina v Cameroon	0-1	Cameroon v Romania	2-1
USSR v Romania	0-2	Argentina v Romania	1-1
Argentina v USSR	2-0	Cameroon v USSR	0-4

	P	W	D	L	F	A	P
Cameroon	3	2	0	1	3	5	4
Romania	3	1	1	1	4	3	3
Argentina	3	1	1	1	3	2	3
USSR	3	1	0	2	4	4	2

Group C

Brazil v Sweden	2-1	Sweden v Scotland	1-2
Costa Rica v Scotland	1-0	Sweden v Costa Rica	1-2
Brazil v Costa Rica	1-0	Brazil v Scotland	1-0

	P	W	D	L	F	A	P
Brazil	3	3	0	0	4	1	6
Costa Rica	3	2	0	1	3	2	4
Scotland	3	1	0	2	2	3	2
Sweden	3	0	0	3	3	6	0

Group D

U A Emirates v Colombia	0-2	W Germany v U A Emirates	5-1
W Germany v Yugoslavia	4-1	W Germany v Colombia	1-1
Yugoslavia v Colombia	1-0	Yugoslavia v U A Emirates	4-1

	P	W	D	L	F	A	P
West Germany	3	2	1	0	10	3	5
Yugoslavia	3	2	0	1	6	5	4
Colombia	3	1	1	1	3	2	3
U A Emirates	3	0	0	3	2	11	0

Group E

Belgium v South Korea	2-0	Belgium v Uruguay	3-1
Uruguay v Spain	0-0	Belgium v Spain	1-2
South Korea v Spain	1-3	South Korea v Uruguay	0-1

	P	W	D	L	F	A	P
Spain	3	2	1	0	5	2	5
Belgium	3	2	0	1	6	3	4
Uruguay	3	1	1	1	2	3	3
South Korea	3	0	0	3	1	6	0

Group F

England v Rep of Ireland	1-1	Rep of Ireland v Egypt	0-0
Holland v Egypt	1-1	England v Egypt	1-0
England v Holland	0-0	Rep of Ireland v Holland	1-1

	P	W	D	L	F	A	P
England	3	1	2	0	2	1	4
Holland	3	0	3	0	2	2	3
Rep of Ireland	3	0	3	0	2	2	3
Egypt	3	0	2	1	1	2	2

Second Round

Czechoslovakia v Costa Rica	4-1	West Germany v Holland	2-1	Italy v Uruguay	2-0
Cameroon v Colombia	2-1	Brazil v Argentina	0-1	Rep of Ireland v Romania	0-0

Spain v Yugoslavia 1-2
England v Belgium 1-0
Rep of Ireland won 5-4 on penalties

Quarter-Finals

Yugoslavia v Argentina	0-0
Argentina won 3-2 on penalties	
Italy v Republic of Ireland	1-0
West Germany v Czechoslovakia	1-0
England v Cameroon	3-2

SEMI-FINALS

Italy	1	Argentina	1
		Argentina won 4-3 on penalties	
West Germany	1	England	1
West Germany won 4-3 on penalties			

3rd & 4th PLACE PLAY-OFF

Italy	2	England	1

FINAL

West Germany	1	Argentina	0

(Brehme pen)

Illgner, Brehme, Kohler, Augenthaler, Berthold (Reuter), Buchwald, Hassler, Matthaus, Littbarski, Voller, Klinsmann

Goycoechea, Lorenzo, Sensini, Serrizuela, Ruggeri (Monzon), Simon, Basualdo, Burruchaga (Calderon), Maradona, Troglio, Dezotti

Below
Franz
Beckenbauer steps
out for the New
York Cosmos.

When Joao Havelange took over the presidency of FIFA in 1974, it was on the basis of his promises to the African nations that they would receive a greater share of the places in future World Cup finals. That had largely been achieved by increasing the number of finalists from sixteen to twenty-four, a change that had taken eight years to come into effect. Of course, it was not only the African nations who benefited, for FIFA had also increased the places for all federations bar Oceania in subsequent competitions. With increased participation in the finals, it was not long before those same federations were asking for an opportunity to host the competition as well.

As we have seen, for many years Europe and South America, by far the most successful and thus influential federations had effectively taken it in turns to host the finals. With the 1990 competition being awarded to Italy, it was

initially felt that the competition would return to South America. Joao Havelange had other ideas, eager to open up new territories for the world's most popular sport. Key amongst these was the United States of America, the richest country in the world and, as well as one of the largest, one of the last to have caught the football buzz.

There had been attempts in the past. Just as they were to do in the other three corners of the world, British immigrants had introduced football into the country at the end of the nineteenth century. In the 1930s the standard of football in America was of sufficient quality to have helped the country reach the semi-finals of the World Cup in 1930. Since then the USA had won only one World Cup finals match, in 1950 against England! After that interest in the game waned, with American football, basketball and baseball becoming the dominant sports in the country. There had been a concerted effort in the 1960s and 70s to re-introduce the game to the nation, with a host of former stars joining the professional league that sprung up, including the likes of Bobby Moore, George Best, Franz Beckenbauer and even Pele lending their weight to the effort. It proved to be in vain – 'Tell the Kraut (Beckenbauer) to get his ass up front; we don't pay a million bucks for a guy to hang around in defence' was one piece of 'encouragement' offered to Beckenbauer by a club owner totally oblivious to the fact that Franz Beckenbauer had made his name as one of the best sweepers in Europe!

Twenty or so years later, Joao Havelange felt it was time for a renewed attempt. Alan Rothenberg, a long-time football official in the United States felt so too and in February 1987 informed FIFA that the USSF (United States Soccer Federation) had an interest in staging the competition finals. Also competing were Morocco and Brazil, but despite Brazil's pedigree in the competition, Morocco was seen as the major threat to the USA. However, on the apt date of 4th July 1988, the choice of the United States to host the 1994 finals was duly ratified by FIFA, the USA collecting ten votes, Morocco seven and Brazil two.

In many ways the United States was both an obvious and yet strange choice. As the richest nation on earth, the commercial possibilities of holding the biggest sporting competition in the world (the Olympics may attract more

plans were in place to bring in a new one after the World Cup was over – that was to be the legacy of the World Cup 1994.

Qualification for the finals threw up the usual surprises. The changing political scene in Europe caused FIFA and their European counterparts UEFA one or two problems but, as FIFA had often stated, football was above politics. Thus it was whilst the re-unified East and West Germany now competed under the banner of Germany, the division of Czechoslovakia into (ultimately) the Czech Republic and Slovakia made no difference to FIFA; neither entity was recognised and the pair had to enter as RCS – Representation of Czechs and Slovaks! In all thirty-eight countries entered the competition, although Liechtenstein subsequently withdrew and Yugoslavia, racked by civil war, was suspended. The remaining entrants were placed into six groups, with the top two in each group advancing into the finals.

Scotland were drawn in Group 1, a particularly tough group containing Italy, Portugal and the ever-improving Switzerland. Defeats away to all three did for Scotland long before the final two emerged, and the battle for the two places went right down to the wire. On the final day, Portugal and Italy were joint top of the group with fourteen points, Switzerland third with thirteen, but Portugal were away in Milan whilst Switzerland had a home tie with whipping boys Estonia. Switzerland duly got their win with a 4-0 victory, and a single strike from Dino Baggio seven minutes from time gave Italy top spot in the group.

England were drawn in Group 2 and should have had little trouble qualifying. Once again Poland were in the same group, but England picked up three points against their perennial foes, an away draw being followed by an emphatic home win. The perceived danger came from Holland, and they did indeed finish ahead of England by two points. Unfortunately, however, Holland were a point adrift of Norway, meaning England went out. Whilst much has been made of the two games against Holland, where England dropped a two goal lead at Wembley and picked up only one point, and the return in Rotterdam where England felt they should have been awarded a penalty when Ronald Koeman pulled down David Platt (television replays showed it was outside the area) and that Koeman should have been sent off (he was only booked), Koeman then giving Holland the lead two minutes later, the truth of the matter was that England picked up only one point against Norway and that had seen them eliminated. The failure to qualify did for another England manager, this time Graham Taylor, departing his job shortly after the final qualifying match.

Northern Ireland and the Republic of Ireland were drawn in Group 3, alongside Spain and Denmark, and both Irish sides harboured strong hopes of being able to qualify. Northern Ireland were eventually undone by their inability to turn defeats

competitors and media interest, but the viewing figures for the World Cup surpass this) in the United States made sense. Coupled with this was the potential for opening up a nation of some 250 million to Pele's 'beautiful game.' And yet this was exactly why holding the competition in America made little sense. As has been pointed out by others, many Americans are so insular they think of Europe as one country, hold no passport because they have no intention of ever leaving the country and cannot see the irony in hosting a World Series in baseball when the competition is only open to North American competitors. Whilst cities such as Los Angeles and New York, with their large immigrant populations, were keen football fans, the same could not be said for many of their countrymen. Soccer, as they knew it, was something foreigners did, and just because it was taking place in their own backyard wouldn't and didn't change their attitude. The success enjoyed by the American women's side, who had won the female version of the World Cup on a number of occasions, had not raised the profile of the game. Neither had the limited success of the male team, who qualified for the 1990 competition and would be automatic qualifiers in 1994, the first time they had managed to compete in successive World Cup finals since 1930 and 1934.

The Americans would spare no effort in making sure the 1994 World Cup finals were, in their words, 'the most colourful and exciting in its 64-year history.' Henry Kissinger, more used to sorting out diplomatic problems around the world, was appointed onto the Board of Directors of World Cup USA 1994, Inc. There again, so was Ahmet Ertegun, one of the founders of Atlantic Records, so at least the musical programme promised to be the best ever! And although the old professional League in America had long since vanished,

into draws; four defeats, including home and away to Denmark, left them adrift in mid-table. The Republic of Ireland, however, still managed by Jack Charlton, showed particular resilience, picking up vital points here and there as the competition progressed. On the final day, therefore, Denmark were top of the group with eighteen points, whilst both Spain and the Republic of Ireland were level on seventeen points, although the Spaniards had a better goal difference. The Republic of Ireland were away in Belfast whilst the Danes visited Seville and for an hour the group placings didn't change; Denmark, Spain, the Republic of Ireland. Then Spain scored on 62 minutes to lift them to the top of the group and move the Republic of Ireland up to second by virtue of their better goal difference over Denmark. Then tragedy, Northern Ireland scored on 73 minutes to send the Republic of Ireland back down to third place. Three minutes later Alan McLoughlin equalised, and both Spain and the Republic of Ireland held on for the remaining quarter of an hour to book their places in America.

The final British entrant, Wales, were in Group 4 alongside Romania, Belgium and Czechoslovakia, with Cyprus and the Faroe Islands making up the numbers. Romania and Belgium quickly dominated the group, Romania handing out a five goal beating to Wales in their opening match and the Welsh didn't really recover. Although Belgium finished with the same point tally as the Romanians at the top of the group, fifteen points, they were streets behind on goal difference, the Romanians having rattled in 29 goals in their ten qualifying matches. Wales meanwhile finished fourth, three points adrift of the top two and a point behind Czechoslovakia. There would be no United Kingdom entrants in the 1994 World cup finals.

There were other surprises as well. Hungary missed out in Group 5 and France and Austria trailed Sweden and Bulgaria in Group 6. The French in particular fell at the very last hurdle; drawing 1-1 at home to Bulgaria and needing just a point to qualify, they conceded a last minute goal to suffer elimination. David Ginola was seen as the villain of the piece, giving away the ball from which the Bulgarians raced up the other end and scored the winning goal. Manager Gerard Houllier branded him a murderer, so badly did he take the defeat! Not surprisingly, Houllier never picked Ginola again.

South American qualification saw history made on 25th July 1993 – Brazil lost a World Cup qualifying match for the first time in their history, going down 2-0 in La Paz against Bolivia. Brazil still won the group (Group B), but only one point ahead of the Bolivians who also earned a place in America. That meant Uruguay missed out. In Group A, where only one team would qualify as of right, Colombia proved the team to beat, topping the group without losing a match and registering a 5-0 win over Argentina in Buenos Aires to clinch the automatic place and condemn Argentina to a play-off place against the winners of the Oceania/CONCACAF section.

Oceania, as we have seen, were still not afforded an automatic place in the finals. In 1994, they didn't even have an automatic place in the play-offs, being expected to face the side which finished second in the CONCACAF qualifying section. That turned out to be Canada, runners-up behind Mexico after a complex qualifying competition that involved a pre-preliminary round, preliminary round, a first round divided into Central and Caribbean sections, two groups and then a final round robin group stage!

Australia meanwhile won their Oceania Group, beat New Zealand in the Oceania final 3-1 on aggregate and then triumphed on penalties 4-1 against Canada to earn their tie against Argentina. That the gap between the Australians and the South Americans was closing was revealed in the tightness of the two games, Australia coming from a goal down to draw in Sydney and suffering just a single goal defeat in Buenos Aires in the second leg.

The performances and accomplishments of Cameroon in Italy 1990 had earned the admiration of the whole football world and their continent an extra place in subsequent World Cups (fortunately FIFA chose to overlook their disciplinary record, one of the worst in 1990!), and they duly booked their place with a 3-1 win at home to Zimbabwe in Group C of the African competition. They were joined by Nigeria from Group A, but most media attention was directed towards the goings on in Group B where Morocco and Zambia were involved in a head to head battle that went down to the wire. Zambia's chances were seemingly ended with a plane crash off the coast of West Africa that killed eighteen squad members in April 1993, but somehow the Zambians put together

Above
Diana Ross performs on stage. She would soon realise sticking to her day job would be the best bet.

Above right
Karl Heinz Riedle heads the ball for Germany against Bolivia in the opening game.

something of a scratch side and headed into the final match needing just a point to qualify for the USA. The Moroccans showed no sentiment (and who would have expected them to), winning 1-0 with a goal on 50 minutes to pip the plucky Zambians at the post.

The final places for the finals went to Saudi Arabia and South Korea, who were among the six teams who won their first stage groups and then accumulated enough points in the second stage group to qualify.

Just as they had promised, the Americans threw a spectacular opening ceremony for the launch of the World Cup, with a welcoming speech from President Bill Clinton. The supposed highlight of the opening ceremony went badly wrong; superstar Diana Ross sang a specially written song to the 63,000 plus crowd and billions of television viewers and did it to perfection, but the next part of her duties, which required her kicking an oversized ball into a goal that would then collapse as she ran through the net, saw her miss the goal from just five yards! Fortunately, this being America, every contingency had been covered and a workman pulled a lever that caused the goal to collapse on cue. Hardly supreme, but something of a foretaste of what was to come in the competition. Ceremony over and it was down to the serious matter of the football – an obviously ageing German side struggled to beat Bolivia 1-0 in Group C. Despite the unification of the old East and West Germanys, this side was effectively West Germany under a shortened name, for not one of the old East German players was seriously considered an automatic choice for the first eleven – even Rudi Voller had been called out of retirement!

Germany eventually qualified top of their group, but there were cracks running throughout the team that even the likes of South Korea were able to exploit; in their final group match the Germans raced into a 3-0 lead

and then let slip two goals and were holding on for dear life at the end. The Germans were joined by Spain, who beat Bolivia and earned a point against both the Germans and South Koreans to finish on five points now that FIFA had finally begun awarding three points for a win.

The three points for a win system proved beneficial to a number of sides, most notably host nation the United States in Group A. They had kicked off their campaign with a 1-1 draw with Switzerland in Detroit's Silverdome, the first time a World Cup match had been played 'indoors' (natural turf had to be laid on top of wooden boards as FIFA would not allow the match to be played on artificial turf). On the same day Romania beat the hugely fancied Colombians 3-1, Raducioiu scoring two of the goals but Hagi, who got the other, orchestrating the side. Hagi scored again in Romania's next match, against Switzerland, but the Swiss grabbed four of their own to all but ensure their progress into the second stage. A day later they were joined by the United States, who recorded a 2-1 win over Colombia in Los Angeles in front of 93,000 fans.

One of the USA's goals was an own goal, the only one of the entire competition, turned into his own net by Andres Escobar to give the Americans a single goal lead 10 minutes before half time. Ernie Stewart added to the lead almost 10 minutes after the break, and although Colombia pulled one back through Valencia, there was not enough time left for them to do any further damage – Colombia were out. It didn't matter that they won their final match, 2-0 against Switzerland, for they finished bottom of the group. Top were the Romanians, who beat the USA 1-0 through a Dan Petrescu goal. The failure of the Colombians, who had a wretched tournament, due it was said through fear after death threats had been issued against the players, was the first major surprise of the competition. A few days after they had returned home, Escobar was shot to death by a gunman as he was leaving a restaurant, with the killer supposedly yelling 'goal' each time a bullet hit Escobar's body. It was claimed that Colombian drug barons, who had supposedly bet huge sums of money on Colombia doing well, had extracted the ultimate revenge. Football is often said to be a matter of life and death, but no one expected the saying to become reality.

Brazil had little trouble in Group B, beating both Russia and Cameroon and drawing with Sweden to top the

group. Sweden came second thanks to a further draw against Cameroon and a victory over Russia, enough to earn them five points. The Russians were a major disappointment, having been expected to do well in the tournament and crashing out at the first hurdle. Their final match, a 6-1 thrashing of Cameroon and in which Oleg Salenko set a new record with five of his side's goals and took his own personal tally to six, was scant reward. History was made by the scorer of Cameroon's consolation effort, Roger Milla becoming the oldest World Cup finals' goalscorer at the age of 42 (although as was noted previously, Milla may have been even older than he claimed).

Argentina were favourites to win Group D, based more on the country's pedigree than actual form (they had had to rely on winning a play-off with Australia to qualify for the finals), and had they won their final match they would have been able to register a 100% record. An easy 4-0 victory over Greece, with Diego Maradona netting one of the goals, seemed to indicate Argentina were on their way back, but the manic stare Maradona gave to the television cameras after scoring his goal seemed to tell a different story. In their second match they came from behind

Above
Romario of Brazil runs towards his team-mates after scoring a goal against Russia in their first-round match.

Above right
Diego Maradona pleads his innocence to the referee and the supporters during Argentina's match with Greece.

Right
Roger Milla back to his old-tricks again, as he celebrates scoring against Russia.

against this tournament's surprise African package, Nigeria, thanks to two goals from Caniggia, allowed to play against the opposition unlike his experiences four years previously. That left Argentina top of the group and assured of a place in the next stage, but a day after the game came the bombshell news that a player had failed a mandatory drug test and, should a second test also prove positive, then that player would be expelled from the competition. Media speculation on who the actual player was raged around the world until the official FIFA announcement – the player was Diego Maradona, the second test had proved positive and Maradona was on his way back home to Argentina, his international career in tatters. Argentina's hopes might well

have accompanied Maradona on the plane home, for a lacklustre performance in their final match, where they went down 2-0 to Bulgaria, saw them removed from the top of the group and into third place. Although Nigeria, Bulgaria and Argentina finished level on points, Nigeria took topplace thanks to a one goal advantage over their rivals and Bulgaria got second place by virtue of their head to head record against Argentina.

Qualification out of Group E was even closer, all four sides finishing level on four points, having won, drawn and lost a match apiece! Mexico topped the group, their victory coming over the Republic of Ireland, thanks to having scored three goals (and conceded the same number) in their three matches. The Republic of Ireland took second place, their victory over Italy enough to give them the higher placing after both countries had scored and conceded two goals. Italy took third place, leaving Norway the side to miss out by the narrowest of margins.

The final group, Group F resulted in another three way tie between Holland, Saudi Arabia and Belgium, with Morocco the group's whipping boys. The Saudi

Arabians were undoubtedly a revelation, scoring the goal of the tournament through Saeed Owairan in the match against Belgium (he collected the ball in his own half and beat four opposition players before slotting the ball home) and deserved their place in the next round. They were only just pipped for top spot in the group by Holland, who came from behind to beat the Saudis in their opening match. Belgium suffered the same fate as Argentina as far as group placings were concerned; top of the group with a 100% record going into their final match (and with qualification already achieved) they suffered their first defeat and dropped to third place.

Three days later Belgium suffered their second defeat and were eliminated from the competition, beaten by Germany in the second round. An early Rudi Voller goal was quickly cancelled out by Georges Grun two minutes later, but the Germans added two more before half time through Jurgen Klinsmann and a second for Voller to leave the Belgians with a

Above
Roy Keane of the Republic of Ireland is chased by Giuseppe Signori of Italy.

Left inset
Maradona faces the press, after he is tested positive in a drugs test.

Below left
Saeed Owairan of Saudi Arabia celebrates after scoring in their first-round game against Belgium.

mountain to climb. They managed to pull one back, through Philippe Albert, but there was too little time left on the clock for them to get a third.

Spain finally began showing promise in their second round match, proving too strong for Switzerland as they ran up a three goal win. Similarly, a day later Sweden overcame Saudi Arabia 3-1, the Saudis falling behind on just six minutes and trying to play catch up for the remaining 84 minutes.

On the same day came the first major casualty. Deprived of Diego Maradona's prompting in midfield and his inspirational abilities elsewhere, Argentina were not even a shadow of their former selves. Romania took full advantage, running out 3-2 winners, but in truth the Romanians, with Gheorghe Hagi and Ilie Dumitrescu who scored the three goals, goalkeeper Florin Prunea and Gheorghe Popescu, had a side with quality running throughout and would have been a match for anyone on their day.

Honest graft rather than individual ability had seen the Republic of Ireland get through to the second round, where they were ultimately

found out against the Dutch. Dennis Bergkamp got the first and Wim Jonk added a second before half time and the Irish had little answer during the second period, the match finally finishing a 2-0 win to Holland.

Host nation the United States gave Brazil a scare or two in their clash in San Francisco. The Brazilian cause was not helped by the dismissal of Leonardo for deliberately elbowing Tab Ramos, a sickening strike that left the American with a fractured skull. The USA were unable to make their extra player advantage pay however, for Fernando Clavijo got himself sent off to even up the numbers and Bebeto grabbed the only goal of the game 15 minutes from the end. That they had pushed the Brazilians so close was indicative of how far the USA had come in the last four years – that progress was to be maintained over the next twelve.

Whilst Brazil were never in any real danger of slipping out against the Americans, the same could not be said for one of the other favourites to win the competition, Italy. Fortunate to have qualified out of the group stage, they were lethargic and almost disinterested in their second round match against Nigeria. Emmanuel Ammunike gave the Africans the lead shortly before half an hour and it was

Above
Luis Enrique of Spain is happy to have scored against the Swiss.

Above right
Jose Basualdo of Argentina is booked during Argentina's loss to Romania.

Right
Dennis Bergkamp of Holland is tackled by Paul McGrath of the Republic of Ireland in their second-round encounter.

they rather than Italy who looked likeliest to add to the score as the game began to draw to a conclusion. Then, with barely three minutes on the clock, Roberto Baggio seemingly remembered he was European and World Player of the Year and required to play as such and grabbed a vital equaliser to send the game into extra time. A second Baggio strike, this time from the penalty spot, took Italy into the quarter-finals but it was a close run thing.

The final second round match, between Mexico and Bulgaria stretched out beyond extra time, becoming the first match of the competition to be settled by a penalty shoot out. Hristo Stoitchkov gave Bulgaria the lead on seven minutes, only for the Mexicans to equalise from the penalty spot 11 minutes later from Alberto Garcia Aspe. With no further goals scored in either the remaining time or extra time, it was left to penalties to settle matters. Despite their earlier experience, the Mexican penalties were disastrous, scoring only once, whilst the Bulgarians netted three to earn their place in the quarter-finals.

Having left it late before seeing off Nigeria in the second round, Italy were made to go the distance again in their quarter-final clash with Spain. An Italian opener from Dino Baggio after just short of half an hour settled the Italians down but Spain refused to give up, hitting the equaliser virtually on the hour mark. Roberto Baggio again returned from his slumbers to net the winning goal with two minutes left and Italy held on to reach the semi-finals.

The match of the round took place in Dallas where Holland faced Brazil. A first half of much enterprise but little end result saw half time reached still goalless. The match exploded into life in the second half, Romario and Bebeto, the Brazilian strike force, netting a goal apiece to give Brazil a two goal advantage and with less than half an hour left to play. Holland responded well, reducing the deficit through Bergkamp two minutes later and deservedly drawing level through Aron Winter and we had a real game on our hands. The Dutch were level for just five minutes, Branco netting what proved to be a winner with a stunning free kick nine minutes from time.

Above
Romario of Brazil surges past Alexi Lalas of the USA.

Above right
Alessandro Costac can't believe his eyes that Nigeria have scored.

Left
Bebeto of Brazil is tackled by Frank Rijkaard of Holland.

Bulgaria, netting twice in a five minute spell in the first half. Stoitchkov, who else, pulled one back shortly before half time from the penalty spot, but the Italians held firm in the second half to finish 2-1 winners and make the final for the fifth time in their history.

The extra day recuperation enjoyed by the Brazilians before their semi-final meeting with Sweden gave them a slight

Despite taking lead shortly after half time with a Lothar Matthaus penalty, the Germans' ageing side ran out of steam well before the end of their match with Bulgaria. Stoitchkov and Iordan Letchkov got the goals that took them into the semi-final, easily the best ever performance from the East Europeans, but most interest was aimed at the performance of the Germans, who had been expected to do so much better.

The final place in the semi-finals was claimed by Sweden, who were involved in a tense struggle against Romania. Tomas Brolin gave Sweden the lead with a little over 10 minutes remaining, Florin Raducioiu equalising as the game entered its final minute. Raducioiu gave Romania the lead in the first half of extra time, Kennet Andersson grabbed a vital equaliser five minutes from the end. That sent the game into a penalty shoot out which the Swedes won 5-4.

Roberto Baggio was alert much earlier in the semi-final clash with

Above
Letchkov of Bulgaria heads the ball, beating Thomas Hassler of Germany.

Right
Dejection for Romania, as they bow out to Sweden.

Bulgaria had seemingly given their all in their efforts to reach the final in their match against Italy, for having built their progress on a solid defence in earlier matches, it all but collapsed in the third and fourth place play-off with Sweden. Sweden were four goals ahead by the break and seldom troubled in the second half to register their best ever performance in the competition.

And so to the final, featuring two of the sides with the best pedigree. Italy were in their fifth final, having won the competition three times. Brazil had also won the trophy on three occasions and been runners-up once – one side would move ahead of the other in the rankings after 1994. The match itself was something of a disappointment, although little criticism can be levelled at those who took part. With Brazil having adopted a more European approach, they were always going to be difficult to score against. Unfortunately, they came up against a side who were past masters at defending, and so the match headed towards stalemate almost as soon as it started. The Brazilians had much more of the play and in Romario and Bebeto the more likely match

Left
Robert Baggio of Italy celebrates with the crowd after scoring in their World Cup semi-final against Bulgaria.

Below
Romario scores the winning goal for Brazil in their semi-final against Sweden.

edge, but Sweden ran them close. It took until the 80th minute before Romario grabbed what proved to be the only goal of the game, with the Brazilians worthy winners at the end.

winners, but there was always a suspicion that Roberto Baggio might pop up at any moment and score a winning goal for the Italians.

Unfortunately, no one managed a goal in more than 120 minutes of action, meaning the World Cup final would be settled by a penalty shoot out for the first time in its history. Franco Baresi stepped up first for Italy and saw his shot sail over the bar. Marcio Santos' effort was then saved by Gianluca Pagliuca. Demetrio Albertini finally got the scoring underway to give the Italians the advantage. Romario responded with a Brazilian goal, although the ball hit the post before hitting the back of the net. Alberigo restored Italy's lead, Branco brought the tie level. Daniele Massaro's effort was saved by Taffarel and Dunga gave Brazil the lead for the first time in the competition. Up stepped Roberto Baggio, needing to score to keep the Italians in the competition. With

Above
Branco of Brazil is brought down by Apolloni of Italy in the World Cup final.

Above right
The Rose Bowl Pasadena, California is the scene for the 1994 World Cup final.

Right
Franco Baresi of Italy misses his penalty in the shoot-out.

Far right
Brazilian players run to join their teammates as Roberto Baggio bows his head in disappointment after missing his penalty kick giving Brazil a 3-2 victory in the shoot-out.

a certain irony in the fact that a competition that began with a missed penalty by Diana Ross should be settled by one missed by Roberto Baggio. The Americans couldn't have planned it better as far as drama was concerned!

Left
Dunga of Brazil displays the World Cup.

the whole of the football world watching, his shot zipped up and over the goal – Brazil were world champions for the fourth time.

Whilst the Brazilians were undoubtedly worthy winners on the day, the manner of their victory lacked the flair and sparkle of earlier victories, especially their previous final clash with Italy in 1970. Penalties is a dreadful way of finishing a match, especially a cup final. Perhaps playing on until one side scored, so at least the matter was settled by football rather than a lottery, would be a better option for the future. There again, there is

RESULTS

Group A

USA v Switzerland	1-1	USA v Columbia	2-1
Columbia v Romania	1-3	USA v Romania	0-1
Romania v Switzerland	1-4	Switzerland v Columbia	0-2

	P	W	D	L	F	A	P
Romania	3	2	0	1	5	5	6
Switzerland	3	1	1	1	5	4	4
USA	3	1	1	1	3	3	4
Columbia	3	1	0	2	4	5	3

Group B

Cameroon v Sweden	2-2	Sweden v Russia	3-1
Brazil v Russia	2-0	Russia v Cameroon	6-1
Brazil v Cameroon	3-0	Brazil v Sweden	1-1

	P	W	D	L	F	A	P
Brazil	3	2	1	0	6	1	7
Sweden	3	1	2	0	6	4	5
Russia	3	1	0	2	7	6	3
Cameroon	3	0	1	2	3	11	1

Group C

Germany v Bolivia	1-0	South Korea v Bolivia	0-0
Spain v South Korea	2-2	Bolivia v Spain	1-3
Germany v Spain	1-1	Germany v South Korea	3-2

	P	W	D	L	F	A	P
Germany	3	2	1	0	5	3	7
Spain	3	1	2	0	6	4	5
South Korea	3	0	2	1	4	5	2
Bolivia	3	0	1	2	1	4	1

Group D

Argentina v Greece	4-0	Bulgaria v Greece	4-0
Nigeria v Bulgaria	3-0	Greece v Nigeria	0-2
Argentina v Nigeria	2-1	Argentina v Bulgaria	0-2

	P	W	D	L	F	A	P
Nigeria	3	2	0	1	6	2	6
Argentina	3	2	0	1	6	3	6
Bulgaria	3	2	0	1	6	3	6
Greece	3	0	0	1	0	10	0

Group E

Italy v Republic of Ireland	0-1	Mexico v Republic of Ireland	2-1
Norway v Mexico	1-0	Italy v Mexico	1-1
Italy v Norway	1-0	Republic of Ireland v Norway	0-0

	P	W	D	L	F	A	P
Mexico	3	1	1	1	3	3	4
Rep of Ireland	3	1	1	1	2	2	4
Italy	3	1	1	1	2	2	4
Norway	3	1	1	1	1	1	4

Group F

Belgium v Morocco	1-0	Belgium v Holland	1-0
Holland v Saudi Arabia	2-1	Morocco v Holland	1-2
Saudi Arabia v Morocco	2-1	Belgium v Saudi Arabia	0-1

	P	W	D	L	F	A	P
Holland	3	2	0	1	4	3	6
Saudi Arabia	3	2	0	1	4	3	6
Belgium	3	2	0	1	2	1	6
Morocco	3	0	0	3	2	5	0

Second Round

| Spain v Switzerland | 3-0 | Saudi Arabia v Sweden | 1-3 | Brazil v USA | 1-0 | Nigeria v Italy | 1-2 |
| Germany v Belgium | 3-2 | Romania v Argentina | 3-2 | Holland v Republic of Ireland | 2-0 | Mexico v Bulgaria | 1-1 |

Bulgaria won 3-1 on penalties

Quarter-Finals

Italy v Spain	2-1
Holland v Brazil	2-3
Romania v Sweden	2-2
Sweden won 5-4 on penalties	
Bulgaria v Germany	2-1

SEMI-FINALS

Bulgaria	1	Italy	2
Sweden	0	Brazil	1

3rd & 4th PLACE PLAY-OFF

| Sweden | 4 | Bulgaria | 0 |

FINAL

| Brazil | 0 | Italy | 0 |

Taffarel, Jorginho (Moraes), Branco, Aldair, Marcia Santos, Mazinho, Dunga, Zinho (Viola), Bebeto, Romario

Pagliuca, Benarrivo, Maldini, Baresi, Mussi (Apolloni), Albertini, D Baggio (Evani), Berti, Donadoni, R Baggio, Massaro
Albertini, Evani

Brazil won 3-2 on penalties: *Romario, Branco, Dunga*

Below
1998 official World
Cup poster.

France were one of the early runners in the race to host the 1998 World Cup finals, announcing their intention to submit an application in 1988, a good ten years before the tournament was due to take place. Their eventual selection, which would coincide with the sixtieth anniversary of the only other occasion they had hosted the finals, was duly ratified in 1992.

The finals were to be the last under the FIFA presidency of Joao Havelange. President since 1974, Havelange had overseen the growth of FIFA into a hugely successful, commercial organisation. True to his word, he had increased the number of finalists from sixteen when he took over to twenty-four in 1982. The success of the four tournaments since, at least financially, had convinced Havelange and others within the FIFA hierarchy that the larger format worked. If it worked for twenty-four teams, perhaps it could also work as well with thirty-two. Thus Joao Havelange's parting shot at FIFA was a further increase in the number of finalists to thirty-two. This was certainly well received by the so-called minnow nations, for their federations received an increase in the number of final places, although others did not do quite so well – Oceania still received no automatic place.

1998 FRANCE

When France first hosted the competition in 1938, the fifty-seven member countries produced thirty-six entries for the competition. Sixty years on, FIFA had grown more than three fold – the 193 members produced 174 entries, easily a new record. Europe received fourteen automatic places, plus France as hosts. Asia received three places and a possible fourth via a play-off with the winners of the Oceania group, who had no automatic place allocation. CONCACAF had three places, Africa five and South America had four plus Brazil as holders.

Australia had little trouble winning the Oceania group, registering a 13-0 home victory over the Solomon Islands in the group stage. Even the final, home and away ties with New Zealand were little more than a walkover, Australia winning 3-0 away and 7-0 at home. The reward for their efforts was a home and away play-off against whoever finished fourth in the Asian group.

Two rounds of mini Leagues decided Asian qualification – the top team in each of the ten groups in the first round were put into two groups in the second round and played each other home and away. The top two sides won automatic qualification, the two runners-up played off to decide who earned the third automatic place, with the runner-up getting a second tilt via a play-off with the winners of the Oceania competition, Australia. The two group winners turned out to be Saudi Arabia and South Korea, who just pipped Iran and Japan respectively. The play-off between Japan and Iran, decided in a single match, saw Japan win in sudden death 3-2. For long spells it looked as though Iran were heading for elimination in their play-off against Australia as well. After a 1-1 draw in Iran, Australia, managed by former England manager Terry Venables, led by two goals in the second leg, but two late strikes from the Iranians saw them draw level and earn qualification on away goals.

A complex system of knockout ties and a final League settled matters in the CONCACAF federation, with Mexico, the United States and Jamaica's reggae boys taking the top three

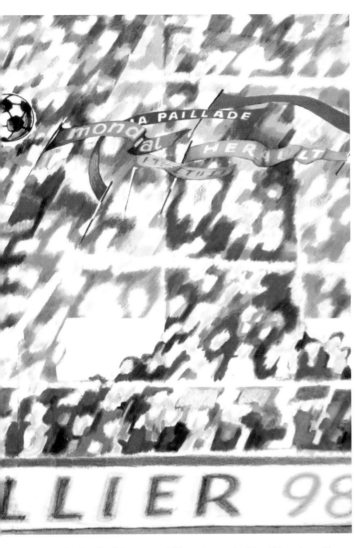

in Poland and Georgia. The two points dropped in Georgia, on the same night England hammered Moldova 4-0 gave England the advantage for the first time in the competition and meant that a draw in Rome would be enough to gain automatic qualification for England and condemn Italy to the lottery of the play-offs. A sterling defensive display, despite provocation on and off the field, earned England the 0-0 they needed.

Scotland too had a seemingly difficult draw on paper, up against the Austrians and Swedes, with Latvia, Estonia and Belarus completing the line-up in Group 4. For once Scotland started brightly, earning a commendable goalless draw in Vienna and wins away in Latvia and at home to Sweden. In between the Latvia and Sweden matches Scotland were also involved in something of a farce in Tallinn against Estonia. A row over the quality of the floodlights, even though the match was being played mid-afternoon, saw the Estonians refuse to play, with the Scottish players, their fans and the match officials the only people present in the stadium. There was a symbolic kick off before the referee abandoned the game. Initially the match was awarded to Scotland but following a FIFA investigation it was decided to replay the match, in Monaco! Scotland were held to another goalless draw, one that might prove costly in later stages. As it was Scotland went into their final match in second position two points behind Austria, but most crucially two points ahead of Sweden. A win against Latvia and it didn't matter what the Swedes did, Scotland would at least earn a place in the play-offs. As it was it got better than that, with their 2-0 win enough to earn them the automatic qualification spot as the best European runner-up.

Wales had no such luck in Group 7, drawn against Holland, Belgium and the emergent Turks, with San Marino making up the numbers. Wales' only two victories came against San Marino (5-0 away and 6-0 at home), their only other point at home to Turkey and a final position of fourth in a five team group. The group was won by Holland, a point ahead of Belgium, the crucial effective decider coming with a 3-1 Dutch victory over Belgium in Rotterdam.

Northern Ireland had even less luck, drawn alongside Germany and Portugal in Group 9. Whilst these two sides were expected to dominate the group, Ukraine managed to split them, finishing second behind Germany, but even German qualification wasn't as clear cut as they might have expected, requiring a last minute goal at home to Albania to ensure they topped the group.

The Republic of Ireland were seldom a threat to Romania, who ran away with Group 8, winning nine and drawing the other of their ten matches. But the Republic of Ireland managed to see off the challenge of Lithuania to finish runners-up and earn a play-off place. The remaining groups saw Denmark, Norway, Bulgaria and Spain top the groups, with Croatia, Hungary, Russia and Yugoslavia taking the play-off places.

The Republic of Ireland were pitched against Belgium and managed a 1-1 draw at home despite taking the lead. They fell

spots in the final League. Africa also opted for this mix, with the thirty-eight entries being reduced to twenty for the group stages. These were then put into five groups of four, with the top team progressing to the finals. Nigeria, Tunisia, South Africa, Cameroon and Morocco won their respective groups, with the likes of Egypt and Zaire, both of whom had previously qualified for the finals, missing out.

With fourteen places up for grabs in Europe, qualification was a relatively straightforward process. Placed into nine groups, the group winners and best runner-up would earn automatic qualification, with the other eight runners-up then being drawn in pairs to play off for the remaining four places. England had a particularly tough draw, pulled out of the hat with Italy and Poland (again!), with Georgia and Moldova making up the numbers. England managed to bury their Polish jinx, winning 2-1 at home and 2-0 away in what quickly became a straight battle between England and Italy to win the group. The Italians gained an early advantage, winning 1-0 at Wembley thanks to Zola's goal, but whilst England won just about every match other than that, the Italians dropped points

behind in the second leg, equalised through Ray Houghton and then fell behind a second and final time. Had they managed a second goal, qualification would have been theirs on away goals. Hungary would have welcomed the opportunity of getting close to achieving an away goals victory, but a shock 7-1 home defeat in the first leg against Yugoslavia ended any interest they might have had in qualifying for the finals. It was a night when nothing went right for Hungary; a goal down inside two minutes, three behind after ten and five goals adrift at half time! The second leg was no better, Yugoslavia finishing 5-0 winners to register an unlikely 12-1 aggregate victory.

Goals either side of the break in the first leg in Zagreb gave Croatia a two goal lead to take into the second leg against the Ukraine. Ukraine pulled one back inside four minutes of the second leg through Shevchenko, but a vital away goal from Boksic just after half time left the Ukraine needing three goals to qualify – they failed to add even one.

The final play-off pitted Italy against Russia. The severe weather in Russia at the time Italy were due to play their first leg was initially felt to be to the Russians' advantage, but Italy defended well and scored a priceless away goal through Vieri four minutes after half time. Although their defence was breached once, advantage passed to the Italians. A single goal settled the second leg, Casiraghi scoring on 53 minutes for the Italians to book their place in the finals.

Across the globe in South America, the nine teams entered into the competition (Brazil qualified as holders) were put into a single League for the first time, with each side facing the others home and away, with the top four qualifying for the finals. With the Brazilians out of the way, there was seemingly little to challenge the Argentineans' march to the top of the table, although they finally finished just a point ahead of Paraguay in second place and two ahead of Colombia in third. They did qualify before any of their rivals, a goalless draw at home to Uruguay on 10th September 1997 ensuring they could finish no lower than fourth. Uruguay were the major disappointment in the tournament, finishing a lowly seventh and four points away from qualification. After Paraguay and Colombia had confirmed their qualification for France, the final place came down to a battle between Chile and Peru. Peru had got an early advantage, winning 2-1 against the Chileans in January 1997, but Chile kept picking up points here and there and got their revenge with a 4-0 win over Peru in October 1997. That put Chile ahead of their rivals on goal difference, with both sides having one match left to play. Peru recorded a 1-0 win over the already-qualified Paraguay to bring their points tally up to twenty-five, but on the same day Chile got the better of Bolivia 3-0 to take the last place in the finals.

Brazil as holders kicked off the finals on 10th June and were soon off the mark, opening the scoring after just four minutes against Scotland. This, however, was not a vintage Brazilian team nor performance, for Scotland equalised from the penalty spot shortly before half time and deserved better than to be finally beaten by an own goal. Later the same day Morocco and Norway played out a much more entertaining 2-2 draw, so the damage to Scotland was not as bad as it might have been. Brazil returned to former glories next time out, beating Morocco 3-0, whilst Scotland were required to come from behind again before finally picking up their first

Above
Cesar Sampaio of Brazil celebrates scoring the opening goal of the World Cup against Scotland.

Above right
Rigobert Song in action for Cameroon before he was sent off against Chile.

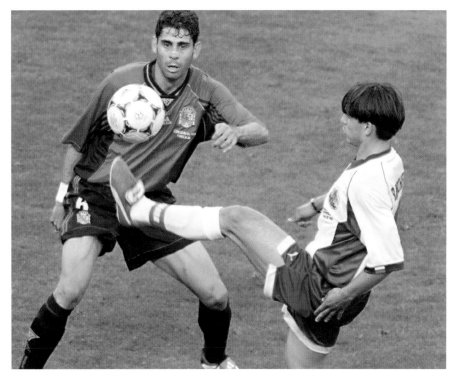

point in the competition in a 1-1 draw with Norway. It proved to be their only point too, for a disastrous 3-0 defeat against Morocco meant Scottish interest in the competition came to an end. The poor Africans went out at the same stage too, for having confidently expected that Brazil would beat Norway, Morocco's four points should have been enough to take them into the second round. Unfortunately, two late goals, the second from the penalty spot a minute from time, gave the Norwegians a 2-1 win over their South American opponents, five points in the group and a one point advantage over their African rivals.

Aside from Italy, who won two and drew the other of their three matches in Group B, any one of the three other sides in the group could have qualified on the final day. As it was qualification went to Chile, whose three draws and three points proved better than the two points apiece Austria and Cameroon were able to collect. Rigobert Song also created a new record, although it was not one he would have liked – he was sent off against Chile, becoming the first player in World Cup history to have been sent off twice following his dismissal against Brazil four years earlier! Once again Cameroon's ill-discipline cost them dearly, for Kalla Nkongo against Italy and Etame, also against Chile, collected red cards.

There was a similar tale in Group C, with the host nation France dominating proceedings and registering three straight wins against Denmark, South Africa and Saudi Arabia to top the group, although at a cost, with Zinedine Zidane being sent off for a stamp on Amin in the second match which earned him a two match ban. The battle for second place was effectively between Denmark and South Africa; France's victory over Denmark in the last match could have let the South Africans in for the next stage. Had they managed one more goal themselves in their meeting with Saudi Arabia, the additional points would have given them a place in the second round by virtue of having scored more goals than the Danes. As it was, Denmark sneaked in through the back door.

Bulgaria were expected to be one of the two qualifiers from Group D, based largely on their performances four years previously in the USA, where they had finished fourth. Little went right for the Bulgarians, however, with Stoichkov no longer his inspirational self, and they finished bottom of the group with only one

Above
Fernando Hierro of Spain challenges Gueorgui Batchev of Bulgaria in their first-round game.

Left
Zidane of France running with the ball against South Africa.

point gained and left to lick their wounds after a 6-1 mauling from Spain. Despite this fine victory, Spain progressed no further either, finding form too late in the day. Instead, almost against the odds, the qualifiers from Group D were Nigeria and Paraguay, Nigeria topping the group with six points after two victories and one defeat and Paraguay coming second after going through the group unbeaten. Paraguay found form when it mattered; their first two points were collected without a goal being scored in either of their two matches, before a 3-1 win over Nigeria enabled them to keep one step ahead of Spain.

Holland and Mexico qualified out of Group E, both with five points following a win and two draws apiece. Their finishing

Germany and Yugoslavia ensured there was no upset in Group F, both beating the minnows of the group, Iran and the USA, and sharing the spoils with a 2-2 draw. Germany ultimately took the group on goal difference. The USA and Iran may have made up the numbers as far as the group was concerned but the match between the two was the epitome of sportsmanship – whilst there had been a considerable amount of bad blood between the two nations politically in recent years, the match itself was a shining example of sport being above politics. The Iranians won the match 2-1, the American side took their defeat in good spirit.

In Group G the initial headlines were grabbed by Paul Gascoigne's omission from the squad (manager Glenn Hoddle felt he was unfit for the tournament), then by supporters of England and Tunisia who, unable to get tickets

Above
Iranian players offer flowers to the USA players as a token of peace before their game.

Above right
Paul Scholes celebrates scoring against Tunisia in the first-round.

Right
Paul Gascoigne with bandaged head in a an England game versus Belgium before the World Cup, in which he did not participate.

Far right
Glenn Hoddle directing proceedings for England against Tunisia.

first and second ultimately squeezed out Belgium, who had expected to do better and should

have at least finished with the same points tally as their two main rivals, but being held to a draw by South Korea in their final group match meant they had to settle for third place and three points.

for the match, had running battles across France anywhere where the match was being shown on television. Those inside the stadium behaved considerably better, largely due to England's eventual 2-0 victory. England slipped up in their second match, pulling level with Romania and then going to sleep in the final minute to allow Dan Petrescu to grab the

winner. That goal was to prove doubly costly, for although England won their final match against Colombia to finish second, it gave them progression into the more difficult half of the draw. Romania topped the group with two wins and a draw, being held by Tunisia in their final match.

The final group, Group H was dominated as expected by Argentina, who won all three of their matches and didn't concede a goal. However, it should be remembered that they registered five of their seven goals in one match, against Jamaica, and could score only once against both Japan and Croatia. The Croatians took second place, beating both Japan and Jamaica, whilst the battle between the minnows saw the reggae boys of Jamaica win over the crowd with their 2-1 victory.

After the group matches came the straight knockout phase, with Brazil up against their South American compatriots Chile. Largely unimpressive in the group stage, Brazil moved up a gear to win 4-1, Ronaldo at

last showing the form that had him marked down as one of the best players in the world by scoring twice.

Italy managed a single goal victory over the Norwegians, whilst France did similarly to the Paraguayans to move into the quarter-finals. They were joined by Denmark, who punished the Nigerians for some slack defensive play in their 4-1 victory. Mexico matched their German opponents in their meeting and

Above left
Batistuta of Argentina celebrates after scoring a goal past Jamaican goalkeeper Warren Barrett.

Above
Ronaldo scores for Brazil against Chile in the second-round.

Left
Oliver Bierhoff of Germany is congratulated by team-mate Jurgen Klinsmann after scoring the winning goal against Mexico.

even took the lead, but a series of missed chances that might have put the match beyond their opponents gave the Germans hope that they might recover. Jurgen Klinsmann equalised with 15 minutes to go and Oliver Bierhoff grabbed the winner with four minutes to go.

It was equally close between Holland and Yugoslavia, with Edgar Davids netting the winner in the last minute to put the Dutch through 2-1. They had also survived a bit of a scare, with Dennis Bergkamp lucky not to have sent off for a stamping incident that the referee allowed to go unpunished. There was a sending off in the next second round match, that which pitted England against Argentina, in what was undoubtedly the game of the round. Gabriel Batistuta gave Argentina the lead from the penalty spot after David Seaman was adjudged to have committed a foul, although he did not receive the seemingly obligatory red card. Alan Shearer levelled the scores, also from the penalty spot, after Michael Owen was brought down. Six

minutes later Owen scored one of the goals of the tournament, collecting the ball just inside the Argentine half and using both pace and skill to take himself past two defenders. Just when it looked as though the ball might run away from Owen and into

Above
Edgar Davids of Holland celebrates after scoring the injury-time winner in their World Cup second-round match against Yugoslavia.

Above right
David Beckham is sent off by referee Kim Nielsen after lashing out at Diego Simeone of Argentina during their World Cup second-round game.

Right
Michael Owen strides with the ball past Jose Chamot of Argentina, goal bound.

which saw Beckham dismissed. The match went to penalties, the first in this World Cup, with Argentina going first and scoring through Sergio Berti, Juan Veron, Marcelo Gallardo and Roberto Fabian Ayala, only Hernan Crespo's effort, saved by Seaman failing to hit the net. England penalties were taken by Alan Shearer (scored), Paul Ince (saved), Paul Merson (scored) and Michael Owen (scored), before David Batty stepped up to take England's last penalty of the scheduled five and needing to score to keep them in the competition. Instead his penalty, the first he'd ever taken, was saved and England went out once again on penalties.

The final quarter-final place was claimed by Croatia, rapidly becoming the dark horses of the competition, with Davor Suker, ultimately to claim the Golden Boot, netting the only goal of the game from the penalty spot.

Brazil were given a shock in their clash with Denmark, falling behind to a goal after two minutes from Jorgensen,

Below
Sol Campbell (no.2) rises to head the ball into the back of the Argentina net, but the goal is disallowed for Alan Shearer's elbow on goalkeeper Carlos Roa .

the path of the supporting Paul Scholes, Owen hooked the ball past Carlos Angel Roa to put England ahead. Argentina drew level just before half time, England going to sleep at a free kick and allowing Javier Zanetti to strike home virtually unchallenged. There have been countless column inches devoted to the incident that saw David Beckham sent off early in the second half, equally divided between those who felt England would have won had he remained on the field, others bemoaning the fact that Diego Simeone, who Beckham half-heartedly lashed out at, conned the referee and got away virtually blameless. For long spells England played better than their opponents, despite the man disadvantage, and although there was no further score in either the second half or extra time, England could point to a disallowed goal from Sol Campbell that was perhaps a decision even harsher than that

but nine minutes later Bebeto levelled for the holders. Rivaldo put Brazil ahead for the first time on 26 minutes, with Brian Laudrup bringing the game all square five minutes after the

Above
Bebeto of Brazil celebrates with team-mate Leonardo after scoring in their World Cup quarter-final match against Denmark.

Right
Luigi Di Biagio of Italy hangs his head in despair after missing their crucial penalty as Fabien Barthez of France celebrates with his team-mates in their World Cup quarter-final match.

break. Rivaldo put Brazil ahead for the second time after an hour, Denmark pressed hard looking for an equaliser but found the defence, usually Brazil's weak spot, holding firm – Brazil moved menacingly into the semi-finals.

They were joined by hosts France, who eventually overcame the Italians in a penalty shoot out after the two sides had played for 120 goalless minutes. The reintroduction of Zinedine Zidane after suspension had not enabled the French to overcome the Italians in normal time, but Zidane made his impact felt in the shoot out, scoring the first of the four successful attempts the French recorded. For the second consecutive World Cup, Italy were undone in the shoot out, this time Di Biagio being the guilty party with his miss.

A day later came one of the biggest shocks of the

competition, with Germany being completely outplayed in their clash with Croatia. Jarni gave the Croatians the lead just before half time, Vlaovic adding a second with 10 minutes to

play and Suker a third five minutes later. Although the Germans were seemingly in with a shout for lengthy spells, in reality an ageing side that had peaked two years earlier at the European Championships had been well and truly found out.

On the same day Argentina slipped out of the competition, eventually beaten by a piece of sublime skill by Dennis Bergkamp that saw him control a 60-yard pass with his first touch, elude his marker with his second and fire home at the near post with his third, as the game entered its final minutes. Earlier Patrick Kluivert had given Holland the lead on 12 minutes, only for Claudio Lopez to level the score six minutes later. Then came 70 minutes of stalemate, the game only enlivened by Ortega's dismissal two minutes from time. With extra time looking a certainty and the game calling out for a moment of inspiration to settle the tie, up stepped Dennis Bergkamp.

Holland hoped for more of the same in the semi-final against Brazil, but Bergkamp was kept quiet, only finding the net in the penalty shoot out. Brazil

were also somewhat subdued, taking the lead through Ronaldo a minute after the restart for the second half and lacking punch up front for the rest of the game. With three

Above
Davor Suker of Croatia and Lothar Matthaus of Germany stretch for the ball during their World Cup quarter-final match.

Left
Dutch forward Dennis Bergkamp bursts in joy after he scored the victory goal against Argentina in their quarter-final.

minutes to go and Brazil staring the final in the face, Kluivert came to Holland's rescue with an equaliser. With no further goals in extra time the game moved into a penalty shoot out, the third and thankfully last of this particular competition. Claudio Taffarel saved Cocu and Ronald De Boer's efforts to eventually give Brazil a 4-2 win and a place in the final.

Croatia set about proving their victory over Germany in the quarter-final had been no fluke by taking the game to France in their semi-final clash. Suker put the Croatians ahead a minute after half time, stunning the partisan French crowd, but a minute later Lilian Thuram levelled the score. Roared on by the crowd and strengthened by the introduction of Thierry Henry and David Trezeguet, France began to take control and 20 minutes from the end Thuram netted his and France's second goal. The sending off of Laurent Blanc four minutes later put the pressure back on France, but the ten men held out to make the final.

Davor Suker had one more goal in his locker, his sixth of the tournament and the eventual winner in the third and fourth place play-off against Holland, Robert Prosinecki giving Croatia the lead only for Boudewijn Zenden to level eight minutes later. Prosinecki's goal was also historic, allowing him

Above
Wim Jonk of Holland takes the ball past Roberto Carlos of Brazil during their semi-final match.

Above right
The two goalkeepers; Edwin van der Sar of Holland and Claudio Tafferel of Brazil prepare for the penalty shoot-out during their semi-final.

Right
Goran Vlaovic of Croatia is challenged by France captain Didier Deschamps during their World Cup semi-final.

to become the first player to score in World Cup finals for two different nations, having previously found the net for Yugoslavia in 1990.

If David Beckham's dismissal attracted intense media interest, at least as far as the English were concerned, then it was nothing compared to the comings and goings surrounding the Brazilian camp before and after the World Cup final. Sometime during the night, on the eve of the final, Ronaldo, something of a talisman for the Brazilians, announced himself unwell, suffering a fit, according to some sources. He was rushed to hospital and, irrespective of the outcome of the tests conducted on the player, coach Mario Zagalo decided to omit him from the team for the match. Depending on which source you choose to believe, either Ronaldo made a miraculous recovery (unlikely, given the performance he was to put in on the day) or team sponsors Nike insisted he be reinstated (possible, but a sad indictment of the influence of sponsors on such matters as team selection), Ronaldo was named in the starting line-up for the final.

He was not alone in not performing on the day, with only Dunga emerging from the final on the Brazilian side with any sense of at least sustaining his reputation. The rest were as much off the pace as Ronaldo, and Zidane, atoning for his earlier indiscretions, netted twice with headers to put France in the driving seat. As much as they huffed and puffed, Brazil had little or no answer and were seldom in the game once France were two goals ahead. Even the French temporarily pushing the self destruct button, with Marcel Desailly getting himself sent off on 68 minutes, did not inspire or ignite Brazil. In the final moments Emmanuel Petit netted a third, the 1000th goal France had scored in the competition.

Despite their disciplinary record, which saw them have three players sent off in the competition, France were just about worthy winners, aided as they were by the inept performance of the Brazilians at the final stage. Their flamboyancy may have won them fans aplenty in 1982 and 1986 but it had not won them the trophy (although they did collect the European Championship in 1984). A solid and tougher approach may have lost them fans, at least outside their own country, but it did result in them winning the trophy which they were largely instrumental in getting off the ground. Funny old game, as some might say.

France were not the only ones to suffer from disciplinary problems, with a new record of twenty-two red cards being issued, along with 257 of the yellow variety, almost four a game! That it was the likes of Zidane, Beckham and Kluivert who should see red did not present the game in the best possible light but try telling that to countless Frenchmen. Seventy years after the World Cup was brought into being and French sculptor Abel Lafleur had

Above
Laurent Blanc kisses the head of goalkeeper Fabien Barthez before the final begins.

Above right
Barthez jumps over Brazilian Ronaldo.

Above far right
Marcel Desailly is sent off in the final.

Right
Zinedine Zidane scores for France.

Far right
France celebrate with the World Cup.

presented his design to FIFA, his countrymen had finally got their hands on its successor.

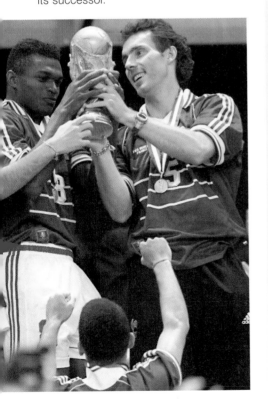

RESULTS

Group A

Brazil v Scotland	2-1	Scotland v Norway	1-1
Morocco v Norway	2-2	Brazil v Norway	1-2
Brazil v Morocco	3-0	Scotland v Morocco	0-3

	P	W	D	L	F	A	P
Brazil	3	2	0	1	6	2	6
Norway	3	1	2	0	5	4	5
Morocco	3	1	1	1	5	5	4
Scotland	3	0	1	2	2	6	1

Group B

Cameroon v Austria	1-1	Italy v Cameroon	3-0
Italy v Chile	2-2	Chile v Cameroon	1-1
Chile v Austria	1-1	Italy v Austria	2-1

	P	W	D	L	F	A	P
Italy	3	2	1	0	6	2	7
Chile	3	0	3	0	4	4	3
Austria	3	0	2	1	3	4	2
Cameroon	3	0	2	1	2	5	2

Group C

France v South Africa	3-0	South Africa v Denmark	1-1
Saudi Arabia v Denmark	0-1	France v Denmark	2-1
France v Saudi Arabia	4-0	South Africa v Saudi Arabia	2-2

	P	W	D	L	F	A	P
France	3	3	0	0	6	3	9
Denmark	3	1	1	1	3	3	4
South Africa	3	0	2	1	3	4	2
Saudi Arabia	3	0	1	2	3	9	1

Group D

Paraguay v Bulgaria	0-0	Spain v Paraguay	0-0
Spain v Nigeria	2-3	Nigeria v Paraguay	1-3
Nigeria v Bulgaria	1-0	Spain v Bulgaria	6-1

	P	W	D	L	F	A	P
Nigeria	3	2	0	1	5	5	6
Paraguay	3	1	2	0	3	1	5
Spain	3	1	1	1	8	4	4
Bulgaria	3	0	1	2	1	7	1

Group E

Holland v Belgium	0-0	Holland v South Korea	5-0
South Korea v Mexico	1-3	Belgium v South Korea	1-1
Belgium v Mexico	2-2	Holland v Mexico	2-2

	P	W	D	L	F	A	P
Holland	3	1	2	0	7	3	5
Mexico	3	1	2	0	7	5	5
Belgium	3	0	3	0	3	3	3
South Korea	3	0	1	2	2	9	1

Group F

Yugoslavia v Iran	1-0	USA v Iran	1-2
Germany v USA	2-0	Germany v Iran	2-0
Germany v Yugoslavia	2-2	USA v Yugoslavia	0-1

	P	W	D	L	F	A	P
Germany	3	2	1	0	6	2	7
Yugoslavia	3	2	1	0	4	2	7
Iran	3	1	0	2	2	5	3
USA	3	0	0	3	1	5	0

Group G

England v Tunisia	2-0	Romania v England	2-1
Romania v Colombia	1-0	Colombia v England	0-2
Colombia v Tunisia	1-0	Romania v Tunisia	1-1

	P	W	D	L	F	A	P
Romania	3	2	1	0	4	2	7
England	3	2	0	1	5	2	6
Columbia	3	1	0	2	1	3	3
Tunisia	3	0	1	2	1	4	1

Group H

Argentina v Japan	1-0	Argentina v Jamaica	5-0
Jamaica v Croatia	1-3	Argentina v Croatia	1-0
Japan v Croatia	0-1	Japan v Jamaica	1-2

	P	W	D	L	F	A	P
Argentina	3	3	0	0	7	0	9
Croatia	3	2	0	1	4	2	6
Jamaica	3	1	0	2	3	9	3
Japan	3	0	1	3	1	5	0

Second Round

Brazil v Chile	4-1	France v Paraguay	1-0
Italy v Norway	1-0	Nigeria v Denmark	1-4
		Germany v Mexico	2-1	Romania v Croatia	0-1
		Holland v Yugoslavia	2-1	Argentian v England	2-2

Argentina won 4-3 on penalties

Quarter-Finals

| Brazil v Denmark | 3-2 |
| France v Italy | 0-0 |

France won 4-3 on penalties

| Germany v Croatia | 0-3 |
| Holland v Argentina | 2-1 |

SEMI-FINALS			
Brazil	1	Holland	1
Brazil won 4-2 on penalties			
France	2	Croatia	1

3rd & 4th PLACE PLAY-OFF	Holland	1	Croatia	2

FINAL	France	3	Brazil	0

(Zidane 2, Petit)

Barthez, Lizarazu, Desailly, Thuram, Leboeuf, Djorkkaeuff (Vieira), Deschamps, Zidane, Petit, Karembeu (Boghossian), Guivarc'h (Henry)   Taffarel, Cafu, Aldair, Junior Baiano, Roberto Carlos, Cesar Sampaio (Edmundo), Dunga, Rivaldo, Leonardo (Denilson), Ronaldo, Bebeto

2002

JAPAN & SOUTH KOREA

Right
Dietmar Hamann of Germany beats Gareth Southgate of England on his way to scoring in their World Cup qualifying game.

Below
2002 official World Cup poster.

Ever since the World Cup came into being, it had only ever been competed for in either Europe or the Americas. On the American continent, the dominance of the South Americans, at least on the field, had seen Uruguay, Brazil, Chile and Argentina host the competition. Mexico, a member of the CONCACAF federation, had twice hosted the finals, stepping in in 1986 to bail out Colombia after they announced themselves unable to organise the finals. In 1994, FIFA took the bold step of awarding the competition to the United States, ostensibly to assist opening up the game to one of the largest nations on earth.

Interest in the game in Asia was known to be massive, although in the absence of any club sides of quality most of the vast continent tended to follow the fortunes of Europe's better clubs – Manchester United are probably more popular

in Thailand than even the Thai national team! European clubs frequently tour the continent, looking to establish a fan base that will religiously buy the new club shirt, even if their chances of ever visiting Anfield, Old Trafford or any other Premiership ground remain slim. This interest was noted by FIFA and, as they had done previously with the United States, an application from an Asian country to host the competition was actively encouraged. But who would make the application? None of the countries in Asia could boast sufficient grounds of the quality demanded by FIFA on their own, leaving a joint application the only conceivable way of actually succeeding. Whilst relationships between Japan and South Korea had been known to be frosty over the years, both nations managed to put their differences to one side and

2002 FIFA WORLD CUP KOREA/JAPAN
31 MAY – 30 JUNE

submit a joint application to host the 2002 finals. They even managed to agree who would host the prestigious final among themselves, proof that football is often above politics.

The joint Japan and South Korea application was duly accepted, although FIFA was quick to point out that this would not set a precedent – future applications to host the competition finals would only be accepted from single nations except under extreme circumstances. The decision to give both countries automatic places in the finals, together with the winners of the previous competition (France), meant that for the first time there were three sides spared the trouble of qualification. It also meant there was one less place for the rest of the world!

Europe's quota remained exactly the same – fourteen places in addition to France. CONCACAF remained exactly the same with three places. Africa also received the same number of places as they had the previous tournament, five. Poor old Oceania still didn't have an automatic place, just the promise of a play-off against a runner-up from another federation. The changes affected both South America and Asia, with Asia gaining rather than losing. Having had three automatic places in 1998, plus a play-off spot with Oceania, Asia was now given four automatic spots, with two of these granted to the co-hosts. South America, which had four qualifying places and Brazil as holders in 1998, now dropped to four automatic places and a place in the play-off with the Oceania competition for the final place in the finals.

Europe opted for the same system it had employed for the 1998 finals; nine groups, with the winners earning automatic qualification together with the best runner-up. The remaining eight runners-up would then be drawn to play off against each other. Whilst this system produced plenty of drama, nowhere

quite matched the battle in Group 9. Pitting long time foes England and Germany together again, the group quickly settled down to a straight battle between two of Europe's biggest footballing nations. England started woefully, losing at home to Germany 1-0 in the last match played at Wembley before the old stadium was pulled down, it also signalled the end of manager Kevin Keegan's tenure, coming out from the dressing room shortly after the game to announce he had taken the team as far as he could. Four days later England could only draw away in Finland to leave themselves five points adrift of the Germans after only two games! A new manager, Sven Goran Eriksson brought new ideas and, if not optimism, at least the belief that England could catch Germany if they started winning. So it proved, for three consecutive victories made the Germans catchable, even more so when Germany faltered to a draw in Finland. The crunch match came in Munich in September 2001, with the Germans taking the lead through Jancker after only six minutes. England fought back, equalising through Michael Owen seven minutes later and taking the lead through Steven Gerrard just before half time. The second half was the stuff of legends, with Owen completing a hat-trick and Emile Heskey adding a fifth to leave England 5-1 victors! An expected victory over Albania meant England had only to beat Greece at home or, in the event Germany were unable to beat Finland, match whatever result the Germans achieved to ensure automatic qualification and

condemn the Germans to the lottery of the play-offs. With news filtering through that the Germans were being held to a goalless draw, England seemingly relaxed, which allowed Greece to take the lead. Teddy Sheringham came off the substitutes' bench to equalise, but two minutes later Greece again took the lead. The German match finished slightly ahead of the England game, which meant England knew they had to equalise to take top spot. In the final minute David Beckham took a free kick that eluded Nikopolidis and got England the draw they needed, but England also had cause to thank the Finns along the way!

Not one of the other home countries managed to qualify, Wales and Northern Ireland finishing second bottom in their respective groups and Scotland an agonising third behind Croatia and Belgium in Group 6. Going into the home straight Scotland still had a chance of qualifying, but a goalless draw at home to Croatia and a 2-0 defeat in Brussels put them out.

Meanwhile, in Group 2 the Republic of Ireland managed to see off the challenge of Holland, the vital result being a 1-0 home win in Dublin with Jason McAteer netting the only goal of the game two minutes into the second half. They also finished level on points with Portugal but had to settle for second place on goals scored and a place in the play-off against the winners of the Asian play-off. Aside from Holland, another major absence was Bulgaria, who finished behind Denmark and the Czech Republic in Group 3.

Right
Thierry Henry of France is pursued by Aliou Cisse of Senegal during the opening match of the 2002 World Cup.

Middle
Raul of Spain passes the ball during their game against Paraguay.

Qualifying as group winners were Russia, Portugal, Denmark, Sweden, Poland, Croatia, Spain, Italy and England, whilst those who made the play-offs were Austria, Turkey, Slovenia, Romania, Ukraine, Germany, Belgium and the Czech Republic. Germany fell behind in their first leg with Ukraine but recovered to earn a draw and then made sure in the second leg with a 4-1 victory. Turkey proved themselves an emerging force with victories home and away against Austria, including a 5-0 hammering in Istanbul. Belgium too won home and away, 1-0 to book their passage, and were joined by Slovenia, who won 2-1 at home to Romania and secured an away draw to take the last European place. They were subsequently joined by the Republic of Ireland, who beat Iran 2-1 on aggregate, thanks to a 2-0 home win in the first leg which had given the Iranians a mountain to climb in the second leg.

South America again put their ten entrants into one League, with the top four going to the finals and the fifth placed nation playing off against the winners of the Oceania competition. There were both surprises and controversy in South America, where Brazil were not the dominant side they had once been, losing six of their eighteen qualifying matches, including defeats by Bolivia and Chile, neither of whom qualified. If at one stage it looked as though the Brazilians were in danger of not making the finals, then they recovered to finish third behind Argentina and Ecuador. Paraguay took the final automatic place, with Uruguay sneaking into fifth place and a play-off with Australia, although the point they picked up in their final match to ensure the play-off spot did arouse suspicion, coming as it did in a 1-1 draw against an Argentina side that had already qualified. Those suspicions were to be raised four years later when Uruguay got a place in the play-off under similar circumstances. Advantage in the play-off first went to Australia, who recorded a 1-0 win in Melbourne in the first leg but found the pace a little quicker in Montevideo and fell to a 3-0 defeat.

After Japan and South Korea qualified automatically as co-hosts, the remaining sides were placed in ten groups with the winners advancing into a second round group stage. The imbalance in quality was nowhere better observed than in Group 2, where Iran recorded a 19-0 win over Guam before Tajikistan hammered the same opponents 16-0. Iran beat Tajikistan by a more realistic score of 2-0 to make the second round stage. Split into two groups of five teams each, the winners were to qualify for the finals whilst the two runners-up would play off to earn the right to meet one of the European

runners-up which, as we have seen, saw the Republic of Ireland beat Iran. The two groups' winners were China, who qualified for the finals for the first time in their history, and Saudi Arabia, with United Arab Emirates the other runner-up who lost in a play-off with Iran.

Central and North American qualification was equally complex, involving zonal rounds and Leagues before six sides met in a round robin League, with the top three all qualifying for the finals. Of the six nations that made this round, only Trinidad & Tobago had yet to qualify for the finals, although the group effectively went with form, with Mexico, Costa Rica and the United States making it through.

Fifty African nations entered the competition, with this number being reduced by half after a first round mini League. The remaining twenty-five nations were then put into five mini Leagues, the winners to qualify for the finals. Cameroon and Nigeria won their groups, as expected, but the surprise came in Group C where Senegal finished ahead of Egypt, Algeria and Morocco to make the finals for the first time. It was not the last surprise they would spring either. African qualifiers were completed by Tunisia and South Africa, the latter despite the suspension of Guinea midway through qualification and the abandonment of their match with Zimbabwe after 82 minutes with the South Africans leading 2-0; the score being allowed to stand.

More than a few sides arrived in Japan and South Korea believing they had a chance of lifting the trophy, with the likes of France, Argentina and Portugal among the favourites to complete the task. None of these sides enhanced their

reputations, for the 2002 World Cup became the tournament of the underdog, with surprises virtually all along the way.

First to falter were France, who lost their opening match with the unknown quantity that was Senegal and never recovered. Indeed, they failed to find the net in their three group matches, this despite being able to boast the likes of Thierry Henry, Zinedine Zidane and others in their line-up. Henry had a wretched tournament, getting himself sent off against Uruguay and therefore forced to sit it out when Denmark knocked them out in the final match. Zidane didn't fare much better, picking up an injury in a warm-up friendly just prior to the competition and was also forced to sit out the first couple of matches. By the time he came back, there was too much to do to try and rescue the group. According to the French, their campaign was hindered by not having had to play competitive matches prior to the competition, qualifying automatically as holders, but this had not hindered any of their predecessors. Senegal were able to capitalise on their opening win, holding both Denmark and Uruguay to draws to finish with five points and second place. Denmark, who could hardly believe their luck, beat Uruguay and France to take top spot.

With Spain dominating Group B, winning all three of their matches, the battle was on for second place. Much was expected of Slovenia, but they crashed to three straight defeats, leaving the unlikely Paraguay and South Africa to contest second spot in the group. It ultimately went to Paraguay on goals scored, the crucial tally being grabbed in the 3-1 win over Slovenia – had they won only 2-1, South Africa would have qualified.

Brazil had little or no trouble in Group C, winning all three of their matches, although Rivaldo was guilty of a dreadful piece of professionalism in clutching his face when Hakan Unsal kicked the ball against his leg in the match with Turkey. Unsal collected his second yellow card and got sent off, Brazil went on to win 2-1, although Rivaldo was later fined by FIFA for his part in the incident. Turkey recovered from the defeat to eventually finish second in the group, although it was another close run thing, their 3-0 win over China whilst Costa Rica were being thumped 5-2 by Brazil enabled Turkey to squeeze in on goal difference. Much of the interest in Group C was directed towards the Chinese, who won friends but no points during their involvement in the competition. The crowd were willing them to score a goal, against anyone, but they failed in this too.

Group D saw one of the host nations, South Korea, and the United States battling it out with two of the supposed stronger European sides in Portugal and Poland. The first round of matches saw the first surprises, South Korea beating Poland 2-0 to set off celebrations the like of which had never been seen in South Korea before. A day later the United States raced into an unbelievable 3-0 lead against Portugal, although the Portuguese rallied and pulled two goals back, laying siege to the American goal in search of the elusive equaliser. Poland were then effectively put out of the competition with a 4-0 defeat by Portugal, on the same day South Korea and the United States took another step towards qualification with a 1-1 draw between the two nations. The final round still had one more surprise, Poland recording a

Above
Rivaldo lies on the ground apparently injured after being struck by the ball in Brazil's game versus Turkey.

consolation win over the USA 3-1 to leave the Americans sweating on the result from Incheon, where Portugal were expected to beat South Korea. A partisan crowd, some fortunate refereeing decisions and a goal from Park gave South Korea the victory, top place in the group and handed the Americans their passport to the next stage.

Interest in Group E was aroused even before the tournament kicked off, with the Republic of Ireland captain Roy Keane being sent home from their training camp after directing a volatile rant against manager Mick McCarthy. Although it robbed the Irish of perhaps their most important player, Irish success in previous tournaments had

Above
Luis Figo takes a corner during the first-round game Portugal played against the USA.

Above right
Robbie Keane of the Republic of Ireland celebrates after scoring against Germany.

Right
Roy Keane of the Republic of Ireland did not play in the 2002 World Cup. He was sent home after falling out with Irish manager Mick McCarthy.

always been based upon a strong team spirit, something the continued presence of Roy Keane would undoubtedly have endangered. Germany kicked off their campaign with an 8-0 mauling of Saudi Arabia whilst Cameroon and the Republic of Ireland shared the spoils in a 1-1 draw. The Irish raised their game against Germany in their second match and grabbed a deserved last minute equaliser through Robbie Keane to give them a perfect opportunity of qualifying from the group if they could beat Saudi Arabia

in their final match. Although never hitting the heights the Germans had, their 3-0 win, with Germany aiding them by beating Cameroon 2-0, got them through to the second round. Roy Keane wasn't particularly missed.

Group F was the one to be billed as the 'group of death', containing as it did Argentina, Nigeria, Sweden and England. The similar styles of England and Sweden cancelled each other out in their meeting in Saitama, Sol Campbell giving England the lead only for a slip by Danny Mills to allow Sweden to equalise. Meanwhile Argentina took pole position in the group, beating Nigeria 1-0 through Batistuta's goal on 63 minutes.

There was plenty of previous history when England clashed with Argentina in Sapporo five days later, England citing the taunts of the Argentineans as they boarded their coach after the victory four years previously as a major incentive to want to avenge that defeat in 2002. Whilst the desire for revenge was collective, no one wanted it more than captain David Beckham. Vilified and established as public enemy number one after his sending off in 1998, his elevation to 'goldenballs' was completed with his penalty strike that ultimately won England the game. Sweden's victory over Nigeria put the

African nation out of the competition but, more importantly, virtually guaranteed England's progress into the next stage, as long as they avoided defeat against Nigeria. A dour goalless draw may not have excited many of those present at the game or the watching millions around the world, but progress was the only thing that mattered – England made it through to the second round. They were joined by Sweden, who held Argentina to a 1-1 draw that saw the much fancied South Americans eliminated.

Their performances in France four years previously, where they had finished third, had led to many predicting perhaps even better things for Croatia. Sadly, they failed to live up to expectations, going down 1-0 to Mexico and Ecuador either side of a magnificent 2-1 win over Italy. It was Mexico's turn to be the surprise team in Group G, gaining a draw with Italy and victories over Croatia and Ecuador to win the group, Italy just squeezing in behind them in second place.

The final group contained the other host, Japan, along with Belgium, Russia and Tunisia. The two European nations were expected to progress with little or no trouble, but this being 2002 and the year of the minnow, things didn't go to plan. After holding Belgium to an exciting 2-2 draw in their opening match, Japan managed to rack up their first ever victories in the World Cup finals with a 1-0 victory over Russia and then 2-0 against Tunisia. The scramble for second place was eventually won by Belgium, courtesy of a 3-2 win over the Russians who again failed to live up to expectations.

Above
David Beckham scores his penalty for England against Argentina. Retribution for the last World Cup.

Above inset
The scorebaord doesn't lie. England have at last defeated Argentina.

Left
The Japanese team celebrate victory over Tunisia.

Short of firing power in their group, where they netted only twice, England found their mark in their second round match against Denmark. A fifth minute opener eventually credited to Rio Ferdinand settled the nerves, Michael Owen and Emile Heskey putting the match beyond the Danes before half time had been reached.

Germany had almost the opposite problem; prolific in their group, which had included an eight goal tally against Saudi Arabia, it took them 88 minutes to breach the Paraguayan defence even once, although they were perhaps aided by the fact that Paraguay seemed content to settle for a goalless draw and rely on a penalty shoot out to decide their ultimate fate. Fortunately Oliver Neuville ensured that penalties weren't needed, at least in this match.

They were, however, required in the Republic of Ireland's clash with Spain, which saw the Spaniards take an eight minute lead and then survive wave after wave of Irish attack until the very last minute when the Republic of Ireland were awarded a penalty. Robbie Keane netted from the spot to take the game into extra time and, when the additional half hour had failed to separate the sides, retained his composure to net again with the opening strike in the penalty shoot out. Sadly some of his team mates were not equal to his efforts, Holland, Connolly and Kilbane either missing or having their shots saved as Spain won 3-2.

Senegal shocked Sweden in their second round tie, recovering from Henrik Larsson giving Sweden the lead after only 11 minutes to equalise before half time through Henri Camara. Extra time brought a Senegalese sudden death winner, again

Above
Michael Owen celebrates as Rio Ferdinand opens the scoring for England against Denmark in the second-round.

Above right
The Republic of Ireland eventually lose to Spain on penalties. Mendieta scores the decisive goal past Shay Given.

Right
Germany's Oliver Neuville celebrates his 88th minute match winning goal against Paraguay.

needed sent an entire nation into raptures. Unfortunately, Ahn's employers at Perugia were not nearly so excited, sacking him from the club almost immediately!

from Camara, as Senegal became only the second African nation to reach the quarter-finals, after Cameroon in 1990, but this was in their first attempt!

Competition favourites Brazil also left it relatively late against Belgium, taking the lead on 67 minutes and only adding a second three minutes before time to take the tie 2-0.

The clash between Mexico and the USA, so often foes in the CONCACAF competition, went the way of the Americans to put them into the quarter-finals too, Brian McBride and Landon Donovan getting the goals either side of the break.

Both host nations were in action on the final day of second round action, Japan against Turkey and South Korea up against the Italians. Japan slipped up against the Turks, Umit netting the only goal of the game. South Korea, meanwhile, upset the form book with a 2-1 sudden death win over Italy that brought even greater celebrations than had accompanied the Koreans' earlier group victories. The primary goal of the South Koreans had been to progress further than Japan, and goals from Seol two minutes from time to send the game into extra time and then Ahn Jung-Hwa four minutes before penalty kicks were

Eagerly anticipated and widely predicted to see the eventual world champions victorious, the clash between England and Brazil lived up to some of its expectations. Michael Owen showed why he was one of the most feared hitmen in the modern game with a typical strike to put England into the lead. The lead didn't survive until the break, however, Rivaldo equalising on the stroke of half time after the Brazilian midfield had reacted quicker to a ball that appeared to be on

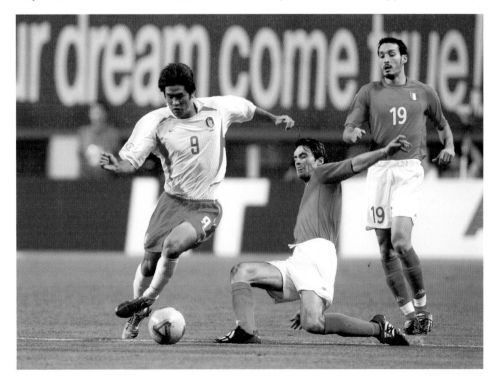

Above left
Henri Camara of Sengal scores the second goal against Sweden in their second-round game.

Above right
USA's Landon Donovan scores off a header past an outstretched Oscar Perez in goal for Mexico.

Left
Hyeon Seol Ki of South Korea takes the ball past Christian Panucci of Italy during their second-round match.

Above
Michael Owen
celebrates with
team-mates David
Beckham and Rio
Ferdinand after
scoring the
opening goal for
England against
Brazil.

Above right
David Seaman of
England can only
watch in horror as
an amazing free-
kick from
Ronaldinho of
Brazil goes in to
the net for the
winning goal in
their quarter-final.

Right
Spain play South
Korea in their
rather controversial
quarter-final.

its way out for a throw in. The goal that settled the game was something of a fluke, a Ronaldinho free kick sailing over the head of David Seaman five minutes after the sides had turned round. Despite throwing on the likes of Teddy Sheringham and Emile Heskey in search of an equaliser, it was England's inability to change how the ball was delivered to the front men that attracted criticism. Ronaldinho was later harshly sent off (his suspension was subsequently amended to only a single game instead of the customary two), but despite the extra space England could not capitalise and slipped out.

The Germans were put under the cosh by the Americans, the match belying the respective rankings of the two sides. However, the Germans had the ultimate match winner, Michael Ballack scoring the only goal of the game six minutes before half time.

A single goal, in sudden death, settled the meeting between two of the underdogs left in the competition,

Turkey finally getting the breakthrough over Senegal in the 94th minute through Ilhan Mansiz. Considering it was the first time Turkey had qualified for the finals since 1954, reaching the semi-finals was beyond expectations.

They were eventually joined by South Korea, who similarly defied form to overcome Spain. However, there was considerable controversy, raised by the Spaniards, over some of the refereeing decisions that had gone the way of the host nation – Spain had two perfectly good goals ruled out by the Egyptian referee and his assistants. The referee, however, was not responsible for Spain's ineptitude from the penalty spot – South Korea won the shoot-out 5-3.

South Korea's reward was a semi-final clash with the Germans, but a Michael Ballack goal 15 minutes from time brought their great adventure to an end. Unfortunately, a yellow card for a professional foul also brought Ballack's World Cup to an end – an earlier yellow card meant he had to sit out the final.

A single goal settled the other semi-final, Ronaldo playing as though he were on a mission to put the disappointment of four years previously well and truly to bed and scoring soon after the break to book Brazil's place in their sixth final.

For many the third and fourth place play-off is little more than an inconvenience, requiring two teams who have suffered the ultimate in World Cup disappointment, elimination at the semi-final stage, to drag their weary bodies and minds through another ninety minutes of football. Neither applied to South Korea and Turkey, perhaps both even astonished to find themselves contesting the match. In something approaching a carnival atmosphere, Turkey finally won 3-2 and then joined their hosts in a well deserved lap of honour.

Since the World Cup was launched in 1930, Brazil had played eighty-six matches in the finals, the most by any nation, and had won the trophy more than anybody else, four times. Germany, taking into account the record of West Germany between 1954 and 1990, were only just behind them on eighty-four final matches and had won the cup three times. Yet the two most successful

nations had never previously met each other! There has often been speculation that the draws over the years had been 'rigged' so that Brazil and Germany appeared in opposite halves of the draw; the only place they could possibly meet was in the final itself, which finally came good in 2002.

Brazil had been in good if not blistering form in reaching the final, their sternest test possibly coming in the quarter-final

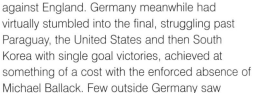

against England. Germany meanwhile had virtually stumbled into the final, struggling past Paraguay, the United States and then South Korea with single goal victories, achieved at something of a cost with the enforced absence of Michael Ballack. Few outside Germany saw anything other than a Brazilian win, but the Germans defied the odds in the opening stages, taking the game to the opposition and initially looking the more likely to open the scoring. Gradually the Brazilians began to exert themselves, the three Rs in Rivaldo, Ronaldinho and Ronaldo dominating the key areas on the field. The game was entering its final stages when Ronaldo at last put the Brazilians ahead, adding a second 12 minutes later. To the relief of the Germans (and no doubt countless watching Englishmen!), his chance of

netting a hat trick disappeared when he was substituted by Denilson in virtually the last minute, although he had won the Golden Boot for netting eight goals in the finals. A few moments later came the final whistle and Brazil were world champions for the fifth time, a feat that had seemed so unlikely during initial qualification that three coaches had lost the job! In winning all seven of their matches, they set yet another record.

The success of Brazil notwithstanding, the 2002 finals will almost forever be remembered for the performances of the so-called minnows. Nearly every manager has claimed there is no such thing as an easy game anymore and not been believed by either the media or his countrymen, but the achievements of South Korea and Turkey, who went further than the likes of Italy and England, and the United States, Senegal and Japan, who surpassed the accomplishments of Argentina, Portugal and France, would give credence to the claim.

Whilst the quality of the football in 2002 sometimes left a lot to be desired, the same could not be said for the enthusiasm and colourfulness of the two hosts. They gave us a tournament to enjoy at the very least. Eight managers

Above
Ronaldo scores his first goal for Brazil in the final against Germany.

Above right
The International Stadium in Yokohama Japan, gears up for the World Cup final.

Right
Ronaldinho pushes the ball past Hamann of Germany.

Far right
Brazil celebrate in style, their fifth title.

RESULTS

Group A

France v Senegal	0-1	France v Uruguay	0-0
Uruguay v Denmark	1-2	Denmark v France	2-0
Denmark v Senegal	1-1	Senegal v Uruguay	3-3

	P	W	D	L	F	A	P
Denmark	3	2	1	0	5	2	7
Senegal	3	1	2	0	5	4	5
Uruguay	3	0	2	1	4	5	2
France	3	0	1	2	0	3	1

Group B

Paraguay v South Africa	2-2	South Africa v Slovenia	1-0
Spain v Slovenia	3-1	Slovenia v Paraguay	1-3
Spain v Paraguay	3-1	Spain v South Africa	3-2

	P	W	D	L	F	A	P
Spain	3	3	0	0	9	4	9
Paraguay	3	1	1	1	6	6	4
South Africa	3	1	1	1	5	5	4
Slovenia	3	0	0	3	2	7	0

Group C

Brazil v Turkey	2-1	Costa Rica v Turkey	1-1
China v Costa Rica	0-2	Costa Rica v Brazil	2-5
Brazil v China	4-0	Turkey v China	3-0

	P	W	D	L	F	A	P
Brazil	3	3	0	0	11	3	9
Turkey	3	1	1	1	5	3	4
Costa Rica	3	1	1	1	5	6	4
China	3	0	0	3	0	9	0

Group D

South Korea v Poland	2-0	South Korea v USA	1-1
USA v Portugal	3-2	Poland v USA	3-1
Portugal v Poland	4-0	Portugal v South Korea	0-1

	P	W	D	L	F	A	P
South Korea	3	2	1	0	4	1	7
USA	3	1	1	1	5	6	4
Portugal	3	1	0	2	6	4	3
Poland	3	1	0	2	3	7	3

Group E

Germany v Saudi Arabia	8-0	Cameroon v Saudi Arabia	1-0
Rep of Ireland v Cameroon	1-1	Cameroon v Germany	0-2
Germany v Rep of Ireland	1-1	Saudi Arabia v Rep of Ireland	0-3

	P	W	D	L	F	A	P
Germany	3	2	1	0	11	1	7
Rep of Ireland	3	1	2	0	5	2	5
Cameroon	3	1	1	1	2	3	4
Saudi Arabia	3	0	0	3	0	12	0

Group F

Argentina v Nigeria	1-0	Sweden v Nigeria	2-1
England v Sweden	1-1	Argentina v Sweden	1-1
Argentina v England	0-1	Nigeria v England	0-0

	P	W	D	L	F	A	P
Sweden	3	1	2	0	4	3	5
England	3	1	2	0	2	1	5
Argentina	3	1	1	1	2	2	4
Nigeria	3	0	1	2	1	3	1

Group G

Croatia v Mexico	0-1	Mexico v Ecuador	2-1
Italy v Ecuador	2-0	Ecuador v Croatia	1-0
Italy v Croatia	1-2	Mexico v Italy	1-1

	P	W	D	L	F	A	P
Mexico	3	2	1	0	4	2	7
Italy	3	1	1	1	4	3	4
Croatia	3	1	0	2	2	3	3
Ecuador	3	1	0	2	2	4	3

Group H

Japan v Belgium	2-2	Tunisia v Belgium	1-1
Russia v Tunisia	2-0	Belgium v Russia	3-2
Japan v Russia	1-0	Tunisia v Japan	0-2

	P	W	D	L	F	A	P
Japan	3	2	1	0	5	2	7
Belgium	3	1	2	0	6	5	5
Russia	3	1	0	2	4	4	3
Tunisia	3	0	1	2	1	5	1

Second Round

Denmark v England	0-3	Sweden v Senegal	1-2	Brazil v Belgium	2-0	Japan v Turkey	0-1
Germany v Paraguay	1-0	Spain v Republic of Ireland	1-1	Mexico v USA	0-2	South Korea v Italy	2-1
		Spain won 3-2 on penalties					

Quarter-Finals

England v Brazil	1-2
Germany v USA	1-0
Senegal v Turkey	0-1
Spain v South Korea	0-0
South Korea won 5-3 on penalties	

SEMI-FINALS

Germany	1	South Korea	0
Brazil	1	Turkey	0

3rd & 4th PLACE PLAY-OFF

| South Korea | 2 | Turkey | 3 |

FINAL

| Brazil | 2 | Germany | 0 |

(Ronaldo 2)

Roberto Silva, Da Silva, Edmilson, Junior, Cafu, Kleberson, Silva, Rivaldo, Roberto Carlos, Ronaldinho, (Juninho) Ronaldo (Denilson)

Kahn, Linke, Ramelow, Metzelder, Frings, Schneider, Jeremies (Asamoah), Hamann, Bode (Ziege), Neuville, Klose (Bierhoff)

who qualified for the finals lost their jobs either during or immediately after. Another, Dutchman Guus Hiddinck, worked miracles in taking the South Koreans almost all the way. There will be one or two eyebrows raised to see if he can do the same in 2006 with Trinidad & Tobago!

Right
The Olympic stadium in Berlin, which has received a face-lift for the 2006 World Cup.

Below
Nelson Mandela was a campaigner for South Africa's 2006 World Cup bid. They have since been awarded the tournament in 2010.

If there had been controversy over the years over the way the host nation was selected for the World Cup finals, then it was nothing compared to the furore that accompanied the eventual decision to award the 2006 finals to Germany. No decision before and, one suspects, in the future will ever divide the world in quite the same way Germany's selection did.

Up until 1994, the competition had effectively alternated between South America and Europe. The 1986 finals had originally been awarded to Colombia, who subsequently withdrew, with Mexico offering to stage the competition so that the finals at least remained on the same continent. Europe, in the form of Italy, staged the 1990 finals. The following competition returned to the American continent, but to the United States. It was back to Europe in 1998 with France, but by this time there were growing calls for the other FIFA federations to be given the opportunity of staging the finals. This call was picked up with the eventual selection of Japan and South Korea in 2002, putting the finals on the Asian continent for the first time. With the precedent now set, South Africa, on behalf of the African continent, submitted the most convincing proposal for staging the 2006 competition.

2006
GERMANY

As much as FIFA's will made itself known to a large number of countries, there were others looking at hosting the competition themselves. Chief among them were England and Germany. The English submission, which did not even get the backing of UEFA (although a working party from FIFA that visited the designated grounds claimed it was by far the best application), managed to alienate Europe, for it was claimed that the English FA and their German counterparts had a gentleman's agreement in place whereby the Germans backed the English application to stage the 1996 European Championships in return for English support for a German application for the 2006 World Cup. The English FA never

commented on whether there was such an agreement and pressed ahead with their application, eventually being voted out of contention early on in the process.

The selection finally came down to a choice between Germany and South Africa, with the South Africans convinced they had enough promised votes to secure the finals. They had also wheeled out their own political heavyweights, such as Nelson Mandela, to support their application. Equally, the Germans had canvassed support and were confident they had enough votes in the bag to win. Eventually, the simple mathematics were that Germany were one vote ahead but that the final vote to be cast, by the Oceania representative Charles Dempsey from New Zealand, had already been promised to South Africa. In the event of a draw, FIFA's executive committee would hold their own vote, and that would also go South

Africa's way. Unfortunately, the Oceania representative ignored his federation's wishes and abstained, leaving Germany winners 12-11. The South Africans were incredulous, the Oceania federation demanded to know why their representative had gone against instructions and even FIFA promised changes in the future in the way host nations were selected. It did not matter for the 2006 finals – they would be staged in Germany for the second time in a little over thirty years.

If the decision to award the finals to Germany had been contentious, then qualification around the various federations was equally covered in controversy. Europe had fifty-two teams enter the competition, with thirteen places (plus Germany) available for the finals. The teams were to be placed into eight groups of varying size, with the group winners earning automatic qualification. The two best runners-up

would also earn automatic qualification, with the six remaining runners-up being drawn in three home and away play-offs where the winners would take the remaining places.

The eight group winners turned out to be Holland, Ukraine, Portugal, France, Italy, England, Serbia & Montenegro and Croatia. The other two automatic places for best runners-up went to Poland and Sweden, leaving the Czech Republic, Spain, Turkey, Norway, Slovakia and Switzerland to battle it out via the play-offs for the remaining three places.

Holland won their group with one of the best records among the European sides, winning ten and drawing the other two of their twelve matches. It was their win in Prague against the Czech Republic that confirmed England would also qualify automatically, at least as one of the best runners-up, should they fail to win their group. Despite that home defeat, the

Above
The 2006 World Cup match ball.

Czech Republic recovered to take second place in the group, seeing off the Romanians by two points.

The tussle for Group 2 was exceptionally tight, with four teams in with a shout of qualifying – Ukraine, Turkey (who finished third in 2002), Denmark and Greece (surprise European Champions in 2004). Four points separated the four teams in the final analysis, Ukraine two points ahead of Turkey in second place, leaving Denmark and Greece out in the cold.

Portugal went through Group 3 undefeated, winning nine and drawing three to finish seven points ahead of their nearest challengers, Slovakia and Russia. Slovakia took second spot on goal difference from the Russians, the crucial match being a goalless draw played in Bratislava in the final round of matches.

Only three points separated four teams in Group 4, a battle between France, Switzerland, Israel and the Republic of Ireland. Too many drawn games looked as though it might cost the French their place in the finals, but a victory in Dublin against the Republic of Ireland put them back on the right track. The Irish missed out at the final hurdle; needing to beat Switzerland in their final match to guarantee at least a place in the play-offs, they were held to a goalless draw. The point Switzerland gained lifted them above Israel into second place behind France.

The Italians were seldom troubled in Group 5, finishing five points ahead of Norway and ten ahead of Scotland. They

could even afford to lose in Celje against Slovenia, who finished fourth well adrift of the front runners. The Scottish had high hopes prior to qualification, but abject performances at home to Norway and Belarus meant that even though they won in Oslo it was always a case of too little too late. Midway through qualification the Scots parted company with manager Bertie Vogts, their experiment with a foreign manager not having the same kind of galvanising effect it had with England. Former Rangers manager Walter Smith, perhaps the one man

Above
Milan Baros for the Czech Republic controls the ball past a Dutch defender in a World Cup qualifier.

Above right
Sergiy Fedorov of Ukraine fights for a ball with Sukur Hokan of Turkey during their qualifying match.

Right
Cristiano Ronaldo celebrates his goal for Portugal against Slovakia.

Middle
Claude Makelele of France vies with Clinton Morrison of the Republic of Ireland in their qualifier.

best suited for the rigours of managing the national side, was brought in to steady the ship and try and prepare the country for qualification for the 2008 European Championships.

All three remaining British Isles sides were placed in Group 6, with England expected to saunter through the group ahead of Poland, Austria, Azerbaijan, Northern Ireland and Wales. This was not a view shared by the English hierarchy, who knew that the Welsh and Irish would be particularly fired up for their matches, as would perennial opponents Poland. For 45 minutes of their opening match, it appeared as though England would saunter through the group, firing into a two goal lead over the Austrians, but mistakes after the break by David James allowed the Austrians to draw level. England redeemed themselves in the second match, a fine 2-1 win in Chorzow over the Poles. An attempt to try a new formation against the Welsh and Northern Irish in away matches backfired spectacularly, with a scrappy 1-0 win in Cardiff being followed by a defeat in Belfast at the hands of the Irish, the first time the Irish had beaten the English since 1972. England's subsequent 1-0 victory over the Austrians, achieved despite the harsh sending off of David Beckham (who achieved the unwelcome distinction of becoming the first England player to be sent off twice) and Holland's victory over the Czech Republic ensured English presence in Germany. A final victory over Poland gave

them the group and, after victory over Argentina in a friendly in Switzerland, elevation into the top eight rankings in the world and subsequent selection as one of the seeded nations.

Whilst Spain had been expected to dominate Group 7, the unknown quantity Serbia & Montenegro proved a surprise package, finally topping the group by two points. Neither side lost a match, but Serbia's six wins and four draws, which

included home and away goalless draws against the Spaniards gave them the edge.

The final European group, Group 8 was a two horse race between Croatia and Sweden, meaning Bulgaria and Hungary missed out. Croatia finally won the group by virtue of their better head to head results against Sweden, but the Swedes earned automatic qualification as one of the two best runners-up across the eight groups.

Spain made up for their group disappointment with a convincing 5-1 home win in the first leg of their play-off with Slovakia, effectively ending the contest, a 1-1 draw in the second leg ensured their eventual passage 6-2 on aggregate. The Czech Republic were equally impressive in their two matches with Norway, winning both legs 1-0 for a 2-0 aggregate win. The real drama came in the other play-off between Switzerland and Turkey. Turkey were widely expected to emerge on top over the two legs but slumped to a 2-0 defeat in Berne, leaving themselves a mountain to climb in the second leg. They managed to claw back the two goal deficit, but in winning 4-2 they allowed the Swiss to progress on away goals. Having endured considerable provocation before and during the match, the Swiss were made

to run a gauntlet of hate when the final whistle blew, with all manner of missiles raining down from the stands as the players left the field. There were also reported fights between the two sets of players in the tunnel, leaving one Swiss player Stephane Grichting requiring hospital treatment. As this was not the first time the Turks had been involved in incidents during and after important qualifying matches (think England

Above
Spain's Vicente Rodriguez tackles Serbia and Montenegro's Djordevic during their World Cup qualifying game.

Above right
Henrik Larsson of Sweden vies with Niko Kovac of Croatia during their qualifier.

Right
Swiss players run to the tunnel in reaction to a hostile crowd, after they win the tie on away goals to Turkey.

in the European Championship qualifiers in 2003), FIFA promised swift action that could include banning the Turkish FA from competing in the 2010 competition.

Asian qualification similarly ended with controversy, although without two sides attempting to kick lumps out of each other. The original forty-four entrants into the qualification process were playing for four automatic places in Germany and, for a fifth side, a place in a play-off with a side from the CONCACAF federation. Myanmar were subsequently suspended and ineligible to enter the competition, with a further six sides, Bhutan, Brunei, Philippines, Cambodia, Nepal and Guam subsequently dropping out of the competition because they couldn't afford the expense of competing! Unfortunately, two of these sides had been drawn against each other in the preliminary round, Guam being given a free passage into the first round but subsequently withdrawing themselves when they realised the cost of staging at least three matches in the first round group matches! Thus Laos, who had lost to Sri Lanka in the preliminary round, earned themselves a reprieve as a 'lucky loser' by virtue of only having a minus three goal deficit, ahead of Bangladesh with minus four, and were reinstated into the competition.

The first round stage saw the remaining thirty-two countries put into eight groups of four teams each, with the winners of each group going forward to the third round stage. This was another group stage, two groups of four teams with the top two in each group going to Germany and the two third placed sides playing off against each other, the winner then playing home and away against the fourth placed side in the CONCACAF tournament in an intercontinental play-off.

Despite their reprieve, Laos were unable to make any further progress in their group, finishing bottom after six successive defeats. The group was won by

Iran, five wins and a single defeat leaving them three points ahead of Jordan. Uzbekistan had a similar record in Group 2 and were five points ahead of Iraq, although Iraq had more pressing domestic problems to contend with rather than concentrate on football. Japan, one of the surprises of 2002, were too strong for Group 3, winning all six of their matches, conceding only one goal in the process. Kuwait won Group 4 by the narrowest of margins from the People's Republic of China – both sides won five and lost one of their six qualifying matches. Their defeats came in their away matches with each other, 1-0, and they were also level on goal difference, so Kuwait took the group by virtue of having scored more goals than the Chinese, 15 compared with 14. North Korea won Group 5, a point ahead of the United Arab Emirates, and were subsequently joined by their biggest rivals across the border, South Korea in Group 7. In Group 6 Bahrain were four points ahead of Syria, whilst the final group saw Saudi Arabia register a 100% record and finish eleven points ahead of Turkmenistan.

Saudi Arabia were unable to maintain their 100% record in Group A of the next stage but still finished four points ahead of South Korea. Both sides gained automatic qualification for Germany, with Uzbekistan finishing third and just about hanging on for a place in the play-off. In Group B Japan and Iran dominated and took the automatic places, Bahrain finishing third.

It was the play-off between Uzbekistan and Bahrain that saw the first controversial incident in Asian qualification. Uzbekistan won the first leg 1-0 but, after protests and a FIFA investigation, the result was declared void owing to a referee error and subsequently replayed. Bahrain managed a 1-1

Above left
Czech Pavel Nedved and Tomas Ujfalusi celebrate their victory over Norway in their World Cup qualifier match.

Left
Japan play Iran in a qualifier game.

three teams qualifying for Germany and the fourth placed side off to meet Bahrain in a play-off.

After eighteen matches therefore, the United States, Mexico and Costa Rica finally made it through to the World Cup finals, the USA finishing level on points with Mexico but being awarded top spot in the final group by virtue of their head to head record against the Mexicans. Costa Rica in third place were six points adrift of the Americans and Mexicans, and three points below them were Trinidad & Tobago in fourth place, who took the play-off place ahead of Guatemala.

Both Bahrain and Trinidad & Tobago were attempting to qualify for the World Cup finals for the first time in their histories and, after two close matches, it was Trinidad & Tobago who earned their place in Germany, but not before more controversy. Trinidad & Tobago won the first leg in Bahrain 1-0, but Bahrain the better of the second leg. Going into the final moments, it was level at 1-1, giving Trinidad & Tobago a one goal advantage, but Bahrain had the ball in the net to seemingly give them the tie on away goals. The referee however had other thoughts,

draw second time around, the goal they scored proving vital when the two sides played out a goalless draw in Manama in the second leg – Bahrain advanced to meet the CONCACAF representatives in another two legged play-off.

There were three rounds of qualifying in the CONCACAF tournament, with thirty-four teams competing for three automatic places and a play-off with Bahrain for Asia for a possible fourth place. The first preliminary round saw the thirty-four sides divided into twelve groups – ten of these had three teams, the remaining two had two sides. In the case of the three team groups, the two weaker sides (according to FIFA rankings) would meet home and away, the winner progressing to meet the third (and supposedly better side according to FIFA) home and away. Eventually, the twelve group winners would progress into the semi final round, where there would be three groups of four teams each. Each side would play the other home and away, the top two teams in the group advancing to the final round, a six team group, again playing each other home and away, with the top

Above
Ronald Gomez of Costa Rica runs at the crowded Mexican defense in their World Cup qualifying game.

Right
Bahrain's Rashed Abdul Rahman vies with Dwight Yorke of Trinidad and Tobago.

disallowing the goal for presumably a high kick by one of the Bahrain players.

South America opted for a straight league format for their ten entrants for the third consecutive occasion. The top four would automatically qualify for the finals, the fifth placed side would earn a play-off against the winners of the Oceania competition. Brazil (despite being holders Brazil were required to qualify) and Argentina were neck and neck in the running for the top two spots, Argentina winning more matches but also losing two more than their nearest rivals – their final defeat would be another that attracted considerable controversy. Brazil finally won the group on goal difference, netting 35 goals in their 18 matches. Third and fourth places were also settled by goal difference, Ecuador finishing four goals better off than Paraguay. Fifth place, which would earn the recipients a play-off with the winners of the Oceania competition, was finally taken by Uruguay after a tense struggle against Colombia and Chile. Just as they had in 2002, Uruguay went into their final match against Argentina needing a positive result in order to continue in the competition – in 2002 they needed a point and got it, in 2006 they needed all three and got them in a 1-0 win. Once again eyebrows were raised at the Argentineans, who had already made sure of their qualification, seemingly helping their nearest rivals.

Uruguay's opponents in the play-off would be Australia, who emerged from the Oceania group for the last time. The

lack of an automatic place for the World Cup finals, combined with the lack of any meaningful competition (Australia had once beaten American Samoa 31-0), apart from New Zealand,

Above
Argentine Fabricio Coloccini and Brazilian Adriano go for the ball in their qualifier.

Left
Fabian Carini of Uruguay watches the ball flash by as Marco Bresciano of Australia scores.

had prompted both countries to announce to Oceania their intention to leave the federation and join the Asian block on 1st January 2006. Oceania decided that the qualifying competition would also double as the Oceania Nations Cup, a decision that meant New Caledonia competed in the competition even though they had not entered the World Cup! Fortunately they progressed no further than the first round. Australia and New Zealand were exempt until the second round, a mini League of six teams that played each other once during the course of a little over a week in Australia. The top two, expected to be Australia and New Zealand, would then play each other home and away to decide who topped the Oceania group and would go on to play Uruguay. Defeats by Australia and Vanuatu wrecked New Zealand's hopes, leaving Australia and the Solomon Islands on top.

withdrawing. Nine sides received byes into the second round (those who had qualified for the 2002 finals plus the top four according to FIFA ranks), with the remaining sides playing home and away ties to reduce the numbers for the second round to thirty teams. These were then placed in five groups of six teams, each playing the others home and away and the group winners qualifying for Germany. Togo, who were one of the sides who had to play in the first round, finally emerged triumphant in Group 1, seeing off Senegal into the bargain, to make the World Cup finals for the first time after a 3-2 win against the Congo confirmed their victory.

They were joined by Ghana from Group 2, another side that made the finals for the first time. The big losers in their group were South Africa, expected to do so much better, especially as they would be hosting the next competition in 2010. There was a similar shock in Group 3, with Cameroon missing out by one point to the Ivory Coast. The crucial matches were the last ones, Ivory Coast

Fourteen months later these two sides played their final, Australia winning the home leg 7-0 and the away leg 2-1 to earn the right to play Uruguay. Whilst the gap between the two nations had been a big one some twenty or so years previously, the same could not be said in 2005, with Australia holding the Uruguayans to a single goal lead after the first half in Montevideo. The Australians made the most of the situation in the second leg, equalling the single goal win and then emerging triumphant after a penalty shoot out 4-2 to earn their place in Germany. According to the Uruguayan players, the result was of little surprise, the Australians having prepared better for the play-off, flying in and out of Uruguay on board a specially chartered plane whilst the Uruguayans flew on scheduled aircraft!

The final qualifying section came from Africa, where fifty-two of the continent's fifty-three members entered the competition, with only Djibouti missing from the start and the Central African Republic later

Above
Michael Essien of Ghana celebrates after their World Cup qualifying match between Cape Verde.

Right
Angolan player Maieco Fabrice (left) is tackled by two Rwandan players in their World Cup game.

Left
The impressive Allianz Arena in Munich which illuminates at night.

Below
The draw for the 2006 finals is made, and displayed on a giant screen.

winning in Sudan at the same time Cameroon were held to a 1-1 at home to Egypt – Cameroon missed out by one point.

It was even closer in Group 3, with Angola pipping Nigeria to top spot by virtue of their head to head record – a 1-0 home win and 1-1 away draw – after the two sides had finished with the same number of points. The final group was won by Tunisia, a point ahead of Morocco, with the two sides clashing in the final group match, a 2-2 draw.

The draw for the finals was made on 9th December 2005 in Leipzig (chosen as that was where the German FA had originally been formed). England joined Brazil, Germany, Italy, Mexico, Argentina, France and Spain as the seeded nations. England manager Sven Goran Eriksson expressed his hope that England might avoid Holland and Australia in the group stages – they drew Paraguay, Trinidad & Tobago and, for the second time in succession, Sweden! The draw soon had bookies installing England as second favourites behind Brazil, but as we have seen on numerous occasions during the history of the World Cup, the favourites

don't always win and results don't always go as expected. Despite almost constant tampering with the format of the World Cup, its sheer unpredictability is what makes it the greatest sporting spectacle in the world.

EXTRA TIME

TOP GOALSCORERS

1930 Guillermo Stabile (ARG)	8
1934 Oldrich Nejedly (CZE)/Angelo Schiavo (ITA)/Edmund Cohen (GER)	5
1938 Leonidas Da Silva (BRA)	8
1950 Ademir (BRA)	9
1954 Sandor Kocsis (HUN)	11
1958 Juste Fontaine (FRA)	13
1962 Drazan Jerkovic (YUG)	5
1966 Eusebio	9
1970 Gerd Muller (GER)	10
1974 Grzegorz Lato (POL)	7
1978 Mario Kempes (ARG)	6
1982 Paolo Rossi (ITA)	6
1986 Gary Lineker (ENG)	6
1990 Salvatore Schillaci (ITA)	6
1994 Hristo Stoitchkov (BUL)/Oleg Salenko (RUS)	6
1998 Davor Suker (CRO)	6
2002 Ronaldo (BRA)	8

ATTENDANCES

YEAR	COUNTRY	GAMES	TOTAL	AVERAGE
1930	URUGUAY	18	434,500	24,139
1934	ITALY	17	395,000	23,235
1938	FRANCE	18	483,000	26,833
1950	BRAZIL	22	1,337,000	60,773
1954	SWITZERLAND	26	943,000	36,269
1958	SWEDEN	35	868,000	24,800
1962	CHILE	32	776,000	24,250
1966	ENGLAND	32	1,614,677	50,459
1970	MEXICO	32	1,673,975	52,312
1974	WEST GERMANY	38	1,774,022	46,685
1978	ARGENTINA	38	1,610,215	42,374
1982	SPAIN	52	1,766,277	33,979
1986	MEXICO	52	2,407,431	46,297
1990	ITALY	52	2,517,348	48,411
1994	UNITED STATES	52	3,587,538	68,991
1998	FRANCE	64	2,785,100	43,517
2002	JAPAN AND SOUTH KOREA	64	2,705,197	42,269

MERIT TABLE

COUNTRY	P	W	D	L	F	A
Brazil	87	62	11	14	191	82
Germany/West Germany	85	53	15	17	176	106
Italy	70	39	14	17	110	67
Argentina	60	33	8	19	102	71
France	44	23	4	17	86	61
England	50	22	13	15	68	45
Spain	45	20	9	16	71	53
USSR/Russia	37	17	6	14	64	44
Sweden	42	16	10	16	71	65
Yugoslavia	37	16	7	14	60	46
Uruguay	40	15	10	15	65	57
Hungary	32	15	3	14	87	57
Holland	32	14	8	10	56	36
Poland	28	14	5	9	42	36
Austria	29	12	4	13	43	47
Belgium	36	11	8	17	46	63
Czechoslovakia	30	11	5	14	44	45
Mexico	41	10	9	22	43	79
Romania	23	8	3	10	30	32
Chile	25	7	6	12	31	40
Denmark	13	7	2	4	24	18
Portugal	12	7	0	5	25	16
Switzerland	22	6	3	13	33	51
United States	22	6	2	14	25	45
Croatia	10	6	0	4	13	8
Paraguay	19	5	7	7	25	34
Turkey	10	5	1	4	20	17
Cameroon	17	4	7	6	15	29
Scotland	23	4	7	12	25	41
Bulgaria	26	4	7	15	22	53
South Korea	21	4	5	12	19	49
Peru	15	4	3	8	19	31
Nigeria	11	4	1	6	14	16
Republic of Ireland	13	3	6	4	10	10
Northern Ireland	13	3	5	5	13	23
Colombia	13	3	2	8	14	23
Costa Rica	7	3	1	3	9	12
Morocco	13	2	4	7	12	18
Norway	8	2	3	3	7	8
Senegal	5	2	2	1	7	6

MERIT TABLE continued

COUNTRY	P	W	D	L	F	A
East Germany	6	2	2	2	5	5
Algeria	6	2	1	3	6	10
Japan	7	2	1	4	6	7
Saudi Arabia	10	2	1	7	7	25
Wales	5	1	3	1	4	4
South Africa	6	1	3	2	8	11
Tunisia	9	1	3	5	5	11
Cuba	3	1	1	1	5	12
North Korea	4	1	1	2	5	9
Iran	6	1	1	4	4	12
Ecuador	3	1	0	2	2	4
Jamaica	3	1	0	2	3	9
Honduras	3	0	2	1	2	3
Israel	3	0	2	1	1	3
Egypt	4	0	2	2	3	6
Australia	3	0	1	2	0	5
Kuwait	3	0	1	2	2	6
Bolivia	6	0	1	5	1	20
Dutch East Indies	1	0	0	1	0	6
Canada	3	0	0	3	0	5
China	3	0	0	3	0	9
Greece	3	0	0	3	0	10
Haiti	3	0	0	3	2	14
Iraq	3	0	0	3	1	4
New Zealand	3	0	0	3	2	12
Slovenia	3	0	0	3	2	7
United Arab Emirates	3	0	0	3	2	11
Zaire	3	0	0	3	0	14
El Salvador	6	0	0	6	1	22

NOTES:

Germany includes West Germany results.
Russia includes USSR results.

Where a match finished drawn but was decided by a penalty shoot out, the team that won has been awarded a victory, the team that lost a defeat.

IMAGES SUPPLIED COURTESY OF:

GETTY IMAGES
101 Bayham Street, London NW10AG

EMPICS
www.empics.com

DESIGN & ARTWORK: Kevin Gardner • **PROJECT EDITOR:** Vanessa Gardner

IMAGE RESEARCH: Ellie Charlston & Kevin Gardner • **PROOFREADER:** Jane Pamenter

WRITTEN BY: Graham Betts